To Lendre:
Great to see

handwritten signature

Al-Qaeda's Armies

Armies

*Middle East Affiliate Groups &
the Next Generation of Terror*

by

Jonathan Schanzer

*Foreword by
Ambassador Dennis Ross,
Director, The Washington Institute for Near East Policy*

SPECIALIST
PRESS
INTERNATIONAL
New York

The Washington Institute
for Near East Policy

Washington, D.C.

For further information, contact:

99 Spring Street, 3rd Floor
New York, NY 10012
Tel: (212) 431-5011
Fax: (212) 431-8646
E-mail: *publicity@spibooks.com*
Visit us at *www.spibooks.com*

10 9 8 7 6 5 4 3 2 1
First Edition

Library of Congress Cataloging-in-Publication Data available.
ISBN: 1-56171-884-x

Contents

Al-Qaeda's Middle East affiliate groups, as described in the U.S. State Department's "Patterns of Global Terrorism 2003."

Al-Qaeda's Middle East affiliate groups, as listed in Executive Order 13224 on September 23, 2001, and subsequent additional designations.

Testimony of George J. Tenet, former Director of Central Intelligence, before the Senate Select Committee on Intelligence, discussing al-Qaeda, the affiliate phenomenon, and "stateless zones."

Foreword

By Ambassador Dennis Ross
Director, The Washington Institute for Near East Policy

On September 11, 2001, I was giving a lecture at the Johns Hopkins School of Advanced International Studies. My lecture was on the lessons of peacemaking in the Middle East. At the conclusion of the lecture, my hosts informed those assembled that two planes had flown into the World Trade Center towers and another had crashed into the Pentagon – and all the buildings were burning. Like everyone there, I was stunned.

My questions were no different than anyone else's: How could this have happened? How could that many planes be hijacked at the same time? How many conspirators must have been involved and for how long had they been living here among us to pull off such a plan? How could we have been so catastrophically surprised?

The one thing I did not question was the Middle East connection. I knew instinctively that there was such a connection. I knew it because the terrorists had attacked the very symbols of American power, influence, and affluence. Middle Eastern terrorists, infused with a radical Islamic impulse toward martyrdom, were the ones most likely to be driven to suicidal attacks of such a scale. Further, the terrorist forces in the Middle East had been bred to believe that the United States was the source of evil, contaminating their faith, destroying their culture with materialism, "propping up" corrupt and oppressive regimes, and supporting the intruders, the Israelis, in their midst.

In the days after September 11, our desire as Americans to search for rational explanations of an irrational, unthinkably horrific act led some inevitably to suggest that the root cause must be the absence of peace in the Middle East. If only there was peace in the Middle East, they seemed to be saying, this would not have happened. But September 11 did not happen because of the absence of Middle East peace. Osama bin Laden and his al-Qaeda network had been planning this attack even when it looked like we were about to succeed in producing a solution to the core of the Arab-Israeli conflict. Indeed, had we succeeded either at Camp David or at the end of 2000 with the Clinton parameters for resolving the existential conflict between Israelis and Palestinians, Osama bin Laden and the al-Qaeda terrorists would have been even more determined to carry out the attack.

Theirs was an attack on us, on civilization and modernity itself, on our support for the Saudi and Egyptian regimes – regimes they believe betray Islam. They reject Israel's existence; for them, the very concept of peace with Israel is an anathema. To be sure, the absence of peace and the *intifada* (with its images of Palestinian youngsters taking on Israeli tanks) soured the climate for moderation in the area and created a more fertile breeding ground for anger and resentment – the stock in trade of Osama bin Laden and the terrorist networks.

Unfortunately, anger, resentment, and frustration have deep roots in the psychology of the Middle East. Bin Laden, in an early videotape after September 11, spoke of eighty years of humiliation, implicitly referring to the broken promises and the imposition of colonial regimes and borders after World War I. The psychic landscape of the Arab Middle East is shaped by an overwhelming sense of betrayal and humiliation, principally by the West. There is an abiding sense of rights and destiny denied; of being constantly victimized; of being entitled, but never responsible. All these perceptions contribute to an Arab mindset that makes defiance of the powerful attractive to a broader audience that feels alienated and powerless. This is the appeal of bin Laden – and Saddam Husayn before him, and Khomeini before him, and Qadahfi before him, and Nasser before him.

The litany of those who have sought to be the hero, of those who have sought to play on the desire to defy the powerful, is a reminder that all those who have sought this role – in Nasser's words, "the role in search of a hero" – have failed. They have failed because they played only on resentment. Their efforts were geared toward destruction, not construction. In the end, leaders must produce, not only defy.

The weakness of most current leaders in the Middle East is that the power they seek is usually an end in itself. They seek to hold it, not to use it for good. While their people fall farther and farther behind, the revolution in global communications and technology shows their people the prosperity that seemingly everyone else has, and what they lack. The Arab public lacks opportunity for advancement, for participation, and for expression of their grievances. They know who holds power and who benefits from it. They are allowed to express their frustration and anger only with regard to Israel and the United States, not against their own governments. And yet, the expression of frustration yields no result because Arab governments, while paying lip service to the cause of Palestine, have done very little to actually support it.

Peace in the Middle East would remove one source of real grievance. But it would not be a panacea. The sources of domestic instability would remain. The socioeconomic failings would have to be addressed. Political participation would have to be broadened beyond narrow elites. The requirements of modernity would have to be embraced, not resisted. In a word, responsibility would have to be assumed.

Some Arab observers recognized this in the aftermath of September 11, 2001. In an article entitled "It's Not All America's Fault," Lebanese journalist Hazem Saghiyeh wrote that it was up to the Muslim world to rethink "its relation to modernity," to Arab and Muslim leaders to resolve "the question of political legitimacy," and to Arab intellectuals to "encourage change," not continue to fail, "in that role." Saghiyeh's plea was for the Arab world to look to itself for answers and not simply blame others.

Others began to echo Saghiyeh. A number of Arab intellectuals drafted the first "Arab Human Development Report" in 2002, which explained why the Arab world has lagged behind the rest of the globe in the quest for modernity. More recently, after the demise of Saddam Husayn's regime and the collapse of Baghdad in the war, other reformers, like academicians Shafeeq Ghabra from Kuwait and Hala Mustafa from Egypt, have addressed the ills that plague Arab regimes. Their recommendations for addressing what is wrong in the area include: introducing a rule of law; developing an independent judiciary; fighting corruption; fostering transparency and accountability; promoting tolerance; supporting women's rights; and emphasizing responsibility.

None of this can emerge overnight. All of this is necessary to create the basis for building governments that can be more representative of their societies and more decent toward their publics. Democracy can emerge from an environment in which civil society and institutions are developed from within, not imposed from without.

Why do I mention this in the foreword to a book entitled *Al-Qaeda's Armies*? For one thing, it is essential for understanding the roots of hostility toward America that terrorists exploit. Anger toward the United States in the Middle East preceded September 11 and, judging by extensive polling, it has, if anything, worsened since that time. I don't subscribe to the view that there is only one cause, but I do believe the perception of an American double standard certainly contributes to hostility. America's support of Israel is certainly another explanation for that perception. But there is another factor that should not be underestimated in this regard: the widespread view throughout the Arab and Islamic world that we use democracy as a weapon against those regimes we don't like, but never against those regimes that we consider to be our allies.

It has therefore become their perception that we support regimes that serve our interests, even while they oppress their own people, who foster deep resentment toward us. The answer is not suddenly to withdraw our support from U.S. strategic allies. But we do need to be clearer with all our allies in the region that we stand for certain values, that those Arab liberals/reformers that embody these values will have our support, and that we will not be silent when they are suppressed.

Acting in this way would begin to address the issue of double standards, and, as importantly, create an environment in which reformers would stand a better chance of having an impact in the region. If we cannot begin to defuse Arabs' anti-American anger – as well as the alienation from the local regimes – there will continue to be a rich pool of recruits for bin Ladenism and local Islamists. The Bush administration has changed the rhetoric on reform and democracy in the region. It has implied that we will not turn a blind eye to the tyranny of those we have considered to be friends. That is a welcome departure from the past. To be credible, it will have to be reflected in behavior and not just in speeches.

Indeed, after 9/11, we now know that how local regimes are dealing with the need for change is no longer strictly their concern alone. It will affect our security as well. We have a stake in how they treat their people, and whether they are fostering a sense that change is possible. Given the demographics of countries like Saudi Arabia, where 75 percent of the population is under the age of twenty-five, it is precisely the need to demonstrate that change is possible that is so important. A youthful population that is increasingly alienated can be transformed, not by dramatic promises, but by demonstrations of change and by proof that inclusion is possible. In the struggle going on between the Crown Prince of Saudi Arabia in favor of reform and members of the Royal family who oppose it, the U.S. should not be neutral. The fledgling steps toward municipal elections are important, especially if they are part of a credible process designed to create real inclusion and transparency.

None of this suggests that we should be focused only on soft forms of power in combating the terror that produced September 11. On the contrary, for bin Laden, al-Qaeda and its off-shoots, there is only a military answer. They understand only power – and those who might otherwise be attracted to someone who defies the West must clearly see that bin Laden's philosophy produces only defeat and further humiliation.

Here it is essential that we understand what we are dealing with, and that is why I believe that Jonathan Schanzer's book is so important. He takes a fresh look at the al-Qaeda problem. He looks at several Middle East terrorist groups with ties to al-Qaeda that have received little attention in the press since the launch of the war on terror. This is the al-Qaeda that you probably don't know. Jonathan points out that the al-Qaeda network relies less on leaders like bin Laden, and more on its expanding orbit of dangerous, local Islamist groups spanning numerous countries. That is certainly one of the reasons why the necessary military struggle against al-Qaeda intersects with the crucial battle for hearts and minds.

Ultimately the war on terror can succeed not through military or intelligence or law enforcement means alone. As important as they are, as important as it is to cut off the financial flows of terror groups and their safe havens, it is also critical to try to discredit what they claim to represent. So long as terror is promoted and accepted by some as a legitimate instrument for pursuing a cause, we will not win this battle. So long as violence against Israeli civilians is justified as a form of resistance and not terror – and suicide bombers are glorified as martyrs rather than murderers – we stand little chance of delegitimizing acts of terror in the Middle East or elsewhere. If terror is legitimate for a cause in one part of the world, it will be legitimate elsewhere.

In the end, the struggle against terror and the philosophy that produced September 11 must employ all the instruments available to us. We must employ hard power and soft power. We must defeat the groups and their leaders when necessary and possible. We must enlist others – including political and religious leaders in the Middle East – in discrediting the use of terror in any circumstances. We must try to deal with – at a minimum defuse – the Israeli-Palestinian conflict, particularly given its resonance in the area and its use as a rallying point for those who embrace terror. We must stand for our values and promote far greater inclusion with our friends in the Middle East.

Creating hope is the best antidote to the anger and frustration that the bin Ladens of the world prey upon. We must create models of success to prove that there is a different pathway – and that it works. In this sense, we have an enormous stake in demonstrating that we actually have liberated Iraqis and helped them to create a better life for themselves, and a political and economic future that they own. Ultimately, it is the power of America's example as much as America's military power that will determine the future.

Introduction

America's "War on Terror" has completely consumed the attention of U.S. foreign policy analysts. Countless man-hours have been expended in the pursuit of sensible policies for what will undoubtedly be a protracted and asymmetrical war. Surprisingly, many analysts have yet to come to the inevitable conclusion that this war is inappropriately named. As I wrote with analyst Daniel Pipes in the *New York Post* on April 8, 2002, "Since September 11, America has waged war against a tactic. When President Bush declared a 'war against terrorism,' he ignored the real enemy - militant Islam, a brutal, totalitarian ideology."[1]

The United States is not battling terrorism, because no military can win a war against a tactic. America is not battling Islam (as some wrongly asserted in the wake of the 9/11 attacks), because one monolithic Islam cannot be extracted from the numerous offshoots, branches, and sects that make up the world's estimated population of 1.3 billion Muslims. Islam is just as ideologically, religiously, and politically fractured as the other two monotheistic faiths: Christianity and Judaism.

It can, however, be established that we are fighting against the forces of militant Islam, an expanding minority outgrowth of the faith that exudes a bitter hatred for Western ideas, including secularism, capitalism, individualism, and consumerism. It rejects the West and much that it has to offer (with the exception of weapons, medicines, and other useful technologies) seeking instead to implement a strict interpretation of the Qur'an (Islam's holy book) and shari'a (Islamic law). America, as radical Muslims see it, is the primary impediment to building an Islamic world order.

How this radical offshoot grew within Islam is worth briefly noting. The history begins with the birth of Islam in the year 610, when the prophet Muhammed received his divine mission and accepted Allah's instructions for a new religion that commanded belief in one God. For the next 22 years, Muhammed served as a transmitter of Allah's message, and his Muslim empire grew to encompass most of the Arabian Peninsula. After the prophet's death, the Muslim empire continued to expand until the 17th century, when Muslims were unquestionably the world's greatest military force, having conquered extensive territory and converted millions throughout the Middle East and Southern Europe. Islam had also achieved unmatched advances in architecture, art, law, mathematics, and science.

During this period, with the exception of battling Christian Crusaders, most Muslims had little to do with the West. Ottoman Turkey, the dominant Islamic power in the 16th century, viewed the West as an inferior culture with inferior religions. By the 17th century, however, the West achieved military superiority. In 1769, the Russians handed the Turks their first sound defeat, pointing to a new and difficult road ahead for Islam. Instead of conquering, the Muslims were the conquered.

The empire soon unraveled. In 1798, Napoleon Bonaparte led his expedition into Egypt. In 1830, the French seized Algeria. Nine years later, the British co-opted Aden (in modern Yemen). In 1881, the French occupied Tunisia, and in 1882 the English tightened their grip on Egypt. In 1911, Russia captured parts of Persia. That same year, Italy announced the annexation of Tripoli, leading to the eventual creation of the modern state of Libya. In 1912, the French extended their influence to Morocco. By the end of World War I, the Ottoman Empire had lost the Middle East, as France and England carved up the Muslim empire as spoils of war. The Muslim world could do little more than look on helplessly.

The Muslim world today is painfully aware of their losses and the subsequent ubiquitous influence of the West. This includes advancements in practical and physical sciences, modern weaponry and military reform, mass communication, law, and political reform, not to mention shopping malls and fast food.

These Western concepts and institutions, when transplanted to the Muslim world, were often destabilizing. They threatened the status quo, and were often too radically different to fit comfortably within a deeply rooted, traditional, and generally static Muslim culture.

While many Muslims adapted to the fast-paced changes common to Western industrialization and modernization, many also rejected them. The rejectionists created a rigid ideology imbedded in the traditional values and laws of the Koran. This is the phenomenon known today as militant Islam. While there may be some merit to the notion that the radicals fight the West because they oppose Western policies, that explanation ignores the fact that adherents to this fundamentalist ideology have long struggled to return to the glorious days when Islam reigned supreme. Their ideology represents a yearning for the return of "pure" Islam as practiced by the prophet, and the return of Islamic power.

The forces of radical Islam have been attacking non-Muslims for centuries. More recently, they have been attacking the United States, its interests and its allies since the late 1970s. The Tehran hostage crisis of 1979, Hizbullah's suicide bombing of a Beirut Marine barracks in 1983, the first World Trade Center bombing of 1993, the bombing of the U.S. embassies in Kenya and Tanzania in 1998, and the attack on the U.S.S. *Cole* in 2000 are just some of the more salient examples. These terrorist attacks were carried out by different actors (the Islamic Republic of Iran, Hizbullah, al-Qaeda, etc.), but they all shared a utopian vision of Islamic power.

Thus, when the U.S. government responded to the attacks of 9/11 by declaring a "war on terror," it used the wrong nom enclature. Washington was right, however, to focus most of its energies on al-Qaeda, the terrorist network founded by Osama bin Laden. Al-Qaeda is responsible for the lion's share of the high-profile attacks against America since 1992. On December 20,

2002, the U.S. government issued a report of nearly 900 pages ("Joint Inquiry into Intelligence Community Activities Before and After the Terrorist Attacks of September 11, 2001"), citing intelligence that demonstrated how al-Qaeda planned and executed the September 11 attacks.[2]

But just as the word "terrorism" is an oversimplification in defining America's war, so is the primary target known as "al-Qaeda." Many Americans are under the false assumption that if U.S. Special Forces caught al-Qaeda's top leaders, the terrorist threat would simply dissipate. The reality, however, is much more complicated. Al-Qaeda has become more of a phenomenon than an organization. Its stubborn and continuing existence lies in the fact that it has long relied upon small and local groups as "subcontractors" for its major terrorist attacks. The network's resiliency stems from its ability to rely on clandestine cells, as well as "affiliates," which are larger, homegrown, organic Islamist[3] terror groups that later became part of the al-Qaeda matrix. Al-Qaeda may have started as a small core, but an ever-expanding force now fights in its name. The challenge now is to defeat this growing network of affiliates and cells – what amounts to "al-Qaeda's Armies."

This book examines al-Qaeda and its affiliate phenomenon, and attempts to provide an in-depth look at several of the more active – but lesser known – affiliates operating specifically in the Arab world. These groups, located in Lebanon, Yemen, Algeria, Egypt, and Iraq, are unquestionably al-Qaeda's representatives in the region. Open sources in English and Arabic, as well as some sources in French and Turkish, make up the bulk of this book's source material. Face-to-face interviews in Washington, Baghdad, Sulaymaniyya, Sanaa, Aden, Cairo, Paris, and Tel Aviv were also very helpful. Area experts, as well as current and former government officials, who were kind enough to speak with me off-the-record, also helped to fill in the blanks.

A few words of caution are necessary, however. As a Middle East specialist, I did not feel qualified to examine the affiliates of Southeast Asia, which has become another hotbed for groups in al-Qaeda's orbit, and is deserving of increased attention. Good work has already been done in this area by academic Zachary Abuza of Simmons College, journalist Maria Ressa of CNN, Rohan Gunaratna, who authored *Inside al-Qaeda: Global Network of Terror* (Columbia University Press, 2002), and several others. Such studies, coupled with this one, can provide a more global and comprehensive view of the al-Qaeda affiliate phenomenon.

Furthermore, the accounts in this book are far from definitive. They represent an earnest attempt to document stories still being told. It is my hope that this work, along with its sources, can serve as a helpful primer for future study by other scholars and policymakers. More optimistically, this work might arm decision makers with information that is helpful in the dismantling of Middle Eastern al-Qaeda affiliates, so that future studies might constitute a post-mortem, rather than a contemporary analysis.

Interestingly, one of the affiliates in this study – Ansar al-Islam – became a target of the U.S. military during the 2003 Iraq war. While that group continued to execute attacks against the U.S. in post-war Iraq, the assault against it was not a wasted effort. Nor was Cairo's battle against Egypt's al-Jihad and al-Gamaa al-Islamiyya, for that matter, despite the fact that many of their members are today seen as al-Qaeda's core. Military action against affiliates in any form equates to an attack on the sources from which al-Qaeda draws its fighters and therefore diminishes the future strength of the al-Qaeda phenomenon.

Military targeting alone, however, will not be sufficient to destroy al-Qaeda's affiliates. In examining each affiliate in this book, it became clear that the groups were able to spawn and prosper by exploiting areas of weak central authority. In light of this trend, the danger of al-Qaeda's affiliates presents Washington with an opportunity. In keeping with its resolve to promote stronger ties with Middle Eastern states, the U.S. can work to build more robust relationships with states willing to fight their local al-Qaeda affiliates and to help stabilize the problematic areas under their sovereignty.

Failure to assist in the dismantling of local al-Qaeda affiliates, which equates to harboring terror, should result in penalties and sanctions. Conversely, successes should result in increased U.S. assistance to countries that clearly need it. If each relationship is structured carefully, the U.S. could play a supporting role in helping Middle East states weaken their al-Qaeda affiliates, while also helping those governments to project authority in the territories where they need it most.

Finally, it is important to note that the thesis of this book, which emphasizes the threat of al-Qaeda affiliates and the need to strengthen areas of weak central authority where terrorism thrives, is shared by a number of influential analysts who have come to similar conclusions. Former director of Central Intelligence, George Tenet, testified before the Senate Select Committee on Intelligence on February 24, 2004, about the threat of al-Qaeda's "loose collection of regional networks that operate more autonomously...." In that same testimony (excerpts of which are reprinted at the end of this book in Appendix C), Tenet warned that "places that combine desperate social and economic circumstances with a failure of government to police its own territory can often provide nurturing environments for terrorist groups, and for insurgents and criminals. The failure of governments to control their own territory creates potential power vacuums that open opportunities for those who hate."

As Tenet's testimony in 2004 shows, the study of al-Qaeda affiliates and their enclaves is of growing importance. Tenet's job was not to create policy, however, but to present information that would be useful to policymakers. As such, he provided an overview of the information, but declined to recommend how policymakers should move forward. This book provides detailed case studies and a deeper explanation of the challenges that Tenet identified, as well as some policy considerations as we look toward the future.

Notes

1 Daniel Pipes and Jonathan Schanzer, "Is America Winning?" *New York Post*, April 8, 2002. http://www.danielpipes.org/article/155
2 http://www.house.gov/gallegly/9-11Report072403.pdf
3 For the purposes of this book, Islamism and militant Islam will be used interchangeably. An Islamist is one who adheres to the ideology of militant Islam.

Chapter One: Al-Qaeda Evolves

Despite global efforts to destroy al-Qaeda, the network continues to survive and even thrive. According to one estimate, al-Qaeda's strength has diminished from some 4,000 fighters to just a few hundred, while about 80 percent of the operational leadership has been captured or killed.[1] Many fighters, however, eluded U.S. forces in Afghanistan, escaping into the Muslim hinterland to fight another day. A British-based think tank asserts that some 18,000 veterans of al-Qaeda training camps in Afghanistan are probably still operating worldwide.[2] U.S. officials further state that al-Qaeda may still maintain hundreds of operatives around the world.[3] Perhaps half of al-Qaeda's top leadership remains at large,[4] and the network's finances are still ample.[5]

With thousands of U.S. intelligence personnel and Special Forces trying to track down al-Qaeda's leaders, the network may be on the run, but it is no less dangerous. Dozens of plots – both successful and unsuccessful – have been attributed to al-Qaeda in recent years. Some of the successful attacks with strong links to al-Qaeda include: the April 2002 attack on a Tunisian synagogue; the Bali night club bombing of October 2002; the October 2002 assassination of USAID official Laurence Foley in Amman, Jordan; the bombing of Israeli tourists in Kenya in November 2002; the bombing of a French tanker in Yemen in November 2002; the May 2003 bombing of three targets in Riyadh, Saudi Arabia that killed 29; the May 2003 suicide bombings in Casablanca, Morocco that killed 41; the suicide attacks of November 2003 in Istanbul, Turkey; and the coordinated, simultaneous train bombings in Madrid, Spain of March 2004. Al-Qaeda recruited fighters and members of the Abu Musab az-Zarqawi cell plagued Iraq with terrorist attacks in 2004, while a group called "Al-Qaeda in the Arabian Peninsula" posed an alarming threat to the Saudi Kingdom in May and June 2004.

In short, al-Qaeda still poses a threat to international security, even after several spectacular arrests, including the apprehension of Khaled Shaykh Muhammed (the alleged master-mind of the September 11 attacks), Abu Zubayda (a senior logistics officer), and Hambali (the senior operational planner in Southeast Asia). The crackdown forced the already elusive al-Qaeda network to become even more decentralized, making it harder to counter. In the face of U.S.-led counterterrorism operations, the network has carried out an attack, on average, every three months.[6]

Continued attacks are a testament to al-Qaeda's very structure. Before Operation Enduring Freedom, al-Qaeda was somewhat hierarchal and centralized. Now, a new and decentralized *movement* (not an organization) has emerged. As former CIA director George Tenet noted, the U.S. is battling a "global movement infected by al-Qaeda's radical agenda"[7] (see Appendix C). Even if Osama bin Laden lives for another twenty years, he will play a less central role in the organization. Under al-Qaeda's post-Afghanistan structure, its leaders can simply provide ideological inspiration or a small sum of money to individuals who are willing to carry out terrorist attacks on their own. Al-Qaeda already serves as a sort of foundation, providing grants to local terror squads who pledge to carry out attacks in the name of al-Qaeda and its interests.[8]

This concept of unconventional terrorist group structures has been discussed at great length elsewhere. One RAND Corporation study predicted in 1999 that, "'great man' leaderships will give way to flatter decentralized designs. More effort will go into building arrays of transnationally internetted groups than into building stand-alone groups."[9] These groups, the study notes, "consist of dispersed small groups who communicate, coordinate, and conduct their campaigns in an internetted manner, without command."[10] Today, such structures have clearly emerged in al-Qaeda's ranks. Because there is limited contact between groups, which lessens the risk of penetration, they are increasingly effective.

Thus, an al-Qaeda structure does actually exist. The groups that comprise this amorphous network can be broken down into two categories: cells and affiliates. Cells are small, autonomous clusters of al-Qaeda operatives that may either be dormant or active in a host country. Cells are made up of only a handful of committed individuals who operate clandestinely; their activities range from providing financing and logistics to carrying out attacks. Unknown numbers of al-Qaeda cells are thought to exist today in some 80 countries.[11]

Affiliates - the focus of this book - are homegrown, organic Islamist terror groups with nationalist objectives. Their members are often al-Qaeda operatives from training camps, the Afghanistan War, or other al-Qaeda battlefields, and are known to communicate with al-Qaeda's command structure. Another attribute of many affiliates is their affinity for al-Qaeda's ascetic and militant approach to the implementation of Islamic law, and their shared goal of world Islamic dominance. Some of these groups are reluctant to identify explicitly with al-Qaeda, due to the risk that open affiliation might make them the target of increased counterterrorism operations from their host countries, or even the American military. Others, by contrast, brazenly identify with bin Laden, his network, and his goals.

There are, of course, questions as to which organizations and individuals fall under the al-Qaeda umbrella. This question, writes terrorism expert Bruce Hoffman, "provokes more disagreement than agreement in government, intelligence and academic circles..."[12] There are debates surrounding some of the affiliates discussed in this book. It is known, however, that in the late 1990s bin Laden brokered alliances with local Islamist groups worldwide. According to two former U.S. government counterterrorism specialists, al-Qaeda "subsidizes indigenous

Islamist groups in their fight against the 'near enemy.'"[13] This strategy is a testament to the al-Qaeda ideology and its pragmatic strategy of working with diverse organizations.

Ayman az-Zawahiri, al-Qaeda's top ideologue, wrote, "A jihadist movement needs an arena that would act like an incubator where its seeds would grow and where it can acquire practical experience in combat, politics, and organizational matters."[14] Bin Laden, himself, also stated in an audiotape that al-Qaeda implores "good Muslims to help in any way they can to join the forces and... overthrow the leaderships that work as slaves for America."[15] In this way, al-Qaeda seeks to make the struggle of the smaller militant group an al-Qaeda struggle, furthering the utopian, Islamist vision that the world will succumb to Islam one battle at a time. In other words, al-Qaeda gains access to smaller groups by pledging to help them achieve their regional goals, but soon wields them as tools in pursuing its wider aim of global jihad.[16]

To this end, in February 1998, bin Laden announced the creation of an umbrella organization called "The Islamic World Front for the Struggle Against the Jews and the Crusaders." Bin Laden stated that Muslims should "kill the Americans and their allies – civilians and military"[17] wherever they were found. Under this front, bin Laden boasted signatures from representatives of several affiliates, including Egypt's al-Gamaa al-Islamiyya (led by Rifa'i Ahmad Taha) and al-Jihad (led by Ayman az-Zawahiri), the Jihad movement in Bangladesh (led by Fazlul Rahman), Jamiat ul-Ulema e-Pakistan (led by Shaykh Mir Hamza), and the Advice and Reform Committee (a bin Laden initiative designed to undermine Saudi Arabia).[18]

Today, while there are numerous cells and informal al-Qaeda clusters working around the globe, al-Qaeda's affiliates are thought to number between 30 and 40.[19] The average affiliate has about five hundred fighters, which means that there are thousands of fighters in their ranks. Affiliates in the Arab world include:

Asbat al-Ansar (Lebanon), the Salafist Group for Preaching and Combat (Algeria), the Armed Islamic Group (Algeria), Ansar al-Islam (Iraq), and the Islamic Army of Aden (Yemen). Other affiliates that have made headlines in recent years in other parts of the world include, but are certainly not limited to: al-Ittihad (Somalia), Jaysh Muhammed (Pakistan), the Islamic Movement of Uzbekistan, Laskar-e-Taiba (Pakistan), the Moro Islamic Liberation Front (Philippines), Jemaah Islamiya (Indonesia), and Abu Sayyaf (Philippines).[20]

These and other affiliates were listed in President Bush's September 23, 2001 executive order (13224), labeling them as security threats to America (see Appendix B). Since then, the U.S. has backed its legislation with military action. Through cooperation with local forces, the U.S. has steadily weakened Abu Sayyaf in the Philippines. It also pummeled the enclave of the Iraqi Ansar al-Islam during the war against Iraq in the spring of 2003. Still, many other listed groups have gone virtually untouched, and therefore continue to thrive.

Experts now believe that al-Qaeda has adjusted to this restricted environment, however, by relying more on the infrastructure of the surviving affiliated groups and individuals.[21] Under this informal system, an affiliate "shares expertise, transfers resources, discusses strategy and even conducts joint operations" with other like-minded groups.[22] These affiliates also offer "leadership, recruitment, training and logistics to the global network, allowing the organization to function largely undisturbed."[23]

Al-Qaeda has been able to rely on these groups because they are typically considered the second tier of looming al-Qaeda threats. These affiliates are often overlooked because they are relatively small and operate in areas outside the reach of state authority. But the fact that they operate in areas outside of government control should sound an alarm. Al-Qaeda and its affiliates have historically preyed upon areas of weak central authority and weak states. After Afghanistan, remote areas in Pakistan became the network's next staging ground, thanks to a history of unstable governments and military coups. In the meantime, al-Qaeda continues to operate under similar conditions elsewhere, including the unstable and overpopulated nations of Indonesia and the Philippines, the war-torn areas of Chechnya and Kashmir, and the "tri-border area" that joins Argentina, Brazil, and Paraguay. Accordingly, it is important to examine the connection between terror groups and weak central authority.

Much attention has been placed on the notion of "failed states" in recent years. The nightmares of Afghanistan and Sudan clearly demonstrated that failed states could likewise play host to international terror organizations. The definition of a failed state can vary, but it is commonly defined by the inability to achieve the characteristics described by Max Weber in his definition of a state. In addition to authority "over all action taking place in the area of its jurisdiction," Weber writes, "the claim of the modern state to monopolize the use of force is as essential to it as its character of compulsory jurisdiction and of continuous organization."[24] Failed or failing states cannot project or assert authority within their own borders, making them particularly susceptible to internal violence. They are often characterized by deteriorating living standards, corruption, a marked lack of civil society, and fewer services.[25] It should then come as no surprise that terror groups are particularly active in states where the regime cannot or will not properly challenge them.[26]

President George W. Bush, in September 2002, openly recognized that such failed states "can pose as great a danger to our national interests as strong states. Poverty does not make poor people into terrorists and murderers. Yet poverty, weak institutions, and corruption can make weak states vulnerable to terrorist networks and drug cartels within their borders."[27] State failure, then, is a phenomenon that has the potential to threaten global stability. Conversely, the strong nation state has emerged as a primary component for ensuring stability and order.[28]

"Weak states" are a similar concern. The U.S. government describes these nations as those that, "lack the legal framework, training or technical capabilities to fight money laundering. Others do not have the law enforcement, intelligence or military capabilities to assert effective control over their entire territory."[29]

In the war against al-Qaeda and its affiliates, however, the focus cannot be limited to failed states or weak states. Even if a state is relatively strong, if there are pockets of weak government control, terrorism can still proliferate. Thus, it is crucial to address what the U.S. government calls "ungoverned spaces" or "ungoverned territory."[30] The Israeli government calls such areas "X territories."[31]   Similarly, French terrorism scholar Xavier Raufer warned in the 1980s of impending battles in "gray areas." He noted that unruly territories, often colored gray on maps to denote political non-alignment, are "areas from which the nation-state has disappeared for good and where the real power is exercised by coalitions between guerrillas or militias."[32]

While gray areas exist the world over, the Arab world is arguably a region where ungoverned spaces and failed or failing states appear with increasing frequency. It may also be the region where al-Qaeda's cells and affiliates are most deeply rooted. There are several reasons for this. In the Arab world, leaders may control the state through military means, but often the state remains weak. Lebanese journalist Hazem Saghiyeh draws a distinction between *Sulta*, or governance, bolstered by the military, and *Dawla*, or state, which includes education, welfare, and other important services. "In cases where the Sulta is stronger than the Dawla," Saghiyeh explains, "the state is largely confined to the capital and big cities."[33]

In the Arab world, the "gray areas" of the recent past have

become the well-entrenched homes of today's terrorist groups. The Iran-backed Hizbullah, founded in the early 1980s, inhabits the lawless Beqaa Valley, and now southern Lebanon since the Israeli withdrawal in May 2000. Hamas and Islamic Jihad, Palestinian groups that first gained popularity in the *intifada* of the late 1980s, continue to operate relatively freely due to weak central authority in the Palestinian territories. Al-Qaeda, for its part, operated during its formative years in two states (upon the invitation of the local government) known for weak central authority: Sudan (1992-1996) and Afghanistan (1996-2001).

That is not to say that militant Islam derives exclusively from geographical, economical, or sociological reasons, but areas of weak central authority can often offer a safe haven. Accordingly, this book examines the clear connection between areas of weak central authority and the continued expansion of al-Qaeda affiliates in the Middle East.

The affiliates addressed in this work include: Lebanon's Asbat al-Ansar (in the Ein al-Hilweh refugee camp); Yemen's Islamic Army of Aden (in three or more lawless, tribal provinces); Iraq's Ansar al-Islam (in the northern Kurdish enclave); Algeria's Salafist Group for Preaching and Combat (operating throughout Algeria, where the government continues to struggle for control), and a brief account of Egypt's al-Gamaa al-Islamiyya and al-Jihad. Both of these groups grew in Egypt's south, but are today believed to be largely defeated. Their stories, however, illustrate how organic Islamist groups with narrow, local, or national objectives can eventually come under the influence of bin Laden's network. In each affiliate studied in this book, it is clear that a potent combination of al-Qaeda support and weak central authority allowed the groups to exist or expand.

Al-Qaeda's Armies endeavors to facilitate an understanding of the new al-Qaeda by shedding light on the affiliate phenomenon. The origins, histories, and capabilities of these groups help explain how al-Qaeda can exist without its core leadership. Thus, as the U.S. and its allies snipe at the leadership core of al-Qaeda, affiliates will increasingly constitute al-Qaeda's outer perimeter and the pools from which new terrorists can be drawn. Indeed, al-Qaeda affiliates, in the Arab world and beyond, represent the next generation of the global terrorist threat.

Notes

1 Rohan Gunaratna, "The Post-Madrid Face of Al Qaeda," *Washington Quarterly*, Summer 2004, p.93.
2 "Iraq War 'Swells al-Qaeda Ranks'," *Reuters*, October 15, 2003.
3 David E. Kaplan, "Playing Offense: The Inside Story of how U.S. Terrorist Hunters are Going After al-Qaeda," *U.S. News and World Report*, June 2, 2003. Also see Bill Gertz, "Eroded al Qaeda Still a Threat," *Washington Times*, January 16, 2004.
4 Daniel Benjamin and Steven Simon, *The Age of Sacred Terror: Radical Islam's War Against America*, Revised Edition (NY: Random House, 2003), p. 452.
5 Douglas Farah, "Al Qaeda's Finances Ample, Say Probers," *Washington Post*, December 14, 2003.
6 Rohan Gunaratna, "The Post-Madrid Face of Al Qaeda," *Washington Quarterly*, Summer 2004, p. 93.
7 George J. Tenet, "The Worldwide Threat 2004: Challenges in a Changing Global Context," Testimony before the Senate Select Committee on Intelligence, February 24, 2004. http://www.cia.gov/cia/public_affairs/speeches/2004/dci_speech_02142004.html
8 Audrey Cronin, "Al-Qaeda After the Iraq Conflict," *Congressional Research Service*, May 23, 2003, p. 3.http://fpc.state.gov/documents/organization/21191.pdf

9   Ian O. Lesser, et al. *Countering The New Terrorism*, (Santa Monica, CA: RAND, 1999), p .41.
10 Ian O. Lesser, et al., p. 47.
11 David E. Kaplan, "Playing Offense: The Inside Story of how U.S. Terrorist Hunters are Going After al-Qaeda," *U.S. News and World Report*, June 2, 2003.
12 Bruce Hoffman, *Al-Qaeda, Trends in Terrorism and Future Potentialities: An Assessment*, (Washington, DC: RAND, 2003), p. 4.
13 Daniel Benjamin and Steven Simon, p. 452.
14 "Ash-Sharq Al-Awsat Publishes Extracts from Al-Jihad Leader Az-Zawahiri's New Book," *Ash-Sharq al-Awsat* (London), December 1, 2002.
15 Daniel Benjamin and Steven Simon, p. 460.
16 Bruce Hoffman, p. 18.
17 Yonah Alexander and Michael S. Swetnam, *Usama bin Laden's al-Qaida: Profile of a Terrorist Network*. (NY: Transnational Publishers, 2001), Appendix 1B.
18 Yonah Alexander and Michael S. Swetnam, Appendix 1B.
19 Betsy Pisik, "108 Nations Decline to Pursue Terrorists," *Washington Times*, December 2, 2003.
20 Yonah Alexander and Michael S. Swetnam, p. 30.
21 Rohan Gunaratna, *Inside Al Qaeda: Global Network of Terror*, (NY: Columbia University Press, 2002), p. 235. Also see Jessica Stern, Terror in the *Name of God: Why Religious Militants Kill*, (NY: HarperCollins, 2003), p. 269.
22 Rohan Gunaratna, *Inside Al Qaeda: Global Network of Terror,* p. 95.
23 Rohan Gunaratna, *Inside Al Qaeda: Global Network of Terror,* p. 54-55.
24 Max Weber, *The Theory of Social and Economic Organization*, ed: Talcott Parsons, (NY: Free Press, 1964), p. 156.
25 Robert I. Rotberg, "Failed States in A World of Terror," *Foreign Affairs*, July/August 2002 (81:4), pp. 128-129.
26 Jessica Stern, *Terror in the Name of God: Why Religious Militants Kill*, (NY: HarperCollins, 2003), p. 272.
27 President George W. Bush, September 17, 2002.
http://www.whitehouse.gov/nsc/nssintro.html
28 Robert I. Rotberg, "Failed States in A World of Terror," *Foreign Affairs*, July/August 2002 (81:4), p. 130.
29 National Strategy for Combatting Terrorism,
http://usinfo.state.gov/topical/pol/terror/strategy/ (February 2003), p. 20.
30 "Background Briefing with Traveling Press Corps, Santiago, Chile," November 18, 2002.
http://www.defenselink.mil/news/Nov2002/t11192002_t118bkgd.html . See also, National Strategy for Combatting Terrorism,
http://usinfo.state.gov/topical/pol/terror/strategy/ (February 2003), p. 22.
31 Author's interview with Israeli official, Tel Aviv, June 24, 2003.
32 Xavier Raufer, "New World Disorder, New Terrorisms: New Threats for the Corporate, Computer and National Security," Center for the Study of Contemporary Criminal Menace, November 1998.
33 Author's interview with Hazem Saghiyeh, Washington, DC., March 8, 2003.

Chapter Two: Learning from Upper Egypt

It is too simplistic to assert that any group with financial or logistical ties to al-Qaeda is an affiliate. After all, it has been established that members of Hizbullah and Hamas have had ties to individual members of the al-Qaeda network through joint training exercises and financial "charities," but this does not necessarily make them affiliates.[1] Nor should we assume that the occasional meeting or communication constitutes al-Qaeda affiliation. To properly grasp the characteristics of al-Qaeda affiliates, it is helpful to review the cases of Egyptian al-Jihad al-Islami and al-Gamaa al-Islamiyya, two of the al-Qaeda network's first affiliates. These groups developed over three decades, launching a terror campaign that killed more than 1,500 people, including government officials, military personnel, tourists, and indigenous Coptic Christians.[2] During the 1990s, both groups began to carry out attacks against Western interests in Egypt and abroad, due in part to expanding ties with al-Qaeda. Eventually, factions of both groups declared open affiliation with the al-Qaeda network.

Unlike the subsequent studies in this book, this chapter is, by design, relatively brief and less comprehensive. The Egyptian affiliates have been thoroughly studied elsewhere.[3] For the purposes of this book, aspects of al-Jihad and al-Gamaa present a particularly useful framework for understanding the al-Qaeda affiliate concept, and its dangerous precedent.

Exploiting Weak Central Authority

While Egypt is undoubtedly a strong state relative to others in the Middle East, the southern area of the country, known as Upper Egypt (the region is known as "upper" because the Nile River flows from the south to the north) remains an area of considerably weaker central authority relative to Egypt's north, which is home to both Alexandria and Cairo.

While today the numbers of al-Jihad and al-Gamaa have dwindled and lack the strength they had at their most active periods in the 1970s, 1980s and 1990s, their traditional stronghold was Upper Egypt, also known as the "Sa'id," the string of poverty-stricken towns along the Nile River stretching south from the pharaonic pyramids to the Aswan Dam. They include Beni Suif, Minya, Mallawi, Asyut, Sohag, Qena and Luxor – areas that are traditionally less developed, less educated, and less influenced by the outside world. French scholar Gilles Kepel writes that before the government took measures there, "the state's presence was barely perceptible at the local level, where private interests controlled everything, and this, in turn, encouraged pockets of dissidence that had a long history in this environment."[4]

It is important to note here, however, that the roots of radicalism in Upper Egypt grew from the Muslim Brotherhood, or al-Ikhwan al-Muslimin, a movement that formed in the Nile Delta in Lower Egypt. The Brotherhood was founded by Hassan al-Banna in the late 1920s, and received further impetus from radical ideologue Sayyid Qutb in the 1950s and 1960s. Both men were based in the north. Over time the movement migrated south where al-Gamaa and al-Jihad thrived. While radical Islam still exists throughout Egypt, the movement undoubtedly took root in Upper Egypt more than in any other area, due to the weaker government authority there.

Radical, Local, and Organic

Affiliates are traditionally independent, grass roots Islamist organizations first. Often after several years of contact with the al-Qaeda leadership, they join the broader al-Qaeda network as affiliates. In some cases, however, new affiliates are born with the assistance of al-Qaeda leadership, which can come in the form of financing, weapons, or ideological indoctrination. These affiliate groups can also be built upon the infrastructure of previously existing groups.

Al-Gamaa al-Islamiyya, for its part, emerged as a loose grouping of independent Islamist organizations in Upper Egypt in the early 1970s, almost two decades before al-Qaeda was formed. They received additional support after Saudi Arabia launched a multi-million dollar, global Islamist campaign to counter communism and atheism.[5] This campaign, supported by Egyptian President Anwar as-Sadat, primarily sought to weaken the influence of communism at universities.

By 1976 and 1977, al-Gamaa secured leadership in student unions throughout Egypt.[6] Driving them was a strong, ascetic interpretation of militant Islam, backed by grass roots schools, health clinics, mosques, and other civic services, which were not sanctioned by the state, but were absolutely vital for creating sympathy, legitimacy, and a fertile environment for recruitment.[7] Some students of al-Gamaa began to agitate for "change by force" against the authoritarian, secular Egyptian regime. At the Universities of Minya and Asyut, clashes erupted between moderates and radicals.[8]

By 1979, around the time when Sadat signed the Camp David Accords with Israel, al-Gamaa's groups united under a single banner, and were led by Asyut-based cleric Omar abd ar-Rahman.[9] Concurrently, in the late 1970s, another group emerged in Upper Egypt named al-Jihad al-Islami (al-Jihad). They too rejected peace with Israel, and cooperated closely with al-Gamaa. But while al-Gamaa sought to carry out small-scale violence, al-Jihad sought a strategy of more spectacular attacks. It would still be years before either group became affiliates of al-Qaeda.

Training in Afghanistan

In 1979, the Soviet Union invaded Afghanistan, installing a communist puppet regime. The Muslim world was enraged, prompting irregular fighters from around the world to flood

Afghanistan and fight the communists. Conscription to fight the Soviets was popular throughout the Arab world, and Egypt in particular. In February 1979, Islamists held a conference at the University of Minya, imploring Egyptians to enlist.[10] The airport in Qena was said to be a depot for weapons and volunteers.[11]

A young Islamist named Ayman az-Zawahiri, under pressure from the Egyptian government for his anti-regime activities, soon left Egypt for Afghanistan, where he would be able to operate more freely. He met Osama bin Laden there in 1986, and their terrorist collaboration began.[12] Az-Zawahiri later became the leader of al-Jihad, and the second-in-command of al-Qaeda.

Other Egyptians went to Afghanistan in three waves over the following decade. Official sources claim that some 600 Egyptians were mujahedin.[13] Other estimates suggest the number may have been three times that. According to the Islamist lawyer from Egypt, Montasser az-Zayyat:

> Many young people traveled to Afghanistan to take part in fighting the Soviets and freeing Kabul from communist occupation. Az-Zawahiri, whose relationship with Osama bin Laden was very good, could offer a good reception to young travelers arriving in the camps that bin Laden had established. There he offered them training and mental and political preparation for their battle. This atmosphere facilitated az-Zawahiri's efforts to tighten control over newcomers and recruit them into his new movement which he hoped will achieve the aim that he had worked toward all his life: toppling the regime in Egypt."[14]

In Afghanistan, the lawyers, doctors, engineers and military men from Egypt brought a degree of sophistication and organization to the jihad. Many of these fighters, in keeping with az-Zawahiri's vision, eventually returned to their home countries and, using lessons from the battlefield, organized small jihadi organizations that would eventually become some of al-Qaeda's affiliate groups. Afghanistan was the origin of the connection between the future al-Qaeda core leadership and local Islamist fighters from Egypt and elsewhere. When the jihad ended, the fighters returned to their respective home countries, but maintained strong connections with their brothers-in-arms. In this way, a global matrix was born.

Attacking the "Near Enemy"

Affiliate groups usually form in opposition to the local regime, which the members see as corrupt, too secular, non-representative, or otherwise illegitimate. Accordingly, these groups originally set their sights on local targets. Al-Jihad and al-Gamaa were no exception. On October 6, 1981, Egyptian Army Lieutenant Khaled Islambouli assassinated Sadat and seven others with an automatic rifle at close range. Islambouli's 1982 trial revealed that he was part of a 24-man al-Jihad cell from Upper Egypt.[15] Among them were Omar abd ar-Rahman and Ayman az-Zawahiri, the future leader of al-Jihad. After Sadat's assassination, az-Zawahiri was jailed in Egypt on weapons charges for three years.[16]

Interestingly, both al-Jihad and al-Gamaa were involved in Sadat's assassination.[17] Concurrent to the assassination, al-Gamaa launched an uprising in the Upper Egyptian town of Asyut. Cairo maintained control, despite an Islamist offensive that killed "tens of officers and soldiers."[18] New Egyptian president Hosni Mubarak subsequently crushed Islamist groups throughout Upper Egypt, arresting thousands. He cracked down on the unlicensed mosques and implemented a state of emergency that is still in effect to this day, more than two decades later.

Still vowing to overthrow the state, both groups issued radical manifestos in 1984. Al-Jihad issued *The Philosophy of Confrontation* and al-Gamaa published *The Program for Islamic Action*.[19] Abd ar-Rahman, for his part, agitated for an Islamic theocracy, rather than a secular regime that cooperated with Israel.

He also issued an edict authorizing attacks that looted the businesses of Egypt's Christian Copts to help bankroll the ongoing jihad.

Smaller violent incidents were subsequently reported throughout Upper Egypt in the early 1990s, including attacks on liquor stores, theaters, and government mosques from Fayoum to Asyut.[20] By 1992, as ties to the nascent al-Qaeda were established, the terror campaign expanded to include attacks on prominent moderates and tourists, in addition to bank and train robberies, while sporadic attacks continued against the Copts.[21] There were also several higher profile attacks over the span of a few years, including a 1992 attack on a tour bus full of Germans in Qena (designed to debilitate Egypt's tourism industry), a 1993 attempt by al-Jihad to assassinate Egypt's former minister of the interior, Hassan al-Alfi,[22] and a 1994 car bomb attempt on Egyptian Prime Minister Atif Sidqi.[23]

Cooperation between Al-Qaeda and Affiliate Leaders

Every affiliate eventually makes the transition from operating solely as a local terror group to becoming a part of the larger network. In some cases, that transition is marked by increased cooperation between the affiliate's leadership and key al-Qaeda lieutenants and/or operatives.

For Egypt's Islamist groups, the transformation likely began to take form when al-Qaeda established a semi-formal presence in neighboring Sudan, which lasted from 1992 to 1996. Several leaders from Egypt's Islamist groups took this opportunity to establish closer ties with the nascent al-Qaeda network. Among the high profile Egyptians based in Khartoum were az-Zawahiri, the future deputy to bin Laden, and Muhammed Atef, al-Qaeda's deputy chief of operations in the early 1990s.[24] Another prominent Egyptian was Abdullah Ahmed Abdullah, who became a top financial officer.[25] Al-Qaeda's "Manual of Jihad," compiled in

Sudan between 1993 and 1994, was almost certainly written by al-Gamaa members.[26]

When al-Qaeda's core moved from Khartoum to Afghanistan, Egypt's Islamist leaders moved with them, serving as some of the top al-Qaeda lieutenants alongside the Taliban. Even after the U.S. invasion of Afghanistan in 2001, Egyptian nationals were still core figures in al-Qaeda. In a video released in September 2003, az-Zawahiri is seen walking on a rocky hillside with bin Laden, probably in Pakistan.[27]

Attacks Hinting at al-Qaeda Ties

The most salient and dangerous characteristic of al-Qaeda affiliates is their tendency to serve as contractors for al-Qaeda, striking at targets that meet their local goals, as well as the network's global aims.

February 26, 1993 may have been the day that Egypt's affiliates first demonstrated their links to the emerging network of global terror. On that day, militants attempted to destroy the World Trade Center towers in New York (al-Qaeda would only be successful in bringing the towers down eight years later). In that attack, six people were killed, and some 1,000 were wounded. Mohammed Salameh, Mahmoud Abu Halima and Ramzi Yousef, three men implicated in the plot, belonged to a New Jersey mosque where Omar abd ar-Rahman, the al-Gamaa cleric, had been preaching.[28] Abd ar-Rahman, who was incarcerated in Egypt from 1981 to 1984 for his role in the Sadat assassination, was eventually convicted and jailed in the U.S. for conspiracy to carry out terrorist attacks, which included plans to bomb Manhattan's United Nations and FBI buildings, as well as the George Washington Bridge and the Holland Tunnel.[29]

While it is not known to what extent abd ar-Rahman's followers in Egypt knew about the attack at the World Trade Center, a bomb exploded in Cairo's Tahrir Square less than an hour later, killing four and wounding eighteen. Most reports indicate that no group claimed responsibility; however, at least two sources claim that an al-Gamaa spokesman in Upper Egypt took credit for the nearly simultaneous attack.[30] The close timing of the attacks may well have been a coincidence, but they could also have been a harbinger of al-Qaeda's trademark of multiple and simultaneous attacks. (Examples include the 1998 African embassy bombings, the 2001 attacks on the Pentagon and World Trade Center, the May 2003 bombings in Riyadh, and the string of bombs that rocked Istanbul, Turkey in November 2003.)

Cairo responded to the Tahrir Square attack with increased brutality, and reciprocal Islamist violence ensued. More than 600 people were killed in the two years that followed.[31] In response, al-Gamaa resorted to increasingly daring and more international attacks. The group attempted to assassinate Mubarak in Ethiopia in June 1995.[32] Other attacks included the assassination of an Egyptian attaché in Switzerland, the attempted killing of an Egyptian diplomat in Spain, and a thwarted assassination attempt on Mubarak in Poland.[33]

Perhaps the worst attack abroad was al-Jihad's November 1995 detonation of a car bomb at the Egyptian embassy in Pakistan, which killed 17 people and wounded dozens more. Two former National Security Counsel advisors note that, "Egyptian officials accused bin Laden of involvement in the attack, and, in fact, Ayman az-Zawahiri appears to have played a key role. (The [al-Jihad] leader writes in his memoir that the U.S. embassy in Islamabad was the original target, chosen in retaliation for a Pakistani crackdown on veterans of the Afghan jihad, but that it was too well fortified.)"[34]

Fighting with Al-Qaeda Abroad

Another common trait among affiliates is that their members have often gained experience in al-Qaeda training camps or fought in al-Qaeda wars – other than Afghanistan. Some Islamists belonging to existing or future al-Qaeda affiliates fought alongside al-Qaeda in Chechnya, Bosnia, or even with other clusters around the world.

Egypt's Islamists joined these fronts when they fled the country out of necessity. As Cairo fought back with sweeping arrests, they were forced to either migrate abroad or face arrest. Al-Gamaa and al-Jihad fighters found their way to al-Qaeda bases in Afghanistan, Sudan, Somalia, Burundi, Yemen, Bosnia, Croatia, and elsewhere.[35] Additional reports emerged of al-Gamaa members fighting with the Moro Islamic Liberation Front, an al-Qaeda affiliate in the Philippines.[36]

A 1999 trial in Egypt also shed light on al-Jihad's activities in Albania.[37] The evidence extracted is worth reviewing, if only for the fact that al-Qaeda fighters from al-Jihad gravitated to the former communist country while the regime collapsed between 1990 and 1992. They remained there as the country embarked upon the difficult transition to democracy. In other words, al-Jihad and al-Qaeda established new bases of operation by exploiting the weak central authority in Albania. Once established there, some 20 militants worked for Islamic charities while they simultaneously raised funds to set up jihadi training camps. Intimately involved in other al-Qaeda activities around the globe, they trained recruits in bomb making, document forgery, and other illicit activities.[38]

Fighting on Two Fronts

With a traditional focus on domestic targets, coupled with the outside influence of al-Qaeda to focus on global issues, affiliates often fight on two fronts. Indeed, groups associated with al-Qaeda will attack Western interests in the name of the global jihadi network, but often continue to attack targets at home, reflecting the affiliate's original aims of domestic opposition.

By 1996, the Taliban had conquered most of Afghanistan,

and Egypt's two most radical groups followed bin Laden and his lieutenants from Sudan to Afghanistan. The sanctuary provided by the Taliban allowed al-Jihad and al-Gamaa to conduct operations "against targets inside Egypt, while their leadership was beyond the reach of retaliation."[39] Radical groups from other parts of the Muslim world that sought refuge in Afghanistan also influenced al-Jihad and al-Gamaa. Indeed, contact with these groups served to widen their scope of violence and hatred toward the West.

While al-Jihad and al-Gamaa were linked to spectacular attacks abroad, significant violence continued to occur in Egypt; some 195 fatalities were reported in 1997 alone.[40] The radicals, for their part, targeted Coptic Christians,[41] tourists, and even fellow Muslims.[42] On November 17, 1997, al-Gamaa carried out a grisly attack that was both local and international in nature; terrorists entered a popular tourist site in the southern Egyptian town of Luxor, killing 62 tourists in cold blood. The killers walked calmly through the Temple of Hatshepsut for 45 minutes, shooting Swiss, Japanese, German and British visitors one by one. A statement found amidst the dead left little doubt that the culprits belonged to al-Gamaa. The effect was chilling: a blow to Egypt's lucrative tourism industry and a strike against the West.

Officially Affiliated?

Most Islamist groups affiliated with the al-Qaeda network would never openly admit their affiliation. Such identification would only provide more ammunition for local governments seeking to destroy them, particularly in a heightened counterterrorism environment. Egypt's affiliates broke the mold, openly affiliating with bin Laden and his network in 1998.

While the horrors of Luxor were still fresh, on February 23, 1998, Egypt's Islamist leaders-in-exile announced their new and radical path. Az-Zawahiri, representing al-Jihad, and Refa'i Ahmad Taha, representing al-Gamaa, joined bin Laden's World Islamic

Front, which publicly declared its goal of waging a holy war "against Jews and Crusaders," imploring all Muslims to "kill the Americans," making both groups official al-Qaeda affiliates in the eyes of the West.[43]

While it is worth noting that Taha later rescinded his name from the Front (or may not have willingly signed it in the first place, as az-Zayyat suggests), it seems certain that many al-Gamaa militants had integrated with al-Qaeda nonetheless.[44] Bin Laden had been funding the travels of al-Gamaa fighters from Egypt to Afghanistan, where al-Qaeda had been based since 1996.[45] Az-Zawahiri, meanwhile, officially resigned from the al-Jihad leadership, keeping some 200 al-Jihad fighters with him in Afghanistan.[46] Today, az-Zawahiri continues to issue radical communiqués, and has published a number of inflammatory writings exhorting Muslims to join al-Qaeda's holy war, including a 2002 book entitled *Fursan Taht ar-Rayat an-Nabi*, or "Horsemen under the Prophet's Banner."[47]

Defeatable

While al-Jihad and al-Gamaa al-Islamiyya were among the first al-Qaeda affiliates to emerge, they were also the first to recede. After three decades of clashes, Cairo managed to crush these radical organizations but paid a heavy price. The government, over three decades, had arrested some 23,000 people, according to estimates by human rights officials. Most were detained for long periods of time without due process of law.[48] Other allegations include torture of suspected militants in prison, threats to the families of suspects, and other heavy-handed measures. These measures have led to a general lack of confidence in the regime, both at home and abroad.

The government achieved something unprecedented, however. It cornered many Islamists in Egypt into promoting nonviolence. Cairo expended a great deal of effort to coerce al-Gamaa's "historical leaders" inside Egypt's jails to call for a ceasefire in 1997.[49] Al-Jihad experienced a different transformation. Harvard University lecturer Jessica Stern notes that, "in May 1997 Zawahiri decided that it would be practical to shift his sights away from the 'near enemy,' the secular rulers of Egypt, toward the 'far enemy,' the West and the United States."[50]

Whereas al-Gamaa and al-Jihad were once seen as archetypical al-Qaeda affiliates, today they are anomalies because they have been largely defeated, with the exception of small cells that still maintain contact with the larger network. Since 1997, Cairo has reported sporadic arrests of Islamist cells, but Egypt has been remarkably quiet.

After 9/11, the U.S. pressured Cairo to step up the fight against al-Qaeda and Egyptian radicals.[51] Mohammed Atta, an Egyptian, held a leadership and operational role in the 9/11 attacks, while az-Zawahiri was heavily implicated in the planning. Indeed, az-Zawahiri appeared at bin Laden's side, along with Abu Hafs al-Masri, on the al-Jazeera television network soon after the attack.[52]

Cairo, meanwhile, continued to press Egypt's Islamists in jail to fully renounce violence. In 2002, the historic membership of al-Gamaa issued a four-volume set of books entitled *Correction of Concepts*, which criticized al-Qaeda's strategy and tactics. In June 2002, al-Gamaa also condemned the September 11 attacks in the government-run *al-Mussawar* magazine.[53] Cairo encouraged the historical leaders to tour Egypt's prisons to explain to other members of the group why al-Gamaa embraced nonviolence.[54] After al-Qaeda bombed a housing complex in Riyadh in November 2003, the traditional leadership issued a statement condemning the attack, calling it "a series of errors," and imploring the leaders of al-Qaeda to "apologize to the parents of the victims."[55] Moderate al-Gamaa member Issam Derbella also published a book in 2003 entitled *Al-Qaeda Strategy: Flaws and Dangers*.[56] Other 2003 publications entitled *River of Memories* and *The Riyadh Explosions– Judgments and Effects* also endorse nonviolence.[57]

Of course, the radical remnants of Egypt's affiliates remain, and could pose a future threat. More importantly, the conditions that allowed for the birth of al-Gamaa and al-Jihad have not been resolved. Despite the fact that these two groups have been militarily defeated, the ideology of radical Islam is still very much alive. Egyptian culture is saturated in Islamism, and Cairo has taken only nominal steps to undermine the message. Evidence of this can be found in the soaring numbers of people supporting the Muslim Brotherhood, Egypt's only legal outlet for opposing the regime under an Islamist banner. Chief among their complaints are the stagnant economy, lack of political freedoms and the near-absence of government transparency. Moreover, suppressing the radical movement was bittersweet. While attacks have diminished, fighters from Egypt's two al-Qaeda affiliates still constitute the core of the world's most dangerous terror organization. In other words, the groups exist in deed, if not in name.

Learning from the Egyptian Paradigm

The broad concepts illustrated by the cases of al-Gamaa and al-Jihad should resonate in the four case studies that follow. Set against this background, al-Qaeda's affiliates in Lebanon, Yemen, Algeria, and Iraq walk the path of their Egyptian predecessors in many obvious ways. They are local and organic Islamist groups with a history of exploiting weak central authority, attacking their domestic governments, training in al-Qaeda's camps and battle-grounds, maintaining ties with the al-Qaeda leadership, expanding their mission to attack U.S. and Western interests, and contributing to the larger al-Qaeda phenomenon. Indeed, they are al-Qaeda's armies.

Notes

1   Matthew Levitt, "Untangling the Terror Web: The Need for a Strategic Understanding of the Crossover Between International Terrorist Groups to Successfully Prosecute the War on Terror," Testimony before the Committee on Banking, Housing, and Urban Affairs, United States Senate, October 22, 2003. http://www.washingtoninstitute.org/media/levitt/levitt102203.htm
2   Nachman Tal, "Islamic Terrorism in Egypt: Challenge and Response," Strategic Assessment, April 1998 (1:1), Jaffee Center for Strategic Studies, pp. 8-9. http://www.tau.ac.il/jcss/sa/v1n1p4_n.html
3   They include: Mustafa Kamel al-Sayyid, "The Other Face of the Islamist Movement," Working Papers (Carnegie Endowment for International Peace), Number 33, January 2003; Gehad Auda and Ammar Ali Hasan, "The Globalization of the Radical Islamic Movement: The case of Egypt," Strategic Papers #120 (Cairo: Al-Ahram Center for Political and Strategic Studies, 2002); Gilles Kepel, *Jihad: The Trail of Political Islam*, (Cambridge, MA: The Belknap Press of Harvard University Press, 2002), pp. 276-298; Hala Mustafa, *Al-Islam as-Siyasi fi Masr: Min Haraka al-Islah ila Gama'at al-Unf*. (Al-Qahira: Gamiya Huquq at-Tab' al-Mahfoutha liMarkaz al-Mahrousa, 1999); Mary Anne Weaver, *A Portrait of Egypt: A Journey Through the World of Militant Islam*, (NY: Farrar Straus and Giroux, 2000).
4   Gilles Kepel, *Jihad: The Trail of Political Islam*, (Cambridge, MA: The Belknap Press of Harvard University Press, 2002), p. 285.
5   Mary Anne Weaver, *A Portrait of Egypt: A Journey Through the World of Militant Islam*, (NY: Farrar Straus and Giroux, 2000), p. 29. Also see Josh Pollack, "Saudi Arabia and the United States, 1931-2002," *MERIA Journal*, Vol. 6. No. 3, September 2002.
6   Gilles Kepel, *Muslim Extremism in Egypt: The Prophet and Pharaoh*, (Berkeley: University of California Press, 1986), p. 144.
7   James Toth, "Islamism in Upper Egypt: A Case Study of a Radical Religious Movement," *International Journal of Middle East Studies*, No. 35 (2003), p. 554.
8   Daniel Pipes, *In the Path of God: Islam and Political Power*, (New Delhi: Voice of India, 1983), p. 210.
9   Montasser al-Zayyat, *The Road to al-Qaeda: The Story of Bin Laden's Right-Hand Man*. (London: Pluto Press, 2004). p. 21.
10   Gehad Auda and Ammar Ali Hasan, "The Globalization of the Radical Islamic Movement: The case of Egypt," *Strategic Papers* #120 (Cairo: Al-Ahram Center for Political and Strategic Studies, 2002), p. 13.
11   Gehad Auda and Ammar Ali Hasan, p. 14.
12   Montasser al-Zayyat, p. 68.
13   Gehad Auda and Ammar Ali Hasan, p. 22.
14   Montasser al-Zayyat, p. 33.
15   Mary Anne Weaver, p. 63.

16   Daniel Benjamin and Steven Simon, p. 103.

17   "Islamism in North Africa II: Egypt's Opportunity," International Crisis Group, Middle East and North Africa Briefing, April 20, 2004, p. 7. See also, al-Zayyat, p. xix.

18   Hala Mustafa, *Al-Islam as-Siyasi fi Masr: Min Haraka al-Islah ila Gama'at al-Unf.* (Al-Qahira: Gamiya Huquq at-Tab' al-Mahfoutha liMarkaz al-Mahrousa, 1999). p. 258.

19   Judith Miller, *God Has Ninety-Nine Names*, (NY: Touchstone, 1996), p. 63.

20   Mustafa, pp. 259-263. Corroborated by a document provided by the United States Embassy in Egypt, June 2003.

21   *Egypt's Endangered Christians 1999: A Report by the Center for Religious Freedom of Freedom House*, (Washington, DC: Center for Religious Freedom, 1999).

22   Lawrence Wright, "The Man Behind Bin Laden: How an Egyptian Doctor Became a Master of Terror," *New Yorker*, September 16, 2002.

23   Lawrence Wright, Sept. 16, 2002.

24   Gehad Auda and Ammar Ali Hasan, p. 42-43.

25   Susan Schmidt and Douglas Farah, "Al Qaeda's New Leaders; Six Militants Emerge From Ranks to Fill Void," *Washington Post*, October 29, 2002.

26   Rohan Gunaratna, p. 72.

27   "New purported bin Laden tape raises fear of new attacks. Audiotape: 'The real battle has not started yet'," *CNN.com*, September 11, 2003, http://www.cnn.com/2003/WORLD/meast/09/10/binladen.tape/

28   Simon Reeve, *The New Jackals: Ramzi Yousef, Osama bin Laden and the Future of Terrorism*, (Boston: Northeastern University Press, 1999), p. 60. Also see: Mary Anne Weaver, p. 74.

29   "US v. Ahmed Abdel Satar, Yassir al-Sirri, Lynne Stewart and Mohammed Yousry," April 9, 2002. *The Al-Qaeda Documents*, Volume 2, (Alexandria, VA: Tempest Publishing, 2003), pp. 81-105.

30   "Afghani Terrorism Around the World," *Executive Intelligence Review*, October 13, 1995. Also see Mary Anne Weaver, p. 109.

31   Muhammed al-Ghumri, *Halat Huquq al-Insan fi Masr: At-Taqrir as-Sanawi 1996*, (Cairo: The Egyptian Organization for Human Rights, 1996), p. 40.

32   "Africa Overview," Patterns of Global Terrorism 1995, (Washington, DC: United States Department of State, April 1996), p. 2.

33   Gehad Auda and Ammar Ali Hasan, p. 31.

34   Daniel Benjamin and Steven Simon, p. 132.

35   Gehad Auda and Ammar Ali Hasan, p. 25.

36   Gehad Auda and Ammar Ali Hasan, p. 30.

37   Susan Sachs, "An Investigation in Egypt Illustrates Al Qaeda's Web," *New York Times*, November 21, 2001.

38   Susan Sachs, Nov. 21, 2001; and Andrew Higgins and Christopher Cooper, "A CIA-Backed Team Used Brutal Mean to Crack Terror Cell: Albanian Agents Captures Egyptians, Who Alleged Torture Back in Cairo," *Wall Street Journal*, November 20, 2001.

39   Gehad Auda and Ammar Ali Hasan, p. 36.

40   Muhammed Munib, *Difa'an an Huquq al-Insan: Al-Juz' al-Khaamis*, (Cairo: The Egyptian Organization for Human Rights, 1997), p. 127.

41   Hamza Hendawi, "Fear Among Copts Intensifies in Egypt Over Muslim Militants' Bloody Campaign," AP, March 22, 1997.

42   Salah Nasrawi, "Egyptian Militants Kill 14 in Attack on Mostly Christian Village," AP, March 14, 1997.

43   Alexander and Swetnam, Appendix 1-b. Some analysts have expressed doubt as to whether Taha willingly penned his name to this declaration.

44   See USA vs. Usama bin Laden, Trial Transcript, Day 2, http://cryptome2.org/usa-v-ubl-02.htm

45   Anonymous, Through Our Enemies Eyes: Osama Bin Laden, Radical Islam, and the Future of America, (Washington, DC: Brassey's, 2002), p. 93.

46   Author's interview with Dia Rashwan, Al-Ahram Center, Cairo, Egypt. June 18, 2003.

47   Mustafa Kamel al-Sayyid, "The Other Face of the Islamist Movement," *Working Papers* (Carnegie Endowment for International Peace), Number 33, January 2003, p. 20.

48   Author's interview with human rights officials, Cairo, Egypt. June 22, 2003.

49   According to some reports, al-Gamaa had made such declarations as early as April 1996. For more on that, see: al-Sayyid, p. 15.

50   Jessica Stern, p. 266.

51   Dia Rashwan, "A New Rapprochement?" *Al-Ahram Weekly*, July 4-10, 2002, No. 593, http://weekly.ahram.org.eg/2002/593/op5.htm

52   Daniel Benjamin and Steven Simon, p. 159.

53   Jailan Halawi, "Time for a Historic Reconciliation," *Al-Ahram Weekly*, June 27-July 3, 2002, No. 592.

54   Mustafa Kamel al-Sayyid, "The Other Face of the Islamist Movement," *Working Papers* (Carnegie Endowment for International Peace), Number 33, January 2003, p. 16.

55   Abd al-Latif al-Manawi, "The Egyptian Gamaa Islamiyya Requests the Leaders of al-Qaeda to Apologize to the Parents of the Victims," *Ash-Sharq al-Awsat*, November 14, 2003.

56   "A Book About al-Qaeda Mistakes," *Ash-Sharq al-Awsat*, August 6, 2003. See also "Egyptian Islamist Leaders Fault al-Qa'ida's Strategy," *Ash-Sharq al-Awsat*, January 11, 2004 [FBIS]. www.fas.org/irp/world/para/ig_bk.htm

57   Tom Perry, "Egyptian Islamist Group Drops Guns, Turns to Print," Reuters, November 29, 2003.

Chapter Three: Lebanon

Citizens of Lebanon were reportedly surprised to learn that Asbat al-Ansar, or the League of Partisans, ranked among the first eleven international terror groups that President George W. Bush listed in his executive order (13224) of September 23, 2001 (see Appendix B). Many expected Bush to designate Hizbullah, the Lebanese group linked to the first suicide bombing against Americans in 1983, but few thought that Asbat al-Ansar, a relatively unknown group, would be labeled a threat to U.S. security in the aftermath of 9/11.

Even today, Asbat al-Ansar rarely makes headlines in the U.S., despite the fact that its leaders have direct ties to al-Qaeda's leadership and many of its members trained or fought with al-Qaeda. In recent years, the group has attacked several Western diplomatic and economic interests, as well as numerous Lebanese targets. The lack of attention to this group, despite its record of grisly violence, likely stems from the fact that Asbat al-Ansar is not a direct player in the Arab-Israeli conflict.

Yet, Asbat al-Ansar is inextricably tied to the conflict, even if it does not target Israel. The group's members are predominantly Palestinian, while militants from around the Arab world, as well as veterans of the Afghan war, augment their membership. Asbat al-Ansar thrives because it is headquartered in one of Lebanon's twelve Palestinian refugee camps.[1] Beirut has refused to administrate these camps for more than three decades for fear of upsetting a volatile Palestinian population that suffers under severe government restrictions. As a result, the camps have become twelve lawless zones throughout Lebanon where terrorism thrives.

The Syrian occupation of Lebanon is a primary reason behind the continued existence of these camps and Asbat al-Ansar. Syria prevents the government of Lebanon from asserting its authority in the camps. Indeed, the pockets of weak central authority in Lebanon exist precisely where Syria wants them to exist. Many Lebanese citizens believe that Syria actually arms the Palestinian camps, making them "security islands" by design. Thus, the radicalization of Lebanon's Palestinian refugee camps is a powerful tool that only Syria can effectively control.

Asbat al-Ansar

The name Asbat al-Ansar is steeped in meaning; Ansar refers to the original group of men who converted to Islam and followed the prophet Muhammed. The group's founding ideologue, Hisham Shreidi, was the former leader of a small Sunni group called al-Jama'a al-Islamiyya. His goals were to establish a strict Islamic order in Lebanon, battle Israel, and weaken Lebanon's Christians.[2] In December 1991, Shreidi was killed by a member of Palestinian Authority Chairman Yasir Arafat's Fatah faction. The incident was one battle among many in a long and bitter power struggle inside Lebanon between the Syrians and Arafat.[3] Shreidi's group was subsequently taken over in the mid-1990's by Ahmad Abd al-Kareem as-Saadi (also known as Abu Mohjin), and became known as Asbat al-Ansar.

Abu Mohjin, now on Lebanon's most-wanted list,[4] was "a prominent leader of the Arab Islamic Fighters Battalion in Chechnya" with proven ties to at least one European al-Qaeda cell.[5] While the group rarely speaks of its goals through communiqués or to the press, the State Department reports that Asbat al-Ansar advocates "overthrowing the Lebanese Government and thwarting perceived anti-Islamic influences in the country," which is clearly in line with al-Qaeda's global objectives.[6]

On September 25, 2001, Asbat al-Ansar issued a statement praising bin Laden but denying its links to al-Qaeda.[7] However, U.S. State Department reports note that Asbat al-Ansar "probably receives money through international Sunni extremist networks and Bin Ladin's al-Qaeda."[8] Its members, numbering about 300, fought in Afghanistan, Bosnia, Chechnya and Kashmir.[9] Indeed, several hundred al-Qaeda veterans arrived in Ein al-Hilweh, Lebanon, after the U.S. invaded Afghanistan.[10] For these fighters, the camp was a safe refuge from Operation Enduring Freedom and a place to regroup, far from the reach of coalition forces.

The group's ties to al-Qaeda are many. Asbat al-Ansar members provided logistical support to al-Qaeda conspirators in Abu Musab az-Zarqawi's millennium plot to attack Western and Christian targets in Jordan.[11] According to one report, an al-Qaeda emissary traveling under the name of Salah Hajir met Asbat's leaders in 2002 to discuss future cooperation.[12] Israeli officials note that the group has good ties with other al-Qaeda affiliates around the world, and particularly cells throughout Western Europe.[13]

Ein al-Hilweh

Asbat al-Ansar's home of Ein al-Hilweh is the largest of Lebanon's twelve Palestinian refugee camps, and it is often referred to as the capital of the Palestinian Diaspora. Located about 30 miles south of Beirut, the camp was established in 1948 with an original population of 9,000.[14] Today, 44,133 refugees are registered in the camp,[15] but as many as 75,000 persons may actually reside there.[16] Even after the United Nations Relief and Works Agency (UNRWA) entered the poverty-stricken Lebanese refugee camps in 1952, Ein al-Hilweh was neglected due to lack of funds for nearly two decades, until Yasir Arafat's Palestinian Liberation Organization (PLO) began to invest in it (and other refugee camps) with donations from oil-rich Gulf states.[17]

PLO factions only began serving Lebanon's refugees, including Ein al-Hilweh, after the 1969 Cairo Agreement, which recognized the PLO as a quasi-governing body for the Palestinians inside Lebanon.[18] After Israel expelled the PLO from Lebanon in 1982, however, Ein al-Hilweh and other camps went neglected again, marking a new and difficult period, despite UNRWA's efforts. In 1985, the Shiite Amal (then a pro-Syria militia) attacked Palestinian refugee camps, including Ein al-Hilweh, in a revenge campaign against the Palestinians, whom they blamed for the 1975-1982 civil war and the resulting, painful Israeli military reprisals.

With the eruption of the first Palestinian intifada in December 1987, Hamas gained popularity in Lebanon's camps, but still could not fill the void of the PLO's empty coffers (the PLO was cut off by many Arab financiers when Arafat sided with Saddam Husayn in the 1991 Gulf War). The 1993 Oslo Accords marked the resumption of Arab aid, as well as help from the West, to the PLO. Thereafter, money trickled back into the camp, although not to the extent enjoyed by the West Bank and Gaza. This financial vacuum enabled other factions (such as Hamas) to gain strength inside the camps.

With help from U.S. peace process money during the 1990s, Arafat eventually bought back many of Fatah's loyalists in Ein al-Hilweh.[19] He was never able to regain complete control, however, thanks largely to Syrian efforts that undercut him. In November 2001 a formal security committee was formed in Ein al-Hilweh,[20] with delegates from a patchwork of factions.[21] Even today, while the committee provides a semblance of governance, its component groups regularly engage in turf clashes. They include: Fatah, Ansar Allah (Hizbullah), al-Ahbash (pro-Syria), Hamas, Palestinian Islamic Jihad, and Asbat al-Ansar.[22] In June 2004, yet another hard-line group called Jund ash-Sham was said to have coalesced in Ein al-Hilweh with support from sponsors in Persian Gulf states.[23]

A History of Fragility

The presence of a multitude of factions (and the resulting chaos) in the Ein al-Hilweh camp is a testament to the fractured political makeup of modern Lebanon. Indeed, Lebanon has long ranked among the Middle East's most fragile and unstable states, due largely to its ethnic diversity. Of its 3.6 million citizens, Lebanon's power is shared delicately among more than a dozen

Christian sects (the largest of which are Maronite) and six Muslim sects (the largest of which are Shi'a).[24] Under the French mandate following World War I, Lebanon ratified a 1926 constitution through which its many ethnicities learned to carefully cooperate. In 1943, the Sunni Muslims and Maronite Christians agreed to an unwritten national pact for a multi-ethnic but unified Lebanon, which apportioned government posts based upon numbers from the Lebanese census of 1932. The presidency went to a Maronite, the prime ministership to a Sunni, and the speaker of parliament to a Shi'a, with the Druze and other ethnicities granted lower level posts. Ethnic tensions remain so great (notably, between Lebanese Shi'as and Palestinian Sunnis) that Lebanon's factions still refuse to conduct another census, after more than seventy years, fearing the tumult that change could bring.

The touchy demographic situation was tested in 1948, with the influx of Palestinians fleeing the first Arab-Israeli war. An estimated 150,000 Palestinians squatted in seventeen Lebanese refugee camps, which were consolidated into twelve after Lebanese militias destroyed several during the Lebanese Civil War. The predominantly Sunni Palestinians were allowed to enter Lebanon, but were refused citizenship due to fears of militancy and tipping Lebanon's ethnic and religious balance.

Lebanon maintained its delicate system until civil strife erupted in 1958, prompted by adherents to Egyptian President Gamal Abd al-Nasser's Pan-Arabist ideology.[25] Many Muslims in Lebanon sought to integrate with Nasser's United Arab Republic, forged between Egypt and Syria that year. The pro-Western Maronites, however, were staunchly opposed.

Calm returned, but was short-lived. Internecine violence plagued Lebanon again in 1968, spurred by Palestinian guerrilla groups. When Lebanon-based guerrillas attacked Israel, Israeli reprisals hammered Lebanese targets. Lebanese turmoil was exacerbated when Jordan expelled the PLO in 1970. Under Arafat, the PLO flooded into Lebanon and created a Palestinian mini-state. From Lebanon, the PLO launched attacks against Israel with increased frequency, while simultaneously provoking Lebanon's other ethnic factions. These factions soon armed themselves, leading to vicious street battles. The situation deteriorated into a devastating civil war in 1975.

After a series of particularly painful PLO terrorist attacks, Israel invaded Lebanon in 1978, withdrew, and then invaded again in 1982, eventually expelling Arafat and the PLO to Tunisia. In the process, Israeli forces devastated Beirut, neutralized the Lebanese threat, and then retained a self-declared "security zone" in south Lebanon until May 2000. Meanwhile, Syria intervened in Lebanon in 1976 with the stated purpose of helping to restore calm. That presence became an occupation, and gradually expanded (West Beirut in 1987 and East Beirut in 1990).

Syrian occupation continues to burden Lebanon. The Syrian regime regularly dumps surplus goods on the Lebanese markets, pilfers water, diverts electricity, and uses the country for illegitimate business enterprises.[26] Worse, the Lebanese military has become a lackey of the Syrian military, inhibiting the enforcement of law, particularly in what are now called "security islands" – places that are left almost completely ungoverned. In two such areas (the Beqaa Valley and after 2000, South Lebanon), Syria continues to support and facilitate the activities of Hizbullah, an Iranian-funded terrorist group that has since forced Lebanon into battles with Israel on more than one occasion. The Ta'if agreement, drafted in 1989, was supposed to have ended the occupation long ago. Endorsed by Syria, the agreement called for Lebanese independence, small changes in the power-sharing agreement, and the redeployment of Syrian troops. These stipulations have yet to be enforced.

Another concern for Lebanon is its burgeoning Palestinian population. A constitutional amendment in 1990 stipulates that there may be "no settlement of non-Lebanese in Lebanon."[27] This amendment was passed for fear of upsetting the delicate balance of Lebanon's religions and ethnicities. Accordingly, suggesting the naturalization of Palestinians, notes Farid al-Khazen, "has become a taboo."[28] Thus, the majority of Lebanon's 370,000 Palestinian refugees reside in twelve teeming camps.[29] Compounding the Palestinians' hardships is the fact that Beirut restricts Palestinian employment in some 70 professions, as well as building, property ownership, education and visas.[30] Large numbers of weapons are still able to freely enter the camps, but materials essential for community development are barred.

Although the Lebanese and Syrian military are posted outside these camps, they will not enter, even amidst unrest. While the roots of this policy date back to the 1969 Cairo Agreement, which ensured "PLO sovereignty over Palestinian military affairs" inside the camps, that agreement means virtually nothing today.[31] Instead, Damascus determines the policies that govern Lebanon, and one of the most dangerous among them is the perpetuation of near-anarchy in the camps, enabling the violence of Asbat al-Ansar (and other factions within the camps) to spiral out of control.

Asbat Violence

Asbat al-Ansar's operational abilities in Lebanon are limited. They are largely confined to Ein al-Hilweh, where the group's record of violence against Lebanese interests is quite bloody. In the early 1990s, the group's predecessors bombed Lebanese nightclubs, theaters, and liquor stores which they believed ran counter to their ascetic vision of Islam. In 1995, the group played a role in assassinating Nizar al-Halabi, leader of the Syrian-sponsored al-Ahbash faction.[32] In 1999, Lebanese military personnel clashed with guerillas affiliated with Asbat al-Ansar (known as the Dinniyeh Group) on the outskirts of Tripoli.[33] An estimated 45 people were killed, including 11 soldiers.[34] These militants were also believed to be behind an explosion at a Customs Department office and the killing of four judges at a courthouse that same year.[35] The Lebanese army eventually put the Dinniyeh Group on the run. Not surprisingly, they sought refuge in the lawless enclave of Ein al-Hilweh.

It was not until 2002, however, that Ein al-Hilweh transformed into a veritable tinderbox. In August of that year, *ash-Sharq al-Awsat* reported, "intense armed presence and reciprocal military alerts between [the] Fatah movement and the Islamic Asbat al-Ansar" in Ein al-Hilweh.[36] There were no fewer than nineteen bombings between September and November, prompting officials to declare a state of emergency in the camp.[37] Asbat's attacks targeted Fatah, the Islamist Hamas (which posed a challenge to Asbat's Islamic authority), Lebanese authorities, and even UNRWA, which provides vital services to residents of the Ein al-Hilweh camp.[38] In May, Asbat's violence reached new heights; the group was responsible for the murder of an American missionary, Bonnie Penner.[39]

Car bombings, shootings, and grenade attacks have become commonplace in Ein al-Hilweh in recent years, but nothing could have prepared residents for the events of May 2003, when Ein al-Hilweh was host to a full-blown battle. The conflict began when Fatah gunmen ambushed the leader of an Asbat splinter faction, Abdullah Shreidi, as he drove home from a funeral. He suffered no fewer than eighteen gunshots to his head, back, and chest.[40] Miraculously, Shreidi survived the attack, and had his kidney removed at a camp hospital. Fatah, however, surrounded the hospital and threatened to storm it. Fearing an incursion, Shreidi's followers

> ...managed to switch electric power off in the camp at night-fall Sunday, and punched a big hole in the hospital's rear wall that allowed 12 of them to sneak into the operating theater. They held doctors and nurses at gunpoint in the corridor while

others lifted their leader onto a stretcher and smuggled him out from the intensive care unit to a small clinic operated by Asbat an-Nur [an Asbat al-Ansar splinter group] in the camp's Safsaf neighborhood, Shreidi's main power base.... Appeals for O-positive urgent blood donations rang out from neighboring mosque minarets to help Shreidi.[41]

Subsequently, a full battle erupted on Ein al-Hilweh's streets. Five hours of clashes on May 19 resulted in the deaths of at least eight, including three Fatah guerrillas and one Islamist,[42] while wounding up to 25.[43] The battles included the use of machine guns, mortar rounds, rocket-propelled grenades, and even armor piercing missiles.[44] Schools and stores were closed, and hundreds of camp residents fled.[45]

On May 20, a ceasefire, brokered by representatives from the camp's many factions, was called so that both sides could bury their dead.[46] At first count, 26 houses were destroyed along with dozens of cars.[47] Shreidi eventually died in February 2004, prompting his surviving Islamist brethren to threaten further violence against the Fatah faction.[48]

Global Terror

While Asbat al-Ansar has been a source of domestic chaos, the group has also targeted international interests inside Lebanon. Fighters from Asbat al-Ansar attacked the Russian Embassy in Beirut with rocket-propelled grenades in January 2000. In 2001, Jordanian and Lebanese security foiled an Asbat attack on the Jordanian, U.S., and British embassies in Lebanon.[49]

In February 2003, according to the *Lebanon Daily Star*, Fatah arrested a North Korean agent named Jim Su Kim, who was suspected of planning to attack U.S. and British targets in Lebanon.[50] Was Kim trying to work with al-Qaeda's Lebanese operatives? There was no follow-up in the Lebanese press, and no official statement from Beirut.

Another alarming incident was reported in March 2003, when Faruq al-Masri – a member of the Egyptian al-Jihad with an established al-Qaeda background – was killed by a car bomb outside a restaurant he owned in Ein al-Hilweh. Al-Masri had lived in the camp since 1997, was a veteran of the Afghanistan war, and was thought to be the head of the al-Qaeda cell that plotted to attack U.S. and Israeli targets in Jordan during the millennium celebrations.[51] Israeli officials further alleged that al-Masri led the faction of Asbat most closely related to Asbat al-Ansar.[52] Al-Masri's position in the al-Qaeda network underscores that the lawlessness of Ein al-Hilweh is not only a Lebanese concern.

Other al-Qaeda operatives from Asbat al-Ansar were believed to be behind other higher profile attacks against international interests in 2003. For instance, Lebanese authorities arrested 22 suspected Asbat members in connection with the April 5 bombing of a McDonald's restaurant in a Beirut suburb. According to the *Lebanon Daily Star*, the suspects took refuge in Ein al-Hilweh.[53] On July 15, Beirut announced the capture of five terrorists from Ein al-Hilweh who allegedly planned to attack a Hardee's restaurant.[54]

Syria's detractors in Lebanon assert that these allegations were Syrian fabrications meant to show the United States that both Syria and its puppet Lebanese authorities were rigorously fighting terrorism, particularly in light of the post-Iraq war tensions between Damascus and Washington.[55] Still, this type of attack against Western fast food restaurant chains is not unusual for al-Qaeda affiliates; it is a signature of the Indonesian affiliate Laskar Jundallah, for example, which attacked a McDonald's in December 2002. A nearby Kentucky Fried Chicken outlet in Indonesia was also attacked the year before.[56] It is certainly conceivable that Asbat al-Ansar was mimicking its Indonesian counterpart.

The *Lebanon Daily Star* later reported that the suspects apprehended for the McDonald's attack were also tied to an attempt to assassinate U.S. ambassador to Lebanon, Vincent Battle, while he was visiting Tripoli.[57] According to the report, they tried to fire an armor-piercing missile at the ambassador's car, but the attack failed.

Again, some Lebanese doubt the veracity of these reports, asserting instead that the plot was concocted by the Syrians to show Washington how committed they were to fighting the war on terror. Still, by mid-May 2003, more than 40 people were held in the bombings and assassination attempt.[58] In December, authorities were still searching for Maheer Saadi, a Palestinian who reportedly received $7,000 from an unspecified source to plan the assassination of Ambassador Battle.[59]

In June 2003, Beirut uncovered a thwarted plot to fire wire-guided rockets against a Russian jetliner at Lebanon's international airport. A few days later, militants launched a successful missile attack against Lebanon's Future TV (FTV) station, owned by Prime Minister Rafik Hariri, and located some 500 meters from his home. Militants fired two timer-rigged missiles from the trunk of a stolen BMW.[60] While Lebanese papers indicated that Hariri was a target because of his strong stand against radical groups, other observers believed the attack bore the hallmarks of al-Qaeda due to Hariri's close ties to the Saudi regime, a long-time target of Osama bin Laden.[61]

Following that attack, Lebanese Interior Minister Elias Murr noted that the "operation must have been planned in one of the country's security isles," a clear reference to the lawless enclave of Ein al-Hilweh. About a month later, Murr told the *As-Safir* newspaper that Asbat al-Ansar was behind the attack, "according to incoming reports from more than one security agency."[62] Not surprisingly, Syria's detractors again asserted that the plot was hatched by Damascus, which harbors a long-lasting animosity toward Hariri.

By autumn, a Lebanese military court accused more than 30

suspects of participating in the "Tripoli Cell" (Khaliyat Tarablus), for attacking the U.S. fast food chains, in addition to a British-owned Spinney's supermarket.[63] As information emerged, the Tripoli Cell was increasingly linked to Asbat al-Ansar. According to the London Arabic daily *al-Hayat*, the cell worked under the direction of Ibn ash-Shahid, a Yemeni member of Asbat al-Ansar, based in Ein al-Hilweh.[64] Also known as Moammar Abdullah al-Awamah, ash-Shahid was arrested in mid-October and was brought to Beirut for further questioning, where it was learned that he paid a number of operatives inside Ein al-Hilweh to execute the McDonald's bombing.[65] Later reports indicated that he also helped plan the attack against Ambassador Battle.[66] The indictment against him, which led to a 25-year jail sentence with hard labor,[67] stated that ash-Shahid had fought alongside al-Qaeda in Chechnya, Bosnia, and Afghanistan, and that he left Afghanistan after the U.S. invaded in late 2001.[68] Several other apprehended members of the Tripoli Cell also admitted to being members of Asbat al-Ansar.

The Aussie Connection

Surprisingly, a linchpin that ties al-Qaeda, Asbat al-Ansar and the Tripoli Cell together is an Australian citizen of Lebanese origin. Bilal Khazal, also known as Abu Suhaib, is head of Australia's Islamic Youth Movement (Ash-Shabab al-Islami), a small but influential group of perhaps 150 members that is suspected of recruiting Islamic radicals.[69] Since 1994, that organization has published a radical, Salafist magazine called *Nidaa ul-Islam* (Call of Islam).

Khazal, according to the *Lebanon Daily Star* and *al-Hayat*, is also a direct "financier" of Asbat al-Ansar and other radical factions inside Ein al-Hilweh. One member of the Tripoli Cell told a Beirut military court that the cell's leader, Mohammed Ka'aki, received cash installments from Khazal for terror attacks.[70] Australian press reports indicate that Khazal has been friends with

Ka'aki since the late 1990s and that Khazal's brother met with Ka'aki in the late 1990s to discuss financing for terror operations in Lebanon.[71] Beirut issued a warrant for Khazal's arrest in June,[72] and a military court later issued him a life sentence in absentia.[73] Beirut subsequently considered extraditing Khazal from Australia, but as of this writing, the matter was unresolved.[74]

Khazal is known to have deeper ties to al-Qaeda's global network of terror. He is believed to be the "organizer" of an illegal weapons training camp several hundred miles outside of Sydney in August 2000.[75] Australian authorities searched his home just before the 2000 Sydney summer Olympics,[76] and in 2001 they confiscated his passport based on the suspicion that he was linked to al-Qaeda.[77] According to a 2002 CIA document that has since circulated in Canberra, "the al-Qaeda leadership has allegedly delegated responsibility" to Khazal in Australia. It cited intelligence, provided by the Palestinian Authority, that he was planning attacks against U.S. targets in the Philippines and Venezuela. The document also claims that Khazal "was in Afghanistan in 1998, where he was affiliated with Ayman az-Zawahiri and Osama bin Laden." [78] Australian authorities now indicate that Khazal is closely linked to Mahmoud Habib, an Australian national incarcerated at the U.S. prison facility in Guantanamo Bay, Cuba.[79] Other intelligence suggests that Khazal met repeatedly with Abu Qatada, a London-based cleric detained in Britain. Formal charges were filed against Qatada in September 2003 for participating in al-Qaeda activities.[80]

The charges against Qatada stem from intelligence that Spanish authorities acquired when they dismantled an al-Qaeda cell in Madrid in November 2001. That intelligence revealed even deeper al-Qaeda participation on the part of Khazal. Court documents revealed that Abu Dahdah (Imad ad-Din al-Yarkas), the cell's leader and a mastermind of the September 11 attacks,[81] was an "important contact" of Khazal's. The Australian Broadcast Corporation reports that Dahdah, who also had close ties with 9/11 terror leader Mohammed Atta, was in "constant contact" with Khazal.[82]   Among other connections, in February 2001, Khazal solicited support from Dahdah to help "a brother" slip into Europe after Italian immigration officials issued him "a stamp prohibiting his entry." Dahdah facilitated the illegal entry and then provided the illegal immigrant with accommodations in Madrid.[83] As of June 2004, Khazal was slated to stand trial in Australia for using the internet to incite religious violence, but was allowed to remain free on bail after friends and relatives posted $200,000 (Australian). If convicted, he could serve 15 years in prison.[84]

The Road Ahead

Attacks continued to be reported regularly in Ein al-Hilweh through 2004, and were generally characterized as tit-for-tat violence between Fatah and Asbat al-Ansar. More worrisome, however, is the threat of violence against international targets. The intersection of Khazal's activities, the Tripoli Cell, and the Madrid Cell demonstrates that Asbat al-Ansar is not the small, insignificant al-Qaeda affiliate Beirut and Damascus would have the world believe. Rather, Khazal's activities establish that the group is inextricably connected to al-Qaeda, with both international links and international targets. Asbat al-Ansar fits the very definition of an al-Qaeda affiliate.

While Israel has its hands full with other threats in the region, including Hizbullah, they note that Asbat al-Ansar could grow if left unchecked. Pentagon and State Department officials admit that they are also less focused on the group given the many other fronts that Washington must face in its war on terror. Accordingly, the U.S. has not sufficiently pressed Beirut, and more importantly Damascus, to take action against Asbat al-Ansar.[85] To date, Lebanon refuses to freeze the assets of Asbat al-Ansar, which is likely a directive from Syria.[86]

In the future, Washington must take Syria to task for its

continued role in the lawlessness of the Lebanese refugee camps. As analyst Habib Malik notes, "the Syrians had until lately perfected the tactic of arming the camps and nurturing radical rejectionist and terrorist groups within them only to step in at the appropriate moment and 'capture' a few of these characters of their own making, so as to signal to the U.S. that they are helping the war on terror."[87]

The Palestinian refugee problem in Lebanon is also central to the problem of Asbat al-Ansar. Beirut and Damascus will not address the issue, insisting that it is an Israeli problem. Their refusal to govern these areas created pockets of weak central authority that al-Qaeda now exploits. They claim that the Palestinian refugee problem inside Lebanon is an integral part of the international Palestinian refugee crisis (which they blame on Israel), and necessitates international solutions. However, it is clear that Asbat al-Ansar is a Lebanese phenomenon and a Syrian problem. The challenge now is for Washington is to push Damascus to clean up the camps and finally rid the region of an al-Qaeda affiliate in the process.

Notes

1   They are: Ein el-Hilweh, Nahr el-Bared, Rashidieh, Burj el-Barajneh, Burj ash-Shemali, Beddawi, Shatila, El-Buss, Wavel, Mieh Mieh, Dbayeh, and Mar Elias.
2   Yael Shahar, "Al-Qaida's Links to Iranian Security Services," International Policy Institute for Counterterrorism, January 20, 2003
http://www.ict.org.il/articles/articledet.cfm?articleid=460
3   Radwan Aqil, "Report on Formation, Growth of Usbat al-Ansar Group in Palestinian Refugee Camp in Lebanon," *Al-Wasat* (London), October 1, 2001 (FBIS).

4   Author's interview with Israeli official, Tel Aviv, Israel. June 27, 2003.
5   Spanish Court Document 35/2000, Central Trial Court #5, Madrid Spain, July 19, 2002. p. 7.
6   "Asbat al-Ansar," http://www.fas.org/irp/world/para/asbat.htm
7   Radwan Aqil, Oct. 1, 2001.
8   "Asbat al-Ansar," http://www.fas.org/irp/world/para/asbat.htm
9   Udo Ulfkotte, "Refuge Lebanon," *Frankfurter Allgemein* (German), February 6, 2002 (FBIS).
10 Damien McElroy, "Al-Qaeda Fighters Set Up Base in Lebanese Refugee Camp," *Daily Telegraph*, June 22, 2003. http://portal.telegraph.co.uk/news/main.jhtml?xml=/news/2003/06/22/walq22.xml
11 Daniel Benjamin and Steven Simon, p. 192.
12 Michael Evans, "Al-Qaeda in Secret Talks with Lebanon Terror Group," *The Times* (London), February 1, 2002.
13 Author's interview/Israeli officials, June 27, 2003.
14 Hilal Khashan, "Palestinian Resettlement in Lebanon: Behind the Debate," April 1994, http://www.arts.mcgill.ca/MEPP/PRRN/papers/khashan.html
15 "Lebanon Refugee Camp Profiles," http://www.un.org/unrwa/refugees/lebanon.html
16 Radwan Aqil, Oct. 1, 2001.
17 Gary Gambill, "Ain al-Hilweh: Lebanon's Zone of Unlaw," *Middle East Intelligence Bulletin*, June 2003, Vol. 5, No. 6., http://www.meib.org/articles/0306_ll.htm
18 "Palestinian Non-Government Organizations in Lebanon" http://www.arts.mcgill.ca/MEPP/PRRN/papers/ajial_center/ngo_lebanon.html
19 Nicole Brackman," Palestinian Refugees in Lebanon: A New Source of Cross-Border Tension?" The Washington Institute for Near East Policy, Peacewatch 263, May 30, 2000.
20 Mohammed Zaatari, "Ain al-Hilweh Committee Issues Security Measures New Council Bans Firing Shots in the Air," *Lebanon Daily Star* Nov. 26, 2001, http://www.shaml.org/ground/ain_al-hilweh/Ain al-Hilweh Committee.htm
21 Mohammed Zaatari, Jun. 5, 2002, http://www.lebanonwire.com/0206/02060507DS.asp
22 Hashem Kassem, "Understanding the Significance of Ain al-Hilweh," Eastwest Record (2003), http://www.eastwestrecord.com/Get_Articles.asp?articleId=480
23 "New Hardline Palestinian Group Jund al-Sham Appears in Lebanese Camp," *An-Nahar*, June 26, 2004.
24 *"Lebanon," CIA Factbook*, http://www.cia.gov/cia/publications/factbook/geos/le.html
25 Habib Malik, *Between Damascus and Jerusalem: Lebanon and Middle East Peace*, (Washington, DC: Washington Institute for Near East Policy, 2000), Policy Paper 45, p. 5.

26   Daniel Pipes and Ziad Abdelnour, *Ending Syria's Occupation of Lebanon: The US Role*, (Philadelphia: Middle East Forum, 2000), p. 2.

27   Farid al Khazen, "Permanent Settlement of Palestinians in Lebanon: A Recipe for Conflict," *Journal of Refugee Studies*, Vol. 10, No. 3, 1997, http://ddc.aub.edu.lb/projects/pspa/khazen.html

28   al-Khazen, 1997, http://ddc.aub.edu.lb/projects/pspa/khazen.html

29   Tareq Y. Ismael, *Middle East Politics Today: Government and Civil Society*, (Gainesville, FL: University Press of Florida, 2001), p. 264.

30   "Lebanese Citizenship: Will it Last?" *Jerusalem Times*, May 22, 2003.

31   Farid el Khazen, *The Breakdown of the State in Lebanon, 1967-1976.* (Cambridge, MA: Harvard University Press, 2000). p. 162. For more on the Cairo Agreement, see pp. 140-175.

32   Daniel Nassif, "Al-Ahbash," *Middle East Intelligence Bulletin*, Vol. 3, No.4, April 2001, http://www.meib.org/articles/0104_ld1.htm Also see, "On Sidon's court shootings," Arabic News.com, June 9, 1999 http://www.arabicnews.com/ansub/Daily/Day/990609/1999060917.html

33   Ranwa Yehia, "Islamists on a Rampage in Lebanon," *Al-Ahram Weekly*, No. 464, January 13-19, 2000. http://weekly/ahram.org.ed/2000/464/re3.htm.

34   Radwan Aqil, Oct. 1, 2001.

35   Radwan Aqil, Oct. 1, 2001.

36   "Lebanon: Rumors Revive Emergency Situation in Ein al-Hilweh Between the Fatah Movement and Islamic Asbat al-Ansar," *Ash-Sharq al-Awsat* (London), August 18, 2002.

37   "Bombing Number 19 in Ein al-Hilweh," *Ash-Sharq al-Awsat*, November 6, 2002; and "Blasts and Intermittent Clashes Return to Ein al-Hilweh," *Al-Hayat*, October 28, 2002.

38   A great number of reports were filed between August and November 2002 that reported Asbat al-Ansar violence. Among them are: "Three Wounded in Inter-Palestinian Fighting in Lebanon Refugee Camp," AP, August 4, 2002; "Lebanon: A New Explosion in Ein al-Hilweh Refugee Camp," *Ash-Sharq al-Awsat*, October 15, 2002; "Two More Blasts in Southern Palestinian Refugee Camp," AP, October 16, 2002; "Fatah Official Targeted in Ein al-Hilweh Bomb Attack," *Lebanon Daily Star*, Oct 21, 2002; "Fateh Accuses Palestinians, Kurds and Lebanese for the Series of Explosions in Ein al-Hilweh Refugee Camp in Lebanon," *Ash-Sharq al-Awsat*, October 22, 2002; "Bomb Damages Coffee Shop in Lebanon's Largest Palestinian Camp," AP, November 4, 2002; "Bombing Number 19 in Ein al-Hilweh," *Ash-Sharq al-Awsat*, November 6, 2002.

39   Nicholas Blanford, "Lebanon Targets Islamic Radicals," *Christian Science Monitor*, May 20, 2003.

40   "Heavy Clashes Rage Between Islamists, Arafat's Loyalists in S. Lebanon," *An-Nahar*, May 19, 2003.

41   "Heavy Clashes…," *An-Nahar,* May 19, 2003.

42   Ahmed Mantash, "Clashes in Lebanon Refugee Camp Kill 5," AP, May 19, 2003.

43   "Al-Qaida, Fatah Engage in Heavy Fighting," Middle East Newsline, May 20, 2003.

44 "Heavy Clashes...," *An-Nahar,* May 19, 2003.

45 "Two Dead, More than 20 Wounded in Inter-Palestinian Clashes in Lebanon Camp," AFP, May 19. 2003.

46 "Calm Restored After Clashes in Palestinian Camp in Lebanon," AFP, May 20, 2003.

47 "Cease-Fire Called to Allow Burial of Dead in Ein al-Hilweh," *An-Nahar,* May 20, 2003.

48 "Osbat al Noor Vows to Murder Arafat's Top Lebanon Representative," *An-Nahar,* February 12, 2004.

49 "Lebanon: Two Detainees Not Al-Ansar Members; 'Dismay' at Jordan's Position Noted," *As-Safir,* October 17, 2001 [FBIS].

50 "Fatah Turns in to Lebanese Army Suspected North Korean Terrorist," *Lebanon Daily Star,* February 6, 2003.

51 "Car Bomb Kills Accused al-Qaeda Man in Lebanon Camp," Reuters, March 2, 2003. Also see: "Al-Qaida Feud Continues in Lebanese Camp," Middle East Newsline, March 2, 2003.

52 Author's interview/Israeli officials, June 27, 2003.

53 "Asbat al-Ansar Suspected in McDonald's Bombing," *Lebanon Daily Star,* April 17, 2003.

54 "Lebanon Announces New Arrest of "Terrorists" Targeting US Interests," AFP, July 15, 2003.

55 Author's interviews with several anonymous Lebanese sources, Washington, DC.

56 Maria Ressa, *Seeds of Terror: An Eyewitness Account of al-Qaeda's Newest Center of Operations in Southeast Asia,* (NY: Free Press, 2003), pp. 95 and 211.

57 "Syria Hands Over 'Terrorist Network' Suspect to Lebanese Authorities," *Lebanon Daily Star,* May 9, 2003.

58 "Lebanon Charges Six More in Anti-Western Bombings," Reuters, May 17, 2003.

59 "Lebanon Charges 10 for U.S. Fast-Food Bombings," Reuters, December 8, 2003. See also "It is Disclosed that the Yemeni was Trying to Escape from Lebanon Just before his Detention," *An-Nahar,* December 9, 2003.

60 "Ansar Allah Claim Missile Attack on F-TV, Hariri Unconvinced," *An-Nahar,* June 16, 2003.

61 Damien McElroy, "Al-Qaeda Fighters Set Up Base in Lebanese Refugee Camp," *Daily Telegraph,* June 22, 2003. http://portal.telegraph.co.uk/news/main.jhtml?xml=/news/2003/06/22/walq22.xml

62 "Lebanon Blames Palestinian Extremists for Future TV Attack," AP, July 17, 2003.

63 Joe Panossian, "Security Forces Arrest Yemeni Member of al-Qaida Group Indicted in Bombings of Western Targets in Lebanon," AP, October 18, 2003.

64 "Scenarios to Bomb the American Embassy and the Convoy of the Ambassador and the Execution of Attacks on Syrian and Lebanese Military Positions," *Al-Hayat,* July 4, 2003.

65 "The Environment of the Takfiri Fatwas in "Bab Altbana" Broadens and Turns the Region into an Exporter of Jihad," *al-Hayat,* December 1, 2003.

66 "It is Disclosed that the Yemeni was Trying to Escape from Lebanon Just

before his Detention," *An-Nahar*, December 9, 2003.

67 "Lebanon: 25 Years of Prison for the Yemeni Ibn ash-Shahid," *al-Hayat*, March 9, 2004.

68   Joe Panossian, "Lebanon Arrests Suspected Terrorist," AP, October 20, 2003. Also see: "It is Disclosed that the Yemeni was Trying to Escape from Lebanon Just before his Detention," *An-Nahar*, December 9, 2003.

69   Author's phone interview with Australian security official, September 30, 2003, and "Australian Islamic Leaders Tied to Alleged al-Qa'ida Leader Jailed in Spain," AFP, September 3, 2003.

70 "Australian 'Sent Cash' to Terror Suspect," *The Advertiser* (Australia), September 29, 2003.

71 Sara Smiles and Linda Morris, "Islamic Youth Leader Charged with Terrorist Links," *Sydney Morning Herald*, September 13, 2003. http://www.smh.com.au/articles/2003/09/12/1063341767994.html

72 "Australia Works with Lebanon on Terror Suspect," Reuters, September 6, 2003.

73 Yousef Diab, "The Verdict on a Terrorist Network in Lebanon that Exploded Restaurants and Enterprises with American Names," *Ash-Sharq al-Awsat*, December 21, 2003.

74 Yousef Diab, "Beirut Considers Extraditing the Two Australian Brothers of Lebanese Origin Accused of Financing a Terrorist Network," *Ash-Sharq al-Awsat*, December 23, 2003.

75 Author's phone interview/Australian official, Sept. 30, 2003.

76 "Profile of Bilal Khazal," *Ash-Sharq al-Awsat*, June 13, 2003.

77 Sara Smiles and Linda Morris, Sept. 13, 2003.

78 CIA Document, "Terrorism: Reported Planning by an Australian-Based al-Qaeda Associate to Attack the U.S. Embassy in Venezuela and U.S. Interests in the Philippines; Presence of al-Qaeda Members in Australia." Dated "Mid-June 2002."

79 Author's phone interview/Australian official, Sept. 30, 2003.

80 Giles Tremlett, "Muslim Cleric Faces Extradition: Spanish Court Charges Qatada with al-Qaida Membership," *The Guardian* (UK), September 18, 2003. http://www.guardian.co.uk/alqaida/story/0,12469,1044344,00.html

81 Sara Smiles and Linda Morris, Sept. 13, 2003.

82 "Australian Islamic Leaders Tied to Alleged al-Qa'ida Leader Jailed in Spain," AFP, September 3, 2003.

83 Spanish Cell Documents, Folio 11811, p. 76; and Folio 11730, p. 33.

84 "Australian Terror Suspect Allowed Bail Again Despite New Laws," AFP, June 24, 2004.

85 Nicholas Nasif, "Nature of Cooperation Between Lebanon, US To Combat Terror Explained," *An-Nahar* (Internet), October 11, 2001 [FBIS].

86 Gary Gambill, June 2003.

87 Email correspondence, January 4, 2003.

Chapter Four: Yemen

Yemen should be seen as a "bus stop" for al-Qaeda, "not a headquarters," notes one senior U.S. official. It's a place "where troops are stashed and smaller operations took place. It's a place where everything went through."[1]

While this may generally be the case, Yemen has nonetheless emerged as one of the more fertile locations for al-Qaeda activity. The primary affiliate in Yemen has scored a number of spectacular attacks against Western interests in recent years. Among other attacks, the Islamic Army of Aden Abyan (IAA) was responsible for the kidnapping of Western tourists in 1998, the bombing of the *U.S.S. Cole* in 2000, and an attack on the French tanker *Limburg* in 2002.

By way of background, the Cole attack was a major al-Qaeda operation, with organization, funding and planning from the al-Qaeda leadership, and with operational support from the IAA. Other local attacks were almost certainly IAA operations from start to finish. Thus, the IAA is a quintessential al-Qaeda affiliate operating on two levels: it is a local phenomenon, harboring local, high-level operatives, while assisting the larger al-Qaeda network in its war against the West.

IAA continues to exist in Yemen because of the country's turbulent history of foreign fighters, local Islamists, and its many areas of weak central authority. IAA is also the legacy of Yemenis who fought against the Soviets in Afghanistan. When they returned home to Yemen from battle, they brought with them the mujahedin's particularly dangerous version of radical Islam. President Ali Abdullah Saleh used these same Afghan fighters to help defeat the communist separatists in south Yemen during the brief, but bloody, civil war in 1994. The core group of these Afghan fighters and veterans of the 1994 civil war eventually came to represent al-Qaeda in Yemen.

More than 14 years after the end of the Afghanistan war and

nine years after the civil war, new generations of militants have spawned. An aggressive young guard now seeks to emulate the warriors who preceded them. Although Yemeni government cooperation with the U.S. over counterterrorism issues has yielded significant arrests and thwarted several plots, the al-Qaeda phenomenon maintains deep roots in Yemen.

Yemeni Lawlessness

Modern Yemen has always been a difficult country to rule. The northern Yemenis are proud that they have never been occupied. Even the Ottoman Turks and the British, who at different points occupied parts of Yemen, knew enough to leave some of Yemen's more unruly areas alone.

The indigenous power structure in Yemen has always been loose. In the 1930s, one British observer noted that "there were about 2,000 separate 'governments' in the Hadramawt" territory alone.[2] But over the years, Sanaa has slowly expanded its reach. Whereas the government in the late 1970s barely controlled the Sanaa-Ta'iz-Hodeidah triangle, its authority is now recognized throughout most of the country. The current government operates through a primordial "federal" system, making the best of the political hand it was dealt.[3] Sanaa projects authority in most of Yemen's towns and cities, as well as crucial transportation and oil infrastructure throughout much of the country. Still, it lacks the resources to effectively control "significant patches of countryside, especially the desert regions near the Saudi border."[4]

This is not to say that Yemen is a country characterized by chaos. Yemeni society has an identifiable rhythm and age-old order, especially in the tribal areas outside city centers. Indeed, tribal structures often run parallel to the government. Powerful patriarchs sometimes ignore parameters set by Sanaa. Rather, they see themselves as highly autonomous partners. Allegiances to these tribal patriarchs often supersede respect for the rule of state law in some Yemeni regions.

This observation is echoed in an International Crisis Group report that states, "Parts of the population continue to resist stronger government authority," and the Yemeni government "has yet to exert full control over tribes in remote areas."[5] The result, according to one Yemeni journalist, is that when tribes are sympathetic to radical elements, "the government finds itself in a deadlock."[6]

The government's lack of control, coupled with a lack of resources and Yemen's rugged terrain, sometimes makes it difficult to capture, arrest, or interrogate suspects. And while all of Yemen's provinces contain rugged areas, Yemeni and U.S. authorities agree that there are three primary governorates of major concern – Marib, Shibwa and Jawf – which are known for their tribal domination, lawlessness, and penchant for harboring al-Qaeda elements. While Abyan and Aden, the governorates where the IAA were first born, have been quiet in recent years, the Marib, Shibwa and Jawf governorates are continued cause for concern.

In Marib, for instance, militants from local tribes damaged oil pipelines with gunfire and explosives at least eight times in 1998, possibly as a means to undermine the government authority, but even more likely as an effort to extort greater financial benefits from the oil company that owned it.[7] Until recently, Marib also suffered from a series of tourist kidnappings. Today, the area of Sirwah, located between Sanaa and Marib, is said to be among the worst of Yemen's badlands.[8]

In northern governorates, clashes often take place thanks to Saudi support to certain Yemeni tribes.[9] For decades, the Saudis paid off local tribes and otherwise worked assiduously to maintain a modicum of power inside Yemen and to keep the Yemeni central government off-balance.[10] Yemenis assert that the estimated 100 kidnappings that took place during the 1990s were likely Saudi-financed.[11] However, at least one senior U.S. official believes that Yemeni tribes carried out most of these kidnappings for their own mercantile reasons.[12] Nonetheless, since the signing of a border agreement between Yemen and Saudi Arabia in 2000, tribal kidnappings have reportedly ceased.[13] But border control will remain a challenge. For example, Yemen has more than 3,500 kilometers of land border with Saudi Arabia and 2,200 kilometers of coastline that it must patrol.[14]

In short, Yemen continues its struggle to control areas of weak central authority which al-Qaeda has undoubtedly exploited. As such, al-Qaeda follows in the footsteps of other foreign powers in Yemen's recent past.

Other Countries' Battles

Yemen has long been unstable because it has, time and again, been a battleground for other countries. The rugged Yemeni character and the continued importing of weapons compound that instability.

After centuries under loose Ottoman control, North Yemen established its independence at the end of World War I under the theocratic Imam Yahya. Yahya ruled for two decades, but could not prevent the British (who had been in Yemen since the 1800s) from establishing "spheres of influence" in Aden in the south. He was killed during a coup attempt in 1948, leading to the accession of his son Ahmed, who sought protection from Egypt against British encroachment from the South.

After 14 years in power, Ahmed died in 1962. His son Mohammed ruled for a week until the army coup of September 26. The coup ignited an eight-year republican revolution, which led to the creation of the Yemen Arab Republic (YAR). During this revolutionary phase in the early 1960s, Yemen's two competing forces – republicans and communists – sought sponsorship from the two major regional powers (and ideologies) in the region: Pan-Arabist Egypt under Gamal Abd al-Nasser and the royalists of Saudi Arabia. The popular, socialist ideas behind Pan-Arabism were commonly regarded as the ideology that would rescue the Arab world from its woes and defeat the state of Israel. Saudi Arabia, Jordan, and other Middle East monarchies were fearful of this socialist ideology; its revolutionary nature challenged the sovereignty of their monarchs. They sought to contain Pan-Arabism in Yemen.

This proxy war took its toll on North Yemen. The Saudis and Jordanians backed offensives on northern tribal areas, which prompted Egypt to bombard northern Yemen and the Saudi Kingdom.[15] By 1965, Egyptian troops in North Yemen numbered about 60,000.[16]

Egypt fought with the republicans in North Yemen until October 1967, after the Six Day War with Israel drained its military resources.[17] A defeated Nasser soon withdrew under cover of an Arab Summit agreement, while Saudi Arabia nominally agreed to halt support to the royalists. Although the Egyptians barely controlled Sanaa when they withdrew from Yemen in December, they left a path of destruction, having bombed hostile tribal areas, laid landmines, and even used chemical weapons.[18]

In 1967, after suffering a campaign of costly guerrilla attacks in the south, the British also withdrew from Yemen.[19] Since 1965, the Libyan-backed Front for the Liberation of Occupied South Yemen (FLOSY) and the National Liberation Front (NLF) had unleashed uncontrollable violence on British forces.[20] In the final tally, the conflict claimed some 200,000 lives.[21]

Yemen soon deteriorated again. By 1972, elements in South Yemen seceded from the rest of the country and created the first Arab Marxist state, the People's Democratic Republic of Yemen (PDRY), a Soviet satellite on the Red Sea. Support came from the U.S.S.R., several Eastern European states, China, and Cuba, as well as Libya and radical Palestinian groups.[22]

Following the declaration of the PDRY, South Yemen launched several invasions into the North between 1972 and

1979.[23] During the most serious of the three in 1979, the U.S. supplied arms and a number of Arab states provided military advisors to the YAR.[24] The conflict was clearly a Cold War proxy battle. U.S. officials were particularly concerned about the presence in the PDRY of some "800 to 1,000 Soviet advisers, about half of whom were regular military personnel, between 500 and 700 Cuban advisers, and more than one hundred East Germans, primarily concentrated on internal security intelligence."[25]

In the end, North Yemen emerged victorious. Over 10,000 were killed in the south during a one-month tribal war of 1988.[26] The purges and executions in that extended coup destroyed much of the country's civil infrastructure.[27] The YAR's post-war reconstruction was boosted when a U.S. company discovered oil in 1984, while the demise of the Soviet Union and the Warsaw Pact left the devastated PDRY without patrons or protectors.[28] This created a political opening for unification. Indeed, unification negotiations went through fruitless fits and starts for nearly fifteen years. A unity agreement, including shared power arrangements and a commitment to creating a constitutional democracy, was finally reached in May 1990. Many dispossessed PDRY leaders, however, resented their loss of power and control in the new Yemen. Their grievances, prompted by Saudi encouragement and funding, later led to yet another conflict: the civil war of 1994.

Fighting Others' Battles

Just as foreign powers used Yemen to further their own particular goals, many Yemenis adopted the cause of the Afghan rebels in their war against the Soviets between 1979 and 1989. When the U.S.S.R. invaded Afghanistan in 1979, the Yemeni government and even the U.S. government, as an extension of the Cold War, prodded many Yemenis to fight as mujahedin against the power that backed the PDRY. While in Afghanistan, these fighters not only exacted revenge against the Soviets, but also gained battle experience and were indoctrinated by al-Qaeda's powerful jihadi ideology.

When they returned to Yemen from Afghanistan in the early 1990s, some began to coalesce into new jihadi groups. These groups were built upon their relationships with the core leaders of the group that would soon come to be known as al-Qaeda. The Yemeni "Afghans" became the basis for the al-Qaeda network that exists in Yemen today. They were also the foundation for a group that would not emerge until 1998: the IAA.

Unification and Weaponization

Yemenis returned from Afghanistan triumphant. Their jihad led indirectly to the crumbling of the Soviet empire, the collapse of the PDRY and the unification of Yemen in May 1990. Unity did not, however, bring Yemen greater stability. While the government based in the north absorbed a flood of PDRY civil servants and took other steps for smooth integration, the security apparatus was overwhelmed.[29] According to Yemen's former Prime Minister Abd al-Kareem al-Iryani, southern radicals "exploited the hazy period between November 1993 and July 1994" by building new camps, reactivating existing ones, and preparing for violence against the regime.[30]

Hostilities soon broke out between the central government and the southern secessionists, who attempted to undo Yemen's unification and reestablish its independence. The ensuing brutal, nine-week civil war in 1994 cost 7,000 lives, but ended in victory for unity.[31] President Ali Abdullah Saleh gained the upper hand, in part, due to his ability to co-opt Islamist fighters intent on defeating the atheist communists.

But the years of fighting in Yemen took their toll. According to Sanaa's governor, Yemen experienced an unprecedented "import of weapons between 1967 and 1994, when the country was home to proxy battles between the superpowers."[32]

As a result, there are today more than three guns for every citizen. One analyst believes there may be as many as 80 million firearms in Yemen.[33] Even if that number is exaggerated, many tribal areas are heavily armed, making passage perilous, even for government forces.

The government announced in 2003 that it was in the process of trying to buy back weapons from the tribal elements in these provinces. According to estimates from Yemen's interior ministry, the initiative would require billions of Yemeni Riyals. Since the late 1990s, the parliament has tried to pass legislation prohibiting the public carrying of certain firearms in city limits.[34] Such changes may be difficult to implement; Yemen's rugged culture has been armed for centuries. The gun, as well as the jambiyah (traditional dagger), is an inextricable part of Yemen's male-dominated culture. Furthermore, the arms trade is a major moneymaker for many Yemenis. The country is seen as an arms "supermarket" for Somalia and other countries in the region, and the profit margin can be as high as 200 percent.[35] In addition, Sanaa continues to import new weapons from the Czech Republic, despite its avowed interest in demilitarization.[36]

Al-Qaeda in Yemen

Given Yemen's history of hosting proxy wars, it is not surprising that al-Qaeda has also used Yemen as a battleground in its war against the West. Al-Qaeda has established bases of operation within Yemen, exploiting the country's long history of instability and fragmented authority. Yemenis returning from Afghanistan began setting up training camps in the late 1980s, purportedly with the help of a tribal patriarch, Tariq al-Fadhi, who may have been involved in the first al-Qaeda attack in Yemen in 1992.[37]

According to terrorism analyst Peter Bergen, bin Laden recognized that Yemen was fertile ground for his network, and even considered moving al-Qaeda's base of operations to Yemen after some 20 Yemeni shaykhs met with al-Qaeda operatives in 1997.[38]

While this base never materialized, it is still estimated that Yemenis are the third-largest nationality represented in al-Qaeda, second only to Egyptians and Algerians.[39]

To account for this, many journalists cite the fact that Osama bin Laden's father, Mohammed bin Laden, hailed from a traditional Yemeni village in Hadramawt. But this alone cannot account for al-Qaeda's presence in Yemen. A more plausible argument is that Osama bin Laden has maintained a strong connection there by "quietly cultivating contacts" with several tribes.[40] These contacts, which often amount to financial incentives, have kept tribes on the al-Qaeda bankroll for a decade. According to scholar Mark Katz, Yemeni tribes have also taken money and assistance from others who seek to influence Yemeni politics, including Marxists, Iraqis, and Saudis, to name a few.[41] This indicates that Yemeni tribes may or may not necessarily be ideologically aligned with bin Laden; his coffers may offer sums that Sanaa cannot.

But the bin Laden message also simply resonates in Yemen. According to one CIA analyst, bin Laden helped found the Islamist-oriented Hizb al-Islah (Reform Party), provided logistical help to send Yemenis to Afghanistan to fight the Soviets, and worked with jihadis to fight the communists of South Yemen.[42] Ever since al-Qaeda was formed, reports of al-Qaeda activity in Yemen have been constant. Analysts believe that in the early 1990s, an al-Qaeda training camp was built in Mudiyah, a village in the southern governorate of Abyan.[43] It is also believed that bin Laden was behind attacks on oil rigs and other strategic assets throughout Yemen.[44]

As the al-Qaeda phenomenon grew, so did its ties to Yemen. Of the 1,100 phone calls made by bin Laden on his satellite phone in the mid-1990s, 221 were made to Yemen.[45] In between 1993 and 1996, bin Laden reportedly shipped loads of weapons between Sudan and tribes in Yemen.[46] The al-Qaeda network also used

Yemen to house some of al-Qaeda's business fronts and safe houses which served as financial, logistical, and passport forgery centers.[47] By early 1999, bin Laden reportedly owned a ceramics manufacturing firm in Yemen.[48] The U.S. Treasury's Office of Foreign Assets Control (OFAC) listed three businesses in Yemen's honey industry, including Al-Hamali bakeries and Al-Nur honey, as terrorist fronts in 2001.[49]

IAA: Local and Global

True to the form of al-Qaeda affiliates, the IAA grew out of the relative weak central authority in Yemen. It began as a small, local group with a domestic agenda, and evolved into a terror organization with global targets, but local attacks never ceased. Although the IAA emerged in 1997, its roots likely date back to 1992, when al-Qaeda affiliated militants bombed an Aden hotel, which was a stopping point for U.S. troops bound for Somalia.[50] The attack failed; the U.S. forces had already left the hotel when the explosion took place. Authorities rounded up some twenty jihadis who claimed to represent the "Osama Group" and the "Islamic Jihad Organization."[51] It is important to note, however, that although many terrorism analysts refer to it as the first-ever al-Qaeda attack, some high-level U.S. officials disagree, asserting that the explosion resulted from the escalation of a local land dispute completely unrelated to bin Laden's embryonic network.[52]

In any event, the IAA did not emerge as an active al-Qaeda affiliate until the late 1990s. In May and June 1998, it made headlines by releasing communiqués criticizing the Yemeni government's policies.[53] The group, led by Zein al-Abidin al-Mihdar (Abu al-Hassan), called for the overthrow of the government. One statement threatened that "if the ambassadors of America and Britain do not leave [Yemen], then our time will come soon and the blow will be painful."[54] After the August 7, 1998 attacks on the U.S. embassies in Kenya and Tanzania, the IAA called the bombers "Heroes of the Jihad."[55] It also repeatedly threatened U.S. Ambassador Barbara Bodine via al-Qaeda spokesman Abu Hamza al-Masri (Mustafa Kamel Mustafa) of London's Finsbury Park Mosque. Al-Masri issued many IAA statements during its first years of activity. He was finally arrested in London on May 27, 2004, when a U.S. court charged him with trying to establish a terrorist training camp in Oregon, and raising funds for the al-Qaeda network.

In the late 1990s, the IAA began to shift its focus to other international targets. Previously, the group had only participated in small al-Qaeda training camps and provided operatives with logistical assistance.[56] On December 23, 1998, however, ten suspects were arrested in the Aden and Shibwa governorates with large quantities of explosives, in addition to IAA leaflets, wool masks, uniforms, and cosmetics for disguises.[57] According to a senior U.S. official, the plot was organized, funded, and directed by al-Masri in London, and only a few of the operatives were Yemeni.[58] Yemeni authorities were praised for disrupting terrorist activities, but IAA still managed to pull off a major attack five days later.   On December 28, IAA militants kidnapped 16 Western tourists in the governorate of Abyan. Al-Masri's 2004 indictment alleged that he played a logistical role in that operation. In the subsequent Yemeni rescue mission, four of the tourists (three Britons and one Australian) were killed, and one American citizen was wounded.[59] Abu al-Hassan stated that the kidnappings were carried out "for the sake of bin Laden."[60]

At the end of the hostage stand-off in December 1998, Yemeni authorities captured several IAA members including Abu al-Hassan. He confessed that the group possessed surface-to-air missiles (SAMs), artillery shells, and anti-tank mines. He also revealed that the IAA used mobile phones provided by Abu Hamza in London,[61] and that it had plans for one team of militants to attack, "Christians during the month of Ramadan and another team to attack the Royal-Caltex Hotel [sic] in Aden... Our objective was to hit the Americans."[62]

IAA members made a plea for their leader's release, then issued a warning that "if negotiations fail, all foreigners in Yemen from Western ambassadors, experts and doctors to tourists have to leave Yemen. The Aden-Abyan Islamic Army will not kidnap them but will kill them."[63] Yemeni authorities executed Abu al-Hassan on October 17, 1999. His successor, Hatem bin Fareed, was also captured.[64] Such successes gave some Sanaa officials an inflated sense of accomplishment. They insisted that the IAA had been defeated, and that it existed "only in the imagination of some people."[65]

Although they may not have felt that the IAA was destroyed, some senior U.S. officials also suspected that its strength was waning. Specifically, they asserted that some of the IAA's claims were clearly fabricated. A number of Abu Hamza's claims about the size, capabilities and scope of IAA operations appeared to be exaggerated.[66] For example, it is highly doubtful that the IAA downed a Yemeni military aircraft that killed 17 officers on August 14, 1999, despite the group's claims that it had done so.[67] Still, the IAA had not disappeared. Rather, Yemeni authorities claimed it was responsible for bombing a number of local targets, including a church and a hotel, and for attempting to bomb the U.S. embassy on at least one occasion.[68]

In January 2000, the IAA adopted a bold, new strategy: attacking high-profile U.S. targets. Together with members of the al-Qaeda core, the IAA failed in its efforts to bomb the *U.S.S. The Sullivans*. Al-Qaeda militant Jamal Mohammed al-Badawi and several accomplices overloaded a skiff with explosives, aligned the vessel to intersect the destroyer, but then watched the boat sink from shore.[69] Months later, other local al-Qaeda militants learned from the failed first effort. On October 12, 2000, suicide bombers actually drove the skiff into their target, rather than bombing by remote control. They attacked with a powerful boat bomb the

U.S.S. Cole, an American destroyer, while it refueled in the poorly guarded Aden harbor. The explosion killed 17 U.S. sailors, injured 39, and inflicted an estimated quarter-billion dollars in damage.[70] Following the attack, Yemeni security arrested six men, all of whom had fought in Afghanistan against the Soviets. One of them told officials that he was trained in al-Qaeda's "Jihad Number One" camp in Afghanistan, and that he had fought with al-Qaeda in Bosnia, too. He further claimed that he was acting on instruction from a high-level al-Qaeda operative named Mohammed Omar al-Harazi.[71]

The IAA claimed responsibility for the *Cole* attack.[72] Two other groups (Jaysh Muhammad and the Islamic Deterrence Force) also claimed responsibility,[73] but it was quite clear that Yemen's al-Qaeda network, including individuals, cells and the local affiliate, were to blame. Al-Qaeda's leadership appeared willing to let the IAA take credit for the attack, but officials in both Sanaa and Washington suggest that most of the planning, funding and logistics for the attack were not local.

Despite mounting evidence underscoring al-Qaeda's involvement in the attack, Yemeni cooperation in the U.S.-led investigation was slow and begrudging. Some U.S. security officials believed that the Yemeni security apparatus was penetrated by al-Qaeda elements. At the very least, some Yemeni security men in the Aden harbor may have been forewarned of the attack.[74]

Tensions between Washington and Sanaa continued through 2000 and 2001. The State Department alleged that Yemen was a safe haven for al-Qaeda affiliated groups, including Egyptian al-Jihad, al-Gamaa al-Islamiyya, and the Algerian Armed Islamic Group, as well as fighters from al-Qaeda, itself.[75] The attacks of September 11 heaped more pressure on Yemen, due particularly to the fact that one Yemeni national Ramzi Bin al-Shibh was identified as one of the key planners. After the attacks, U.S.

officials also established "linkages between the East African Embassy bombings, the U.S.S. *Cole* bombing, and the September 11 attacks."[76] Other leads may have come from the estimated 110 Yemenis imprisoned in Guantanamo Bay, Cuba.[77]

Al-Qaeda's war against the West continued after the invasion of Afghanistan, and Yemen was one of the most active fronts in that war. In April 2002, an explosion rocked the civil aviation building in Sanaa. In August 2002, authorities discovered 650 pounds of Semtex explosives hidden among pomegranates.[78] Some speculated that the explosives were intended for a foreign target, but the Yemeni government viewed the discovery and subsequent arrests as a domestic event.

The most devastating blow for Yemen, however, was the October 6, 2002 attack on the French Tanker *Limburg*, which killed one and injured 17 in the port of ad-Dabbah. The environmental consequences were severe; the attack caused thousands of barrels of oil to spill into Hadramawt's waters.[79] This crippled the already poverty-stricken country, prompting expensive environmental clean up, tourist cancellations, and a sharp drop in port usage due to a 300 percent hike in insurance rates. According to officials, "investment projects which [had] been already implemented at the cost of several millions of dollars were suspended. Thousands of job opportunities were lost."[80]

The losses incurred motivated Sanaa to increase counterterrorism cooperation with the U.S. in an attempt to prevent similar attacks in the future. Even amid this heightened coordination, on November 3, 2002, a group of al-Qaeda operatives attempted to shoot down a Hunt Oil company helicopter. They fired two SAMs (which missed) and a barrage of automatic gunfire, injuring two passengers.[81] The following month, on December 30, 2002, a Yemeni militant smuggled a gun into a Baptist-run hospital in the town of Jibla, where he killed three American missionaries and wounded another.[82]

In March 2003, on the eve of the U.S. war with Iraq, reports emerged that Islamists in Yemen were actively recruited by al-Qaeda to "conduct suicide attacks and other sabotage against the oil fields outside Iraq."[83] As if on cue, a few days later, a Yemeni national opened fire on an American, a Canadian, and a Yemeni working on an oil rig east of Sanaa, and then killed himself.[84]

In April, militant Abed Abd ar-Rezzak Kamel was arrested on suspicion of being part of an al-Qaeda cell.[85] Days later, a judge was killed by a hand grenade in the Jibla courtroom where Kamel was sentenced to death.[86] On June 25, Yemeni forces attacked an IAA hideout in the mountainous Hattat region where IAA's first camps were located.[87] During the raid, 10 militants were killed and more than 20 arrested.[88] Twelve more militants were later captured.[89]

In short, Islamist terror has been a constant in Yemen since the IAA's inception. Before the mid-1990s, attacks by radicals inside Yemen were virtually unheard of. With a relatively high number of international attacks to its credit, the once provincial IAA can no longer be considered a primarily local phenomenon. Rather, this affiliate is a loosely constructed al-Qaeda base in Yemen from which large-scale attacks can be planned against international and local interests alike.

Counter-Counterterrorism?

The October 6, 2002 attack on the French tanker *Limburg* pushed Sanaa to work more closely with the U.S. in the area of counterterrorism, marked by close cooperation with the CIA and FBI. Such cooperation was not without precedent. The State Department's *Patterns of Global Terrorism* report of 2001 noted that Yemeni authorities "arrested suspected terrorists and pledged to neutralize key al-Qaeda nodes in Yemen."[90] As part of its effort to crack down on suspected militants, Yemen had also allowed the United States to deploy Special Forces on its soil after the attacks of September 11.

After the *Limburg* attack, however, the scope of Yemeni-American security cooperation increased measurably, as did cooperation with British Special Forces.[91] Increased domestic efforts included the deportation of hundreds of illegal immigrants and suspected terrorists (although some of these deportations began in 1996). Sanaa upgraded programs that began in 2000 to monitor or even control certain mosques and Islamic organizations,[92] while concurrently launching a public relations campaign urging clerics to purge extremism and warning the public of terrorism's cost to the economy.[93]

The pinnacle of Yemeni counterterrorism was likely November 5, 2002. Based on intelligence from Abd ar-Rahim an-Nashiri, the imprisoned mastermind of the *Cole* attack,[94] the CIA tracked al-Qaeda operatives driving in Marib's desert region. Through a Predator Unmanned Aerial Vehicle (UAV), the CIA launched a Hellfire missile at the vehicle. The missile killed all six people, including one high level al-Qaeda operative who had taken part in the attack on the *Cole*.[95] Also killed in that attack were several IAA members and Kamal Derwish, the alleged leader of the "Lackawanna Six," a Yemeni al-Qaeda cell that was discovered near Buffalo, New York in 2002.[96]

Sanaa authorities estimated that there were at least two other high-level operatives at large in Yemen following that operation, as well as some 32 militants from IAA.[97] Coordinated counterterrorism continued, yielding a number of arrests and kills. On April 5, 2003, the government arrested Fawaz ar-Ribeidi and Nasser Megalli, two high-profile al-Qaeda suspects. Despite the good news, less than a week later, ten suspects from the U.S.S. *Cole* bombing escaped from jail on April 11 by drilling through a bathroom wall.[98] One of the suspects reportedly handed himself over to Yemeni authorities, but others remained on the loose.[99] The report was shocking; jailbreaks almost never occur in the Arab world. The break raised questions as to whether some members of the security services had allowed it to happen.

Nonetheless, Yemeni counterterrorism efforts continued to yield results. In September 2003, the Saudi government handed over to Yemen two men suspected of involvement in the *Limburg* attack in exchange for Bandar bin abd ar-Rahman al-Gambdi, a top suspect in the May 12 suicide bombings that rocked Riyadh.[100] In June, Yemeni forces attacked a hideout of the IAA in Hattat, "with the help of U.S. Special Operations Command forces and included helicopters, artillery and combat vehicles."[101] In January 2004, Sanaa continued to make key arrests, including that of Jaber al-Baneh, a member of the Lackawanna Six who was found hiding out in Yemen.[102] Two months later, amidst a counterterrorism offensive that netted 32 militants in the Abyan region, Yemeni forces nabbed Imam ash-Sharif of the Egyptian al-Jihad group and Abdul Raouf Nassib, a local al-Qaeda figure.[103]

While Yemen made critical progress in its fight against terror, it also made some surprising changes. In a manner entirely consistent with his style of governance but contrary to common counterterrorism practices, President Saleh announced in September 2003 that his government would release dozens of militants with links to al-Qaeda as long as they "pledged to respect the rights of non-Muslim foreigners living in Yemen or visiting it."[104] According to one Yemeni official, the announcement was a means of "feeling out" both the Yemeni public and the U.S.[105] However, a State Department spokesman later stated, "It is not clear whether the U.S. was consulted first."[106]

According to *al-Hayat*, the prisoners slated for release included a number of Yemenis who were suspected of involvement with al-Qaeda and who had been in jail for up to three years.[107] Others were imprisoned IAA members who pledged to halt all militant activities.[108] By late November, Agence France Presse reported that as many as 146 suspects linked to al-Qaeda were slated for release, although the actual numbers were likely smaller.[109]

Yemeni officials insisted that the amnesty would not detract from their overall efforts to fight terrorism. In private, some officials explained that the release should be understood within the context of tribal politics; by releasing the "less dangerous" suspects, Sanaa would maintain relations with influential tribes that play a significant role in Yemeni counterterrorism operations. Officials were also quick to note that the amnesty was the result of increased pressure from nongovernmental organizations that accused Sanaa of human rights violations, since many suspects had not stood trial.[110]

According to one Saleh advisor, some 20 prisoners were released by late November 2003, as Ramadan came to a close. He also stated that the total number released would not exceed sixty. State Department officials believe that none of those granted amnesty had direct links to the *Cole* bombing, the *Limburg* attack, or any other major terrorist operation in Yemen, but were rather Islamist sympathizers with only peripheral links to secondary players in al-Qaeda plots. Sanaa also underscored that the suspects, in front of a senior cleric, renounced violence in the name of Islam and even furnished intelligence to Yemeni officials to help thwart terrorist attacks as a condition for their release. While some of the suspects were trained in mujahedin camps in Afghanistan during the 1980s, Sanaa argued that they were growing older and had not been implicated in any subsequent al-Qaeda attacks.[111]

Yemeni officials also noted that the prisoners were released entirely on their own recognizance; their families had to sign for them, using their homes and businesses as a kind of bail bond. In Yemeni culture, the family's word and honor is the real collateral in such agreements. Still, Sanaa admitted that it did not have plans (or likely the resources) to use Yemeni intelligence services to track the activities of these prisoners after their release.[112]

In the weeks after Saleh announced the amnesty initiative, more than fifty IAA members from the Hattat region reportedly turned themselves in. Yemeni officials cited these surrenders as an indication that amnesty during times of relative calm is an effective policy. Only time will prove or disprove that assumption.

Nevertheless, the amnesty was a creative attempt to achieve the elusive and delicate balance between human rights and counterterrorism in a region that is too often known for its heavy-handed approach. If Yemen's efforts succeed, other Middle Eastern countries that have detained al-Qaeda suspects should take note (including Egypt, which still holds an estimated 16,000 Islamists in custody, most without due process). Yemen's amnesty is also a considerable gamble. If the released suspects resort to violence, the initiative will have damaged Yemeni security, which could prove detrimental to regional and global security.

A Microcosm of al-Qaeda

While the face of Yemeni counterterrorism strategy shifted in the fall of 2003, so too did the leadership of al-Qaeda in Yemen. By September of that year, Yemen appeared to have become a microcosm of al-Qaeda's global presence. Rather than one affiliate, several reports indicated that numerous affiliates were working on behalf of al-Qaeda in Yemen.

The reports emerged after Yemeni authorities alerted the U.S. of a potential new terror threat, directing U.S. citizens to take exceptional security measures.[113] That warning was followed by a foiled car bomb plot against the British embassy and other Western targets in Sanaa.[114] The plot was attributed to a group calling itself "Qaedat al-Jihad," another name that al-Qaeda uses to identify itself through communiqués. According to one newspaper report, "the Qaeda of Jihad organization has been strategically restructured, notably with the merging of five groups - Yemeni Jihad, Aden-Abyan Islamic Army, Egyptian Jihad, Organization of Descendants of Companions in the Arabian Peninsula, and the Algerian Al-Dawa Salafi group."[115]

The coming together of these affiliates, according to

Yemeni officials, was seen in Sanaa as a sign that a new generation of al-Qaeda leaders may have emerged in Yemen. After the announcement, 17 militants from Yemen, Saudi Arabia, and Syria were subsequently jailed.[116] They were found with an explosives manual and documents of financial transactions.[117] The subsequent investigation revealed that they were plotting to attack "foreign embassies in addition to vital government installations and services."[118] The group indicated that it still had more than "48 martyrs" at its disposal. It also rejected attempts at mediation by the Yemeni authorities.[119] Thus, Yemen could face a longer and tougher battle with new al-Qaeda militants in the foreseeable future.

Yemen's Challenges in the Future

When the U.S.S. *Cole* deployed from Norfolk, Virginia in December 2003 after undergoing $250 million in repairs,[120] there was a feeling of change in the air. Perhaps Yemen had turned a corner in the war on terrorism. One month prior, in November 2003, Sanaa announced the impressive arrest of Mohammed Hamdi al-Ahdal, also known as Abu Asem al-Makki, one of the masterminds of the attacks on the *Cole* and the *Limburg*.[121] He was also believed to have plotted to bomb a hotel in Yemen where FBI investigators were staying.[122] One official stated that the arrest "provided important information to Yemeni investigators which implicates important personalities in Arab states regarding financial dealings" with the al-Qaeda network.[123]

The arrest of Shaykh Mohammed Ali Hassan Moayad, a high-ranking figure in Yemen's Islamist-oriented Islah Party, was another victory for U.S. counterterrorism efforts in Yemen. Moayad was caught trying to receive $25 million intended for al-Qaeda activities in a FBI sting operation in Frankfurt, Germany on January 10, 2003.[124] During the sting, he allegedly bragged about a prior meeting with bin Laden, and promised that any funds he received would go to al-Qaeda.[125] Since no extradition treaty existed between Germany and Yemen, a German court subsequently handed him over to American authorities, who put him on trial in Brooklyn.[126] While the Islah Party insists that Moayad was a pious man who provided alms and food to the poor through his activities, Attorney General John Ashcroft called this arrest a "severe blow to al-Qaeda."[127]

Ashcroft's optimism notwithstanding, al-Qaeda will certainly continue to operate in Yemen. The Yemeni government claims that operations are sustained through help from Islah. The party's logo, a rising sun, is ubiquitous throughout the country (appearing on t-shirts, stickers, rock murals, posters, etc.). According to several high-ranking Yemeni officials, roughly 20 percent of the party has ties with jihadis in other countries, particularly through one Islah party leader, Shaykh Abd al-Majeed az-Zindani.[128] The U.S. Treasury, on February 24, 2004, labeled az-Zindani a Specially Designated Global Terrorist (SDGT) under executive order 13224 (see Appendix B). The accompanying report indicated that he had a "long history of working with bin Laden, notably serving as one of his spiritual leaders... including actively recruiting for al-Qaeda training camps... [and in his] role in the purchase of weapons on behalf of al-Qaeda." The report also noted his role as "a contact for Ansar al-Islam," a Kurdish al-Qaeda affiliate in Iraq.[129] Predictably, Islah denied these charges vehemently.[130]

But Islah is not the only mitigating factor in Yemen's struggle with radical Islam. Anti-Americanism remains high, and was particularly evident in the demonstrations that spilled out into Sanaa's streets in the months and weeks leading up to the 2003 Iraq war. In light of America's status on the Yemeni street, quiet military cooperation and behind-the-scenes investment in Yemen's counterterrorism squads is likely to characterize the Yemeni-American relationship in the near term. Continued and repeated threats against American interests make attacks with Predator drones and other "remote control" strategies the safest approach, rather than putting U.S. forces in direct contact with a potentially hostile population.

While military assistance will be crucial for Sanaa's fight against al-Qaeda in Yemen, it will not suffice on its own. It will also be essential to facilitate a sharp increase in basic services, health care, education, and other crucial social welfare needs. In this way, the U.S. can help bolster the central authority in Yemen. An incentive-based strategy would likely prove effective in Yemen because the country is hungry for U.S. aid. Its government has shown that it is eager to rank among the more cooperative Middle East countries in the war on terrorism, and that it is interested in expanding government services in its many areas of weak central authority. Sanaa has signaled that it might even want to take more significant steps to democratize in a region where democracy is scarce.[131] Thus, Yemen could be an ideal test case for implementing new, performance-based approaches to democratization, regaining control of gray zones and counterterrorism, alike. Failure to engage Yemen, conversely, would be an opportunity lost on a crucial front in the battle to neutralize al-Qaeda affiliates around the world.

Notes

1   Author's interview with senior U.S. official, Washington, DC. August 13, 2003.
2   Paul Dresch, *A History of Modern Yemen*. (Cambridge, UK: Cambridge University Press, 2000), p. 37.
3   Author's interview with senior U.S. official, Washington, DC. January 9, 2004.
4   Robert D. Kaplan, "A Tale of Two Colonies," *Atlantic Monthly*, April 2003.
5   "Yemen: Coping with Terrorism and Violence in a Fragile State," International Crisis Group, No. 8, January 8, 2003, p. ii (executive summary).
6   Author's interview with Walid as-Saqqaf, Editor of the *Yemen Times* in Sanaa, Yemen. June 9, 2003.

7 "Oil pipeline explosion in Marib," Arabic News.com, July 13, 1998, http://www.arabicnews.com/ansub/Daily/Day/980713/1998071343.html . More information about these attacks provided by a senior U.S. official, Washington, D.C., January 8, 2004.

8 "Yemen: Coping with Terrorism...," p. 18-19.

9 Ahmed Noman and Kassim Almadhagi, *Yemen and the United States: A Study of a Small Power and Super-State Relationship*, 1962-1994, (NY: I.B. Taurus, 1996), p. 123.

10 Author's interviews with Yemeni officials, Sanaa, Yemen. June 2003. Also, author's interview with senior U.S. official, Washington, DC. January 8, 2004.

11 Author's interview with senior Yemeni official, Sanaa, Yemen. June 9, 2003.

12 Author's interview with senior U.S. official, Washington, DC. January 8, 2004.

13 Author's interview/Walid as-Saqqaf, June 9, 2003.

14 Author's interview with Abu Bakr al-Girbi, Yemeni Foreign Minister, Sanaa, Yemen. June 14, 2003.

15 Ahmed Noman and Kassim Almadhagi, p. 57.

16 Mohammed Ahmad Zabarah, *Yemen: Traditionalism vs. Modernity*, (NY: Praeger Publishers, 1982), p. 99.

17 Ahmed Noman and Kassim Almadhagi, p. 82.

18 Dresch, p. 105.

19 Ahmed Noman and Kassim Almadhagi, p. 66.

20 "Background Notes: Yemen, October 1996," Bureau of Public Affairs, U.S. Department of State, http://www.state.gov/www/background_notes/yemen_1096_bgn.html

21 Robert D. Kaplan, Apr. 2003.

22 Background Notes: Yemen, Oct. 1996.

23 Dresch, pp.124 and 149.

24 Ahmed Noman and Kassim Almadhagi, p. 106.

25 Ahmed Noman and Kassim Almadhagi, p. 109.

26 Robert D. Kaplan, Apr. 2003.

27 Tareq Y. Ismael, *Middle East Politics Today: Government and Civil Society*, (Gainesville, FL: University Press of Florida, 2001), p.403.

28 Ahmed Noman and Kassim Almadhagi, p. 9.

29 Author's interview with advisor to President Saleh, Sanaa, Yemen. June 10, 2003.

30 Author's interview with Abd al-Kareem al-Iryani, Sanaa, Yemen. June 14, 2003.

31 Robert D. Kaplan, Apr. 2003.

32 Author's interview with Abdel Wahed al-Bukhaiti, Sanaa, Yemen. June 9, 2003.

33 Robert D. Kaplan, Apr. 2003.

34 Author's interview with Dr. Rashad al-Alimi, Sanaa, Yemen, June 14, 2003.

35 Report of the Panel of Experts in Somalia pursuant to Security Council resolution 1474 (2003), p. 31. http://www.iprt.org/report_of_the_panel_of_experts_i.htm

36 William J. Kole, "Czechs coming under fire for secretive arms deals to Yemen," AP, December 1, 2003.

37   Jason Burke, *Al-Qaeda: Casting a Shadow of Terror*, (NY: I.B. Taurus, 2003), p. 129.

38   Peter Bergen, *Holy War, Inc. Inside the Secret World of Osama bin Laden*, (NY: Free Press, 2001), pp. 175-176.

39   Rohan Gunaratna, *Inside Al Qaeda: Global Network of Terror*, (NY: Columbia University Press, 2002), p. 139.

40   Simon Reeve, p. 218.

41   Mark N. Katz, "Breaking the Yemen-al-Qaeda Connection," *Current History*, January 2003, p.41.

42   Anonymous, *Through Our Enemies' Eyes: Osama Bin Laden, Radical Islam, and the Future of America.* (Washington, DC: Brassey's, 2002), p. 112.

43   Rohan Gunaratna, *Inside Al Qaeda:...* p.139.

44   Anonymous, *Through Our Enemies'* Eyes... p. 112.

45   Rohan Gunaratna, *Inside Al Qaeda:...* p. 12.

46   This was a previously established smuggling route. Anonymous, *Through Our Enemies' Eyes...* p. 126. Also see: Jason Burke, *Al-Qaeda: Casting a Shadow of Terror*, (NY: I.B. Taurus, 2003), p. 133.

47   Rohan Gunaratna, p. 140. Notably, an Egyptian al-Jihad fighter who stood trial in Cairo in 1999 identified one Sanaa safe house. For more on that, see: Susan Sachs, "An Investigation in Egypt Illustrates Al-Qaeda's Web," *New York Times*, November 21, 2001.

48   Simon Reeve, p. 207.

49   "UK expands freeze on terror funds," October 12, 2001, BBC.com, http://news.bbc.co.uk/2/hi/business/1595740.stm

50   Author's interview/Dr. Rashad al-Alimi, June 14, 2003.

51   Anonymous, *Through Our Enemies' Eyes...* p. 135.

52   Author's interview/senior U.S. official, Jan. 8, 2004.

53   "Background Information on Other Terrorist Groups," Appendix C, *Patterns of Global Terrorism 2001*, (Washington, DC: United States Department of State, 2002), p. 120. http://www.state.gov/s/ct/rls/pgtrpt/2001/html/10254.htm#iaa.

54   "Aden Islamic Army Threatens the American and British Ambassadors if they do not Leave Yemen," March 12, 1999.
http://www.library.cornell.edu/colldev/mideast/feat9en.htm . Verified by a senior U.S. official, Washington, DC. June 9, 2003.

55   Salim Jiwa, "Terror Targets: A Look at Radical Islamic Groups Targeted by Bush's Order," ABC News Online, September 25, 2001.
http://abcnews.go.com/sections/us/DailyNews/WTC_obl_finances010925.html. See also "Abu al-Hassan and the Islamic Army of Aden-Abyan," Al-Bab.com, January 1999, http://www.al-bab.com/yemen/hamza/hassan.htm

56   Author's interview/senior U.S. official, Aug. 13, 2003.

57   *Terror in Yemen: Where To?* (Sanaa: 26th September Publications, December 2002), p.15.

58   Author's interview/senior U.S. official, Jan. 8, 2004.

59   B. Raman, "Attack on USS Cole: Background," South Asia Analysis Group, No. 152, October 16, 2000. http://www.saag.org/papers2/paper152.html

60 Anonymous, *Through Our Enemies' Eyes...* p. 200.

61 "Yemen: Report on Confession of Yemeni Kidnapper," *Ash-Sharq al-Awsat*, January 14, 1999 (FBIS).

62 "Yemen Terrorist Offers Deal to Stop Action," *ash-Sharq al-Awsat*, July 27, 1999 (FBIS).

63 B. Raman, "Attack on USS Cole..." Oct. 16, 2000.

64 "Court Upholds Verdict Against Abu al-Hassan's Successor," *Yemen Times*, April 2-8, 2001, No. 14, Vol. 11, http://www.yementimes.com/01/iss14/front.htm

65 Dhikra Abbas, "Yemeni Aide on Islamic Army, Threats," *al-Majallah*, Nov 21, 1999 (FBIS).

66 Author's interview/senior U.S. official, Aug. 13, 2003.

67 For more see: Anonymous, *Through Our Enemies' Eyes...* p. 202.

68 "Islamic Army Suspect Arrested for Aden Blasts: Police," AFP, January 4, 2001. See also "Patterns of Global Terrorism, 2001," http://www.state.gov/s/ct/rls/pgtrpt/2001/html/10254.htm#iaa

69 David Stout, "2 Yemeni Fugitives Indicted in Qaeda Attack on U.S.S. Cole," *New York Times*, May 15, 2003.

70 Peter Bergen, *Holy War, Inc....* (NY: Free Press, 2001), p. 168.

71 Jason Burke, p. 192-193.

72 Brian Whitaker, "Yemen Bombers Hit UK Embassy," *Guardian*, October 14, 2000. http://www.guardian.co.uk/Archive/Article/0,4273,4076525,00.html

73 "Patterns of Global Terrorism, 2000," http://www.state.gov/s/ct/rls/pgtrpt/2000/2438.htm

74 Author's interview with U.S. officials, Washington, DC. June 2003.

75 "Patterns... 2000."

76 "Patterns of Global Terrorism, 2001," http://www.state.gov/s/ct/rls/pgtrpt/2001/html/10247.htm

77 *Terror in Yemen: Where To?* (Sanaa: 26th September Publications, December 2002), p.63.

78 *Terror in Yemen...* p. 20. Also see: Susan Schmidt, "Yemen Recovers Huge Cache of Explosives from Blast Site," Washington Post, September 11, 2002.

79 *Terror in Yemen...* p. 51.

80 *Terror in Yemen...* p. 55.

81 *Terror in Yemen...* p. 26.

82 Ian Fisher, "Recent Attacks in Yemen seen as Sign of Large Terror Cell," *New York Times*, January 3, 2003.

83 Bill Gertz, "Al Qaeda Recruits Oil-Field Attackers," *Washington Times*, March 11, 2003.

84 "Yemeni Kills 3, Including U.S., Canadian Workers," Reuters, March 18, 2003

85 "Man in Yemen Says He Killed Three American Missionaries," AP, April 21, 2003.

86 "Blast at Yemeni Court," BBC World Service, May 14, 2003.

87 "Yemen: Background on Aden-Abyan Islamic Army," *Ash-Sharq al-Awsat*, January 5, 1999 (FBIS).

88 "Yemeni Authorities Arrest Militants from Jaysh Aden Abyan al-Islami," *Ash-Sharq al-Awsat*, July 10, 2003.

89   Abdel Salaam Taher, "Yemen Arrests Four Suspects, and Strikes at the Remaining Elements of the Hattat Group," *Ash-Sharq al-Awsat*, July 29, 2003.

90   "Patterns... 2001."

91   Christina Lamb, "British Forces Hunt Bin Laden in Yemen," *Washington Times*, November 18, 2002.

92   "The Yemeni Government Studies the Enforcement of Regulation of Activities of Mosques and Preachers," *al-Hayat*, June 9, 2003.

93   Andrew Higgins and Alan Cullison, "The Story of A Traitor to al Qaeda," *Wall Street Journal*, December 12, 2002.

94   David E. Kaplan, "Playing Offense: The Inside Story of how U.S. Terrorist Hunters are Going After al-Qaeda," *U.S. News and World Report*, June 2, 2003.

95   Andrew Higgins and Alan Cullison, Dec. 12, 2002.

96   "Guilty Plea From One Of 'Lackawanna Six'," AP, January 10, 2003. http://www.cbsnews.com/stories/2003/03/24/attack/main545772.shtml

97   "Sanaa Prepares to Present 200 Arrested Men to Court After Ending their Investigations," *Al-Hayat*, July 17, 2003.

98   "Yemen Seeks Cole Attack Suspects After Jailbreak," Reuters, April 11, 2003.

99   "Yemeni Authorities Arrest Extremists, and Investigated with Harithi," *Ash-Sharq al-Awsat*, September 25, 2003.

100   "Two Yemenis Wanted for Attack on French Tanker Extradited from Saudi," AFP, September 25, 2003.

101   "Islamic Group Uses Mercenaries for Attacks," Middle East Newsline, July 9, 2003.

102   Lowell Bergman, "Qaeda Trainee is Reported Seized in Yemen," *New York Times*, January 29, 2004.

103   "Yemen Captures 32 Militants from Qaeda and the Escape of the Most Wanted," *Ash-Sharq al-Awsat*, March 10, 2004. See also, "Yemen Reportedly Nabs Second Militant in Days," Reuters, March 4, 2004.

104   Hassan al-Zaidi, "Prospects of Releasing 70 Terror-Linked Detainees," *Yemen Times*, September 22, 2003.

105   Author's phone interview with Sanaa official, November 25, 2003.

106   Author's phone interview with State Department Spokesman, November 25, 2003.

107   "Ali Saleh announces the release of Islamists and detainees who haven't committed any crimes," *Al-Hayat*, October 15, 2003.

108   "Yemen: Release of Most of Those Accused of Terror," *Al-Hayat*, October 28, 2003.

109   "Yemen Frees or Pardons 146 Suspected of al-Qaeda Links," AFP, November 17, 2003.

110   Author's phone interview with Saleh advisor, November 25, 2003.

111   Author's phone interview/Saleh advisor, Nov. 25, 2003.

112   Author's phone interview/Saleh advisor, Nov. 25, 2003.

113   "U.S. Warns of New Terror Threat in Yemen, Calls for 'Exceptional' Security," AFP, September 29, 2003.

114   "Yemen Foils Attacks on British Embassy," AFP, December 14, 2003.

115   "Militant Groups Merging in Yemen," AFP, October 2, 2003. Also see: "Al-Balagh: Yemen: five Islamic groups merged in 'al-Jihad base',"

http://www.arabicnews.com/ansub/Daily/Day/031001/2003100124.html; and Khaled Al-Mahdi, "Yemen Foils Car Bomb Attacks," Arab News, October 1, 2003, http://www.arabnews.com/?page=4&section=0&article=32857&d=1&m= 10&y=2003

116   "World in Brief," *Washington Post*, October 17, 2003.

117   "Yemen Arrests Five Members from Al-Qaeda and Unveils Money Transfers from an Arab African State," *Ash-Sharq al-Awsat*, October 14, 2003.

118   "Yemen Detains 17 al-Qaida Suspects," UPI, October 16, 2003.

119   "Al-Qaeda Wing Rejects Truce that its Branch Was Offered in Yemen," *al-Hayat*, October 21, 2003.

120   "U.S.S. Cole Deployed; Prosecution of Suspects Delayed," *Yemen Observer*, December 4, 2003.

121   David Ensor, "Yemen Arrests al-Qaeda Leader," CNN.com, November 25, 2003. http://www.cnn.com/2003/WORLD/meast/11/25/yemen.arrest/index.html

122   Ahmed al-Haj, "Yemen Pursuing Another al-Qaida Member Following Arrest of Mastermind of Attacks on USS Cole, French Tanker," AP, November 26, 2003.

123   "Arab Figures Implicated in Al-Qaeda Funding," Reuters, December 6, 2003.

124   Peter Finn, "Sting Hints at U.S. Tactics on Terror," *Washington Post*, February 28, 2003.

125   Dan Eggen, "Cleric Charged with Aiding al-Qaeda; U.S. Says Yemeni Raised More than $20 Million," *Washington Post*, November 18, 2003.

126   "US Warns German al-Qaeda Extradition May Lead to 'Repercussions' in Yemen," AFP, November 17, 2003.

127   Author's interview with Dr. Abdul Hadi al-Hamdani, Sanaa, Yemen. June 15, 2003. See also, "Yemeni Official Accuses Leaders in Islah of Involvement in Terrorism and Criminal Sponsorship," *al-Hayat*, April 28, 2004.

128   Author's interview with Dr. Abdul Hadi al-Hamdani, Sanaa, Yemen. June 15, 2003. See also, "Yemeni Official Accuses Leaders in Islah of Involvement in Terrorism and Criminal Sponsorship," *al-Hayat*, April 28, 2004.

129   "United States Designates Bin Laden Loyalist," U.S. Treasury Press Release, February 24, 2004. www.treas.gov/press/releases/js1190.htm.

130   Author's interviews with Muhammed Kahtan, June 10, 2003 and Muhammed al-Yaddoumi, June 15, 2003. See also, "Az-Zindani Invites the American Ambassador to Visit Him," *Al-Hayat*, April 1, 2004.

131   Faisel Makram, "Ali Saleh: Let us shave our heads before others shave theirs," *al-Hayat*, January 12, 2004.

Chapter Five: Algeria

The Salafist Group for Preaching and Combat (GSPC) has puzzled terrorism analysts since its inception in 1998. Intelligence linking the GSPC and al-Qaeda is bountiful, but always murky. In January 2004, however, at least one leader from GSPC's ranks put an end to the speculation. A high-ranking lieutenant, Nabil Sahrawi (also known as Abu Ibrahim Mustafa), admitted to the daily Arabic newspaper *al-Hayat*, in his first ever interview, that his organization had a "connection to al-Qaeda and the other jihad organizations in the world."[1]

More than two years earlier, on September 23, 2001, President George W. Bush's Executive Order 13224 listed the GSPC as a threat to U.S. national security. The GSPC was also designated a Foreign Terrorist Organization (FTO) by the State Department on March 27, 2002. That report labeled it the "most effective remaining armed group,"[2] and the "largest, most active terrorist organization" in Algeria today.[3]

At this, Sahrawi bristled, "We classified ourselves even before America classified us." He added, "This is a war between the camp of Islam and the camp of the Cross, to which the Americans, Zionists, Jews, their apostate allies, and others belong."[4]

Sahrawi also boasted of the GSPC's fight against the Algerian government, claiming that his group was "fighting the regime in Algiers because of its unbelief and apostasy." He concluded by stating that the "Islamic State will not arise through means of slogans, demonstrations, parties and elections, but through blood, body parts, and [sacrifice of] lives..."[5]

While the interview was revealing in many ways, it failed to mention GSPC's most curious attribute: its sharp dichotomy. Indeed, the GSPC's domestic operatives are uniquely focused on attacking the government and the military; they have yet to hit international targets in Algeria, distinguishing them from many other affiliates that attack Western interests on their soil. By contrast, GSPC cells abroad allocate most of their resources toward attacking Western interests in Europe, with some spillover into Southeast Asia and elsewhere in the Middle East.

Using the international contacts and logistics channels established by the now-weakened Armed Islamic Group (Groupe Islamique Armé, or GIA), the GSPC network now provides recruits, finances, false documents, and technology to support attacks in Algeria and worldwide.[6] GSPC Europe could even be described as one of al-Qaeda's primary European networks. Its global activity makes the GSPC potentially more dangerous than any other al-Qaeda affiliate in the Arab world.

Troubled State-Building

While the GSPC has active arms at home in Algeria and abroad, both wings were born of Algeria's recent turmoil. A brief review of Algerian history shows why Algeria became a breeding ground for the GSPC, which rose from the ashes of other Algerian guerrilla groups including the National Liberation Front (Front de Libération Nationale, or FLN), the Armed Islamic Movement (Mouvement Islamique Armé, or MIA) and the GIA.

Algeria struggled under French colonial rule from 1830 until a brutal, eight-year guerrilla war waged by the FLN (countered by a failed but brutal campaign of French suppression) freed the country in 1962. While many Algerians hoped that the end of occupation would herald increased stability, the result was quite the opposite. Between 300,000 and one million Algerians died, internecine violence prompted internal purges against suspected former collaborators with the French, and the economy was failing.[7]

Independent Algeria's first new president, Ahmed Ben Bella, attempted to revive the country with a combination of nationalist, Arab, and Islamic ideologies, but his regime was corrupt and self-serving. A bloodless coup in 1965 brought

Defense Minister Houari Boumedienne to power. He made significant progress in Algerian state building, and was re-elected in 1976. During his tenure, Algeria's GDP per capita ballooned to roughly twice that of Morocco or Tunisia.[8] Despite this growth, Algeria struggled to rebuild a collective identity. Boumedienne died suddenly in 1978, leading to the accession of Colonel Chadli Benjedid in 1979. Despite new wealth derived from oil and natural gas, corruption, overpopulation, unemployment, unreliable food production, a decrepit transportation system, water shortages, overcrowded schools, and poor health services plagued the country.[9]

In what can only be seen as a classic case in the rise of Islamism, a grassroots Islamist movement emerged in the 1980s, backed by a network of as many as 8,000 unofficial mosques and institutions that filled the social welfare vacuum.[10] While some Islamists attacked hotels, stocks of alcohol, and brothels,[11] the majority provided crucial services to Algeria's suffering masses, including public parks, soccer fields, daycare for children, education, and garbage collection – all services neglected by the regime.[12] In this way, the Islamists benefited from the Algerian government's failings. They also received a boost from the 1979 Islamic revolution in Iran, which provided a successful model for Islamists, suggesting the possibility of an Islamic state in Algeria.

The Islamist Windfall

Algeria's Islamists continued to gain strength in the 1980s because of government failures and falling oil prices, which crippled the country. By October 1988, the social, economic, and political situation bottomed out. Riots swept the country, and Benjedid called in the army to quell the disturbances. Once the riots subsided, he promised reform. In February 1989, the FLN drafted a new constitution, calling for a new multi-party system. As a result, more than 30 political parties were formed, including the Islamic Salvation Front (Front Islamique du Salut, or FIS), a popular umbrella organization for smaller Islamic groups that sought the implementation of Islamic law (Shari'a), led by Abassi Madani and Ali Ben Haj.

It was widely believed that some FIS activities were funded in part by Iran, which made Algiers increasingly nervous.[13] FIS leaders further threatened to bring down the regime if it tampered with the forthcoming national elections.[14] Meanwhile, the political and economic misery in Algeria buoyed the popularity of FIS. In the June 1990 local elections, the FIS won 853 municipalities out of a possible 1,541.[15] That amounted to 54 percent of the electorate, compared to 33 percent won by the FLN.[16]

Compounding the FLN's humiliating electoral defeat was domestic tension over the looming the 1991 Gulf War. As war neared, FIS became increasingly pro-Iraq and anti-U.S., as seen through their slogans, protests, and even training camps for volunteers to fight for Saddam Husayn's Iraq.[17] The U.S. conflict with Iraq was a powerful symbol of FIS's soaring popularity. In the first round of national elections in 1991, FIS took 49 percent of the vote.[18] Out of a total of 430 contested seats, the FIS won 188, with a chance to win 150 more in the next round of voting.[19]

Civil War

Following the FIS victory, Algeria teetered on the brink of civil war. A series of destabilizing changes pushed it over the edge. The first occurred on January 11, 1992, when Algeria's military staged a coup, forcing Benjedid to resign. Fearing an Islamist takeover, the military installed Mohammed Boudiaf as president, cancelled the election results, placed restrictions on the Algerian press, dissolved the national assembly, and imposed martial law.[20] The government interned as many as 12,000 Islamists in prison camps in the Sahara.[21] Among the FIS members arrested were Madani and Ben Haj.[22]

From there, the country fell into total disarray. The MIA,

which was the FIS military wing, and other Islamist groups (including Takfir wa'l Hijra, the Jerusalem Brigades, Hamas, and Hizbullah),[23] declared war on the government. Algiers, in turn, declared a state of emergency. The Islamists, furious over the cancelled elections and widespread corruption, initiated a sustained campaign of secular school burnings, car bombings, and hijackings. They also targeted police, journalists, intellectuals, teachers, religious leaders, and other individuals who opposed their activities.

On June 29, 1992, a gunman in military uniform assassinated Boudiaf. Some observers saw this as an indication that Islamists had infiltrated the military at the highest levels.[24] Another power vacuum was created. Two years of attempts to find a suitable replacement for Boudiaf exacerbated an already dire situation. Algiers finally named Defense Minister Liamine Zeroual as interim president in 1994.

Armed Islamic Group (GIA)

As the authority of the Algerian regime continued to crumble, a powerful Islamist group known as the GIA emerged from the chaos. An al-Qaeda spokesman in London, Abu Hamza Al-Masri, revealed that the GIA officially formed from a cadre of seven senior Arab Afghan leaders in October 1992.[25] Their numbers were augmented when "approximately 900 battle-hardened Afghan veterans returned to Algeria, in three waves up to 1994."[26] Local Algerian Islamists joined them to form a loose network of cells, some of which were tied to the nascent al-Qaeda.[27]

In 1993, GIA militants launched a brutal campaign of assassinations on politicians and intellectuals in Algeria. Their tactics included slitting the throats of innocents, including women and children.[28] According to one report, militants threw acid in the faces of female students wearing Western clothing.[29] As violence intensified, one political observer noted, "We are slipping toward a

Kabul-like scenario, where the Afghans are shooting at each other and everyone else."[30] Indeed, with no government controls, the GIA and other armed groups were free to set up checkpoints along major thoroughfares, often putting civilians in the line of fire. By 1994, rural Algeria was divided into territories governed by GIA "emirs."[31]

In 1995, Liamine Zeroual retained the presidency in a national election. He held a series of polls in 1996 to foster increased confidence and public participation. This bid to restore government authority was not limited to these steps, however. From 1994 to 1997, the government adopted a new, aggressive policy, "terrorize the terrorist," which included the random killing of Islamist suspects and the systematic violation of human rights of suspected sympathizers. Journalists, for example, were often targeted for perceived GIA support.[32] The government created as many as 5,000 civilian militia groups to support the military, but in many instances those groups assaulted Islamists and civilians alike.[33]

As al-Masri recounts in his book, *The Khawaarij and Jihad*, on September 8, 1997, the GIA's radical leader, Antar Zouabri, issued a vitriolic statement alleging that the "Algerian people were *kuffar* [infidels], apostates and hypocrites because they did not support the GIA against the government."[34] Zouabri and his cohorts responded to the government offensive by slaughtering citizens they suspected of collaborating with the government. Thousands of Algerian civilians were massacred.

By 1999, after two years of seemingly interminable violence, the country was exhausted. Internecine violence had claimed as many as 150,000 lives since 1992.[35] Damage to the country's infrastructure exceeded $2 billion.[36] Neither the government nor the Islamist fighters had won. In a move designed to bring about national reconciliation, newly elected President Abdelaziz Bouteflika launched a general amnesty for Islamists. The following January, thousands of militants surrendered their weapons.[37] Al-Qaeda's affiliates – the GIA and a new organization called the GSPC – did not.

Weak Government Authority

The combination of Algeria's troubled history, faltering economy, conflicting regional and tribal allegiances, and a nascent national identity made governing the country extremely difficult. Guerrilla fighting and civil war further weakened the Algerian government's ability to project its authority in the 1990s. Lack of confidence in the government was at an all time high, services to the people were at an all time low, and militants challenged the government at nearly every level.

Of particular concern in the mid-1990s was the so-called Triangle of Death, "a terrorist-infested area between the towns of Blida, Medea and Boufarik, about fifty miles south of the capital in the foothills of the Atlas Mountains."[38] The rugged terrain and cavernous mountains provided good hideouts by day and good bases of operation by night. The Islamists also exploited the thickly forested Mitidja Plain.[39] While this topography greatly assisted the Islamists, violence was certainly not limited to advantageous terrain. Clashes between the government and civilian militias against the Islamists were reported throughout the country, particularly across the northern coastal plain, home to the vast majority of Algerians.

After the 1999 Civil Accord, the areas of conflict shifted, but military and insurgency operations were still regularly reported across the coastal plain. Reports in 2004 indicated that the area of Islamist activity continues to grow, particularly outside the "major urban areas."[40] This trend does not bode well for Algerian stability; nearly all of Algeria's insurgency and counter-insurgency operations take place in the area where more than 90 percent of Algerians live.

Al-Qaeda's Algerian affiliates have staked out certain

territories along the coastal plain. The GIA – the organization from which the GSPC evolved – operates in pockets along the western coastal plain, from Algiers to the border with Morocco. The bulk of GIA activity, coupled with some GSPC attacks, occurs in the regions of Chelf, Relizane and Ain Defla.[41]

The GSPC, since its 1998 inception, has been based in the center of the country and the eastern coastal plain.[42] The areas just east of Algiers, including Boumerdes, Tizi Ouzou and Bouira have been the hardest hit,[43] but other attacks against government targets have been reported on the eastern plain in the Jijel, Skikda, Batna, and Tebessa governorates.[44]

While most attacks occur on the north coast, Algeria's east and south are the weakest areas of government control in the country. Like Egypt's south, the area is underdeveloped, and militants are able to roam freely. The GPSC has exploited lucrative contraband networks south of the coastal plain along the borders with Libya, Mauritania, Mali, Niger, and Tunisia.[45] Recent reports show a spike in terrorist activity, particularly in the eastern provinces of Batna and Tebessa, where least one GSPC emir has been active.[46]

Kabylia is another area of concern. The GSPC continues to exploit this governorate for its own operations (it is one of the group's original strongholds). Government control in this area is weakened by an ethnic Berber secessionist movement, which has been calling for autonomy intermittently since Algerian independence. Led by Ferhat Mehenni, the Movement for the Autonomy of Kabylia has been growing and organizing since June 2001.[47] The push for autonomy has increased in recent decades, particularly after periods of unrest, such as a two-year rebellion in 1963 by the Socialist Forces Front against the new Algerian government; the 1980 "Berber Spring" protests against the government that resulted in mass arrests; and the year-long Berber student boycott in 1994 protesting the exclusion of their Tamazight language from classrooms.[48]

Although modern Algeria is not a failed state, its weak authority is painfully evident. This deficit was particularly apparent in December 2001, when heavy rains flooded many parts of the country. While a national crisis unfolded, Algiers failed to respond, forcing bystanders to assume the role of emergency workers. Some of the worst flooding was a direct result of government security measures in the 1990s; military forces cut down large swaths of the forest and sealed sewer drains where Islamist fighters often sought refuge.[49]

Algerian officials insist that the insurgency is on its last legs. Still, more than 800 Algerians were killed as a result of political violence in 2003.[50] Those numbers are relatively low when compared to the bloodbath of the 1990s, and they may continue to decline, particularly as Algiers receives military assistance from the U.S. and elsewhere. However, due to the ongoing activities of the GIA and the GSPC, terrorism will almost surely remain a source of instability for the foreseeable future.

GIA, GSPC, and al-Qaeda

Al-Qaeda has long been drawn to areas of turmoil; the network seeks to make local conflicts part of its global jihad. Algeria was thus particularly appealing in the 1990s, but an al-Qaeda foothold in the country was not easily established. Although the GIA was born from a cadre of veteran Afghan fighters, it operated relatively autonomously in the early 1990s.[51] By the middle of the decade, however, the group began to receive some financial, ideological, and logistical support from al-Qaeda.[52] Some of that aid was supplied through two known al-Qaeda figures in London: Abu Qatada al-Filastini (Shaykh Omar Mahmoud Othman abu Omar) and Abu Musab as-Suri (Mustafa Setmariam Asnan.[53] During the mid-1990s, it was also reported that bin Laden sent fighters and envoys to join up with GIA leaders in Algeria.[54] One of his emissaries even bribed an Algerian official in 1994 to release an accused terrorist from prison.[55] The GIA also reportedly maintained an official office that was in constant contact with the al-Qaeda leadership in Sudan.[56]

After the GIA under Zouabri declared the Algerian public to be *kuffar* (literally, infidels or disbelievers) for supporting the government in Algiers, Abu Hamza admits that "a major rift" developed between the GIA and al-Qaeda.[57] That rift emerged over the GIA's tactics of civilian massacres, kidnapping, and abusive language in their communiqués.[58] Abu Qatada and Abu Musab denounced Zouabri in 1996.[59] Bin Laden, according to one report, stated that the GIA "had become deviant and lost its reputation."[60] Ayman az-Zawahiri also rejected the GIA's wanton violence in a 1997 communiqué.[61]

This schism motivated al-Qaeda to seek out an alternate representative in Algeria, leading to the creation of the GSPC.[62] In 1998, GIA Emir Hassan Hattab left the group and publicly condemned "shedding the blood of innocent people in massacres."[63] At the age of 30,[64] he reportedly established the GSPC at the prompting of bin Laden, who urged him to attack "legitimate" (i.e. military and government) targets.[65] Several reports suggest that bin Laden may have even suggested the name GSPC.[66] Ironically, the terror network responsible for the most horrendous attacks against civilians in the modern age sought a less violent representative in Algeria in an effort to appeal to the Algerian people. According to several sources, an Algerian Afghan associate of bin Laden named Qamaredin Kharban helped to maintain the logistical and financial lines between al-Qaeda and the embryonic GSPC.[67]

On September 14, 1998, the group released its first communiqué, announcing that former GIA members had established the GSPC with Hattab as its leader.[68] Operating out of the Kabylia region, the GSPC started with an estimated 700 fight-ers.[69] Over the years, it grew to as many as 4,000 fighters, with

1,500 in the Kabylia region alone.[70] Many of them had combat experience with the GIA or had trained with al-Qaeda in Afghanistan.[71]

Like the GIA, the GSPC's tactics included attacks at false roadblocks, as well as raids on military, police and government convoys. The group also financed its activities through extortion, "particularly [of] villagers and shop owners."[72] Under Hattab and deputy Abd al-Azziz Abbi, the GSPC expanded in Algeria's eastern and central provinces.[73] Several French sources explain that this expansion was greatly aided by an alliance with a little known group, al-Baqoun ala al-Ahad.[74] Within a year after the GSPC was founded, the group seized territories in the eastern suburbs of Algiers, as well as the Jijel coast, Kabylia, and areas south of Algiers. By 2004, its presence stretched from the eastern border to the western coastal resort of Tipaza, primarily outside the urban centers, where security was sub-standard.[75]

GSPC Southeast Asia

In addition to its domestic expansion, GSPC activity spilled outside of Algeria. Indeed, journalist Maria Ressa wrote an interesting account of how the group joined forces with al-Qaeda and its affiliates in Southeast Asia.

After the twin U.S. embassy bombings in Africa in 1998, Ressa reported, bin Laden and senior al-Qaeda operative Abu Zubayda contacted Hattab, tasking him to create Algerian training camps for Southeast Asian fighters.[76] According to this account, the GSPC also sent its own operatives to Southeast Asia. Abd as-Selem Boulanour was one of two militants from the group captured in the Philippines in 1999. He was found with a training manual that he wrote for the Moro Islamic Liberation Front (MILF), a Philippine al-Qaeda affiliate. The manual detailed techniques in combat, explosives, weapons, communication, military tactics, and security. According to Ressa, Boulanour was sent by the GSPC to the Philippines "with the intention of providing further assistance to the MILF at the request of al-Qaeda."[77]

GSPC Europe

Whatever ties remain in Southeast Asia, the GSPC is far more active in Europe. Hundreds of Algerian operatives have links to European cells responsible for financing, logistics, and planning attacks for al-Qaeda. When apprehended, many of these European militants confessed their ties to Hattab, the GSPC, and al-Qaeda.[78] As analyst Rohan Gunaratna notes, these European cells generate "propaganda, funds and supplies for their campaign to replace the military government in Algeria with an Islamic state."[79]

To understand these links, one must first understand how this network of cells was established (principally in France, Italy, Germany and Belgium).[80] It is believed that these cells were first created and utilized by the Algerian Afghans during the jihad against the Soviets. The GIA subsequently employed these channels both to supply the guerrilla movement in Algeria,[81] and later to go global with a string of eleven bombing attacks in France in 1995.[82] The attacks were part of a larger strategy to proclaim dominance over other Algerian rebel groups that were negotiating a ceasefire with Algiers.

The GIA unquestionably went global when it hijacked an Air Algerie flight to Spain on February 28, 1994. In July of that year, the group also killed seven Italian sailors docked near Algiers. More ominously, on December 24, 1994, the GIA hijacked Air France flight 8969. The hijackers, who did not know how to fly, intended to force the pilot to fly the plane into the Eiffel Tower in Paris.[83] In the end, the plane was diverted to Marseilles, where most of the passengers were set free, except for three French nationals who were killed.[84] While the GIA deemed that attack unsuccessful, the lessons learned may have been applied on September 11, 2001 by terrorists who actually knew how to fly.

Meanwhile, GIA bombings in Paris from July to October 1995 killed eight people and wounded some 200.[85] Logistics and financing for those attacks clearly came from GIA's European networks. Clues from those attacks led authorities to GIA European cells, which enabled them to establish a definitive connection between the GIA and al-Qaeda.[86] Algerian militant Rashid Ramda was arrested in London for financing the cell that bombed a Paris metro. During the investigation, Scotland Yard uncovered "several financial transfers" from bin Laden's office in Khartoum. Other links were also established "between Osama bin Laden and the Algerian GIA and the Islamic supply networks that are loyal to them in Europe."[87]

Three years later, the GSPC took control of the GIA's European networks. Hattab, who is believed to have controlled these networks before defecting from the GIA, may have facilitated the transition.[88] It is reported that he also received additional assistance from his allies in al-Baqoun ala al-Ahad, which had a vast European network.[89]

Since the late 1990s, an immense amount of GSPC activity was reported in Europe, both in support of the GSPC in Algeria, as well as the broader al-Qaeda network. Concern over these cells was reportedly so high that six months before the attacks of September 11, intelligence officials from the U.S. and several European countries met in Europe to deal with the growing threat.[90] In recent years, dozens of militants were arrested and a multitude of cells were uncovered or dismantled throughout Europe.

Belgium. According to a European Union report, Belgium has long played host to Islamist activities linked to the Afghanistan jihad, particularly after mujahedin opened a recruiting office in Brussels in the 1980s. In the 1990s, Afghan veterans also created "logistical support structures" to help operatives in Belgium.[91]

Since the late 1990s, Belgian authorities have foiled a number of GSPC plots. Algerian Farid Moulouk was arrested in Belgium for his role in planning a 1998 GSPC scheme to bomb the World Cup soccer tournament in France.[92] Tunisian Nizar Trabelso was arrested in September 2001 for his involvement in a Spanish al-Qaeda cell with direct ties to GSPC. Trabelso was found with automatic weapons and chemicals to be used in explosives.[93]

Perhaps the most interesting GSPC story to emerge from Belgium involves two French converts from Catholicism to Islam who were members of GSPC. They provided false passports to two Tunisians who killed Northern Alliance leader Ahmad Shah Massoud. The Tunisians, pretending to be journalists seeking an exclusive interview in Afghanistan, detonated bombs strapped to their bodies, killing Massoud. This attack took place just two days before the attacks of September 11, 2001.[94] Massoud's assassination was likely designed to weaken the Northern Alliance with the full expectation that the U.S. would require its help in the post-September 11 invasion of Afghanistan.

England.   London is a major center for al-Qaeda fundraising and recruiting. It also appears to be the center of GSPC activity abroad. Cells in London play a central role in the production of false passports, identification cards, credit cards, and other counterfeit documents for militants the world over.[95] One British official was "convinced that the [international] base of the GIA and GSPC is in London. Their money and their newspapers are all there."[96] "Their newspapers" included *al-Ansar*, a magazine that documented the exploits of GIA as far back as 1994.[97] Abu Hamza al-Masri of London's Finsbury Park Mosque also served as a spokesman for GSPC activities (in addition to the Yemeni IAA, mentioned in chapter three).

In 2001, seven men belonging to an al-Qaeda cell led by Abu Qatada were arrested on suspicion of membership in GSPC's "English cell." Qatada, for his part, is wanted in Jordan for several attacks in 1998. U.S. authorities froze his assets, and he is listed in at least one declassified CIA document as an affiliate of al-Qaeda and the GSPC.[98] Qatada was the imam of the Four Feathers

Mosque in London, where Algerian officials believe much of GSPC's European activities were planned.[99] The English cell had plans to bomb or use sarin nerve gas at a European Parliament meeting in 2001.[100]

A GSPC recruitment video was discovered in a GSPC safe house in England just before September 11, 2001, depicting "the massacre of Algerian soldiers by exultant Salafis, who are seen cutting the throats and beheading their victims. The camera lingers over the neck wounds so that the pumping arterial blood can be seen clearly."[101] The video exhorts Muslims to join al-Qaeda's global jihad.

More recently, in January 2004, the *Times* of London reported that an undercover operation by British agents penetrated several Islamist terror cells planning an attack in Britain. The operation revealed "details of how members of a cell from the Salafist Group for Preaching and Combat... allegedly discussed possible targets for attack in Britain [in 2003]. The only two men in Britain jailed for links with al-Qaeda were Algerians living in Leicester."[102]

France. Home to a rapidly growing population of Algerians and North Africans, France has been another important center for GSPC's European network. The thwarted plot to bomb the World Cup in June of 1998 is just one example of GSPC's reach in France.[103] Nearly 100 people were arrested as a result of that plot.[104]

Another thwarted bomb plot attributed to the GSPC was designed to disrupt the Paris-Dakar Road Rally in 2000.[105] The threat prompted organizers to airlift the race from Niger to Libya to avoid potential dangers in the Algerian desert.[106] Also in 2000, suspected members of a French GSPC cell were arrested for a plot to bomb a French market on Christmas.[107]

In 2004, French intelligence again discovered a GSPC plot

to attack the Paris-Dakar Rally. This plot was reportedly planned by GSPC emir Amari Saifi in Algeria.[108] Also in 2004, the *New York Times* reported that the GSPC maintains a spokesman in Paris named Abu Bakr Rajab Dazi.[109]

Italy. On April 4, 2001, Italian police arrested a number of GSPC suspects in Milan who were planning to attack the U.S. embassy in Rome.[110] Wiretaps by Italian security revealed discussions about attacking American targets and the desire to attract funding for future attacks.[111] Italian authorities arrested others in October 2003 upon suspicion of providing forged documents and financing to GSPC terrorists coming from Algeria to Italy, en route to other countries.[112] One U.S. report labeled a Milan mosque as an al-Qaeda "station house."[113] In January 2004, a Milan court sentenced Mohammad al-Mahfoudi to 16 months in prison for providing assistance to the GSPC. He was convicted of "association with the aim of international terrorism."[114]

In 2003, the Italian government linked Esside Sami Ben Khemais, a high-ranking GSPC member in Milan, to Ansar al-Islam, the al-Qaeda affiliate operating out of Iraq.[115] While the intersection of al-Qaeda affiliates certainly fits the *modus operandi* of al-Qaeda, the link between the GSPC and Ansar al-Islam should be of particular concern, and not just to Rome. This relationship is a clear indication of other synergies throughout Europe.

In June 2004, the U.S. government labeled six al-Qaeda loyalists operating in Italy as Specially Designated Terrorists. According to the report, "the cell is associated with the Salafist Group for Preaching and Combat," and it "engaged in criminal acts with the intent to profit from clandestine migration and false documentation." One operative raised "funds for extremist activity, most notably for the GSPC."[116]

The Netherlands. In April 2002, Dutch police arrested four members of the GSPC for providing support to the "international jihad." The suspects were accused of providing false identity papers and funds to GSPC operatives around the world.[117] One year later, Dutch authorities arrested several Algerians "accused of supporting terrorist activities" of the GSPC.[118] Their activities, which included drug trafficking and document forgery, continue to concern U.S. and Dutch authorities.[119]

Spain. Several GSPC members apprehended in Spain in recent years had been in communication with Algerian Ahmed Ressam, the al-Qaeda operative convicted for planning to bomb a Los Angeles airport on New Year's Eve 1999/2000.[120] In late September 2001, Spanish police dismantled a GSPC cell of six.[121] Spanish Prime Minister Jose Maria Aznar noted the GSPC cell's "financial connections to the terrorist organization led by bin Laden."[122] The men in that cell sent high-tech equipment and intelligence to Algeria. The cell, which took two years to dismantle, had operatives throughout Spain, including one in the Northern Basque region. Authorities continue to uncover connections between the dismantled cell and other GSPC sleeper cells in Spain.[123]

Most of the operatives in Europe are not necessarily GSPC fighters. They can be better defined now as part of the European jihadi milieu. Indeed, U.S. officials recall instances where GSPC operatives attempted to assert control over the European network and failed.[124] Regardless, this European network of Algerians and other North Africans is extensive. The matrix of connections between the European clusters and the Algerian group are complex and often inconclusive. Still, the GSPC European network ranks among the most active terrorist networks in the world.

International Intrigue at Home

As demonstrated by the vitriolic rhetoric in Nabil Sahrawi's aforementioned January 2004 interview with the London Arabic daily *al-Hayat*, elements within the Algerian GSPC may be contemplating an expanded international role. The spring 2003 GSPC kidnapping of 32 foreigners (including Germans, Austrians, Swiss, a Swede and a Dutchman),[125] led by GSPC emir Amari Saifi (aka "Abd ar-Rezzak al-Para"), indicated the GSPC's intentions to attack foreign targets in Algeria.[126] On May 13, Algerian forces clashed with the kidnappers and recovered some of the hostages near the Saharan city of Tamanrasset.[127] One soldier and nine militants were killed in the subsequent four-hour gun battle.[128] By late summer, the GSPC delivered the remaining hostages to Mali (minus one German hostage who died of heat stroke), where Germany, with help from Libya, finally secured the release of the remaining hostages on August 18.[129] The prevailing rumor was that the Malian government paid a ransom of up to $6 million to GSPC,[130] and that the tourists' home countries promised to pay the Malian government in development aid.[131] Libyan leader Moammar Qadahfi's son, Saif al-Islam, admitted that Libya helped mediate the release, but denied paying the ransom.[132]

Whether Libya contributed to the ransom is still a matter of concern. Many U.S. government officials believe that evidence in support of Libyan involvement is weak, but acknowledge Qadahfi's previous history of paying ransoms to al-Qaeda affiliates, ironically under the cover of a charitable organization with a stated goal of promoting peace. In August 2000, for example, the Philippine Abu Sayyaf group held 25 Western hostages for several months on the island of Jolo. When negotiations stalled between Manila and the terrorists, Qadahfi intervened, offering as much as $5 million per hostage. Abu Sayyaf leaders then spent their enormous ransom on M-16 automatic rifles, grenade launchers, and other weaponry, as well as a speedboat. According to one Australian report, a subsequent recruitment drive "attracted an estimated 2,000 new fighters, with each man paid $2,000 to join."[133]

In addition to possible terror financing from Libya, the

GSPC kidnapping also revealed a possible splinter within the organization. According to several reports, corroborated by French, American and Algerian officials, al-Para likely acted on his own. After a mysterious meeting with what appeared to be a bin Laden envoy, the rogue emir seized foreign hostages without the consent of Hattab or the GSPC's leadership.[134] Perhaps al-Para, a former staff sergeant in the Algerian military,[135] wanted global recognition for his group.

In mid-October 2003, press in Algeria and France reported another power struggle in the top ranks of the GSPC. Whether the dispute stemmed from a personality conflict or a disagreement about strategy was not specified. It was known, however, that Sahrawi was attempting to supplant Hattab. The reports emerged amidst an Algerian army offensive in some of the GPSC's strongholds east of Algiers.[136] At least four GSPC members were brought into custody. They verified that Hattab was still leading the organization, but that differences remained between Hattab and his deputies.[137] Thus, Sahrawi's January 2004 interview in *al-Hayat* declaring the GSPC's ties to al-Qaeda may have been an attempt to gain support for his faction, both at home and abroad. Sahrawi also released a separate statement dated September 11, 2003, reiterating his group's formal ties to al-Qaeda, saying that the, "GSPC announces to the world in general and to Muslims in particular its allegiance to all Muslims and to fighting to the glory of God in Palestine and in Afghanistan under the direction of Mullah Omar... and of the al-Qaeda organization of Osama bin Laden."[138]

Increased U.S. Involvement

Washington's interest in Algeria (and the rest of the Middle East) increased dramatically in 2003. On October 20, the State Department announced the designation of another Specially Designated Global Terrorist Group from Algeria known as Dhamat

Houmet Daawa Salafia. This small group, which previously operated under the name of Katibat al-Ahoual (Horror Squadron), is a known splinter group of the GIA that first emerged after its leader, Mohammed Benslim, left the group. A statement from the State Department indicated that the group "is well organized and equipped with military materiel, and has engaged in terrorist activity in Algeria and internationally. It is responsible for numerous killings since the mid-1990s, and has escalated its attacks in recent years." The statement also explicitly asserted the group's links to al-Qaeda.[139]

Four days later, the U.S. government designated three individuals as terrorists involved with the GSPC. Al-Bakoun ala al-Ahad was also designated as a group that provided "support" to the GSPC.[140] Two months later, in December, Abd ar-Rezzak al-Para was labeled a specially designated terrorist, reflecting a mounting interest in the Algerian theater of the war on terror.[141] In late April 2004, the U.S. Treasury's Office of Foreign Assets Control added yet another four Algerians to its list of specially designated terrorists.[142]

The October designations coincided with a visit by Assistant Secretary of State William Burns to Algiers on October 25 and 26. During his visit, he pledged increased counterterrorism cooperation with Algeria and an additional $700,000 in funds for military training for Algerian security.[143] Not long after that, Secretary of State Colin Powell made his first ever visit to Algeria on December 3. He confirmed that "the relationship between the United States and Algeria has been improving in so many ways in recent years," especially in political, technical, counterterrorism and economic cooperation.[144]

Previously, Washington had largely left Algeria's problems and development in the hands of France for largely historical reasons. Terrorism issues, in addition to Washington's efforts to win hearts and minds in the Muslim world, led directly to the so-called "Pan-Sahel" initiative, a State Department program designed to bolster African security, coordinated by Special Operations Command Europe (Eucom). The initiative called for, among other things, the allocation of $125 million over five years in military operations to weaken the Islamist threat in the Sahara Desert region, and to control the grey areas throughout the Sahel.[145] The plan evolved to include the strengthening of local capabilities, with an aim of weakening the GSPC's most dangerous emir, Amari Saifi (al-Para). To this end, the *New York Times* reported:

> The United States European Command sent a Navy P-3 Orion surveillance aircraft to sweep the area, relaying Mr. Saifi's position to forces in the region. Mali pushed him out of the country to Niger, which in turn chased him into Chad, where, with United States Special Forces support of an airlift of fuel and other supplies, 43 of his men were killed or captured. Mr. Saifi himself got away...[146]

The alarm over al-Para stemmed from his activities in early 2004. After receiving his ransom monies for the kidnapped European tourists, al-Para went to Mali and gathered unprecedented numbers of recruits, vehicles, and weapons (including mortar launchers, rocket propelled grenades and SAMs). According to one U.S. military official, al-Para's ransom money provided his wing of the GSPC with a military budget that was larger than that of many countries in Africa. U.S. military officials considered al-Para the most dangerous GSPC terrorist.

In early June 2004, Chadian rebels captured al-Para.[147] The government of Chad reported that it had killed more than 40 GSPC militants in two days of fighting during the previous March.[148] The Chadians also received some military assistance from the French.[149] Algiers then opened negotiations with N'Djamena to acquire al-Para at a substantial price.

By late June, the Algerian army proudly announced that the GSPC's top leadership was "completely neutralized." This came amidst reports that Sahrawi had been killed in a gun battle east of Algiers. Sahrawi's lieutenant, Abd al-Azziz Abbi was also killed in the firefight.[150] This, according to some estimates, left Mokhtar Bel Mokhtar as the senior GSPC operative in Algeria, particularly if the Chadians were to hand al-Para back to Algiers.

Continued Domestic Violence

Despite increased international activity, the GSPC has not renounced its original domestic agenda. Regular attacks are reported in the traditional GIA strongholds west of Algiers, as well as GSPC's eastern territories.[151] In September 2003, 180 people were killed in battles between government forces and militants from the GIA or the GSPC. In one such raid, the 15 GSPC members suspected of kidnapping the Europeans were killed in hideouts east of the capital, and a significant weapons cache was seized.[152] Another military offensive a few days later killed a number of GSPC fighters, "whose charred remains were found in a cave."[153]

In November, the Algerian government reported the arrest of Rashid Oukali (Abu Turaab ar-Rashid), the leader of the GIA. *Al-Hayat* reported that the arrest occurred after Oukali was injured in a shootout just outside of Algiers.[154] Analysts continued to question the veracity of this and other Algerian reports, given the government's past disinformation during its policy of "total war." Indeed, independent reports indicated that Oukali was still leading GIA operations on the ground. Similarly, press reports in May 2004 indicated that Hassan Hattab was killed in 2003 by his former lieutenants.[155] Subsequent reports refuted Hattab's death, claiming he was "still alive in the Tizi Ouzou region."[156]

Future Prospects

The *modus operandi* for the average al-Qaeda affiliate generally involves attacking Western targets on "home turf." Examples cited in this book include Yemen's Islamic Army of Aden (attacks on the *Cole* and *Limburg*), Lebanon's Asbat al-Ansar (attacks on various foreign embassies and fast food restaurants), and Egypt's al-Gamaa al-Islamiyya (the Luxor massacre). Algeria's GSPC, however, has not attacked Western targets inside Algeria. This is strange in that more than 40 countries maintain embassies in Algiers, including some of al-Qaeda's favorite target countries – the U.S., Britain, Spain, Italy, and France. Other potential targets might include foreign consulates, diplomatic housing, oil and gas companies, as well as foreign airlines. Bechtel, Arco, Exxon, and Mobil are among the major U.S. companies with a presence in Algeria.[157]

Thus, the GSPC's continued and brutal terrorist activities in Algeria are almost entirely local in focus, and do not pose an immediate threat to U.S. security. The "near enemy," the Algerian state, is the primary target mainly because its security apparatus vigorously stalks GSPC fighters, restricting their operating environment. Further, while the U.S. is not popular among the GSPC's ranks, the historical lack of American involvement in Algeria has likely led the group to leave Washington out of its struggle for now.

Meanwhile, GSPC operatives across Europe appear to be focused squarely on attacking European targets. While logistics or fundraising for the local insurgents in Algeria would appear to be part of the mission of the GSPC's European network, the primary focus appears to remain Europe, itself. Algerian government targets, including embassies or consulates, have been left alone.

The reasons for this dichotomy remain unclear. Since the launch of the war on terror, however, the U.S. government has taken a more active interest in the GSPC, both in Algeria and in Europe. Clearly, the European activities of the GSPC pose a threat to Western interests, but for the most part, these activities are a European problem. Nevertheless, Washington and Algiers have expanded ties in recent years, demonstrated by visits from senior diplomats to Algeria in the autumn and winter of 2003. Presidents Bush and Bouteflika also met in 2001 and 2003 to discuss heightened cooperation in the war on terror.

While Washington and Algiers have taken unprecedented diplomatic steps, most U.S. officials admit that tangible progress has been moderate. Highlights include some NGO interaction, military training, and economic cooperation in the petrochemical sector. However, Algeria's ambassador to the U.S., Idriss Al-Jazairy, in a May 2003 speech, stated that his country was "prepared to reinforce cooperation" on the military level, particularly in combat training and other activities.[158]

In his December 2003 visit, Secretary of State Colin Powell affirmed Washington's interest in expanding cooperation with Algeria. However, he also rightly stressed the need for Algeria to "move forward with respect to political reform and with respect to human rights issues."[159] Clearly, Washington should push Algeria to devote more effort toward improving human rights, lifting state controls on the media, and implementing much-needed reform. Reports also indicate a drastic housing shortage, as well as major deficits in health, urban services, and education.[160] Algeria must also take steps to ensure that its income from hydrocarbons (accounting for 97 percent of Algeria's exports) trickles down to the people, rather than simply contributing to the longevity of the ruling elite and the military.

In other words, the U.S. should explore increased counter-terrorism cooperation while also working to shore up Algeria's legitimacy. In this way, the GSPC can be defeated without leaving the conditions in place for yet another radical group to replace it. As Washington reengages with Algiers, caution is needed; too much involvement with an already unpopular government could spark anger against the U.S. in a country where there has been a surprisingly low level of anti-American sentiment. The immediate U.S. goal should be to act quietly as a force for change in the areas of counterterrorism and political reform.

Finally, U.S. counterterrorism initiatives should include precautions to ensure that other neighboring countries are prepared to assist in ongoing security efforts, particularly along their porous borders. Indeed, with the help of U.S. forces, effective Algerian counterterrorism could create new dangers. It could force the GSPC out of Algeria, pushing the group's areas of operation into new countries. The group has already spilled over into Mali, Chad and Libya.[161] So, while clearing the GSPC from Algeria could help Algiers in its battle against al-Qaeda affiliates, such operations could also create new and unforeseen terrorism problems for other countries in the region.

Notes

1   "Interview with Algerian Terror Leader Associated with Al-Qa'ida: The Islamic State Will Arise Only Through Blood and Body Parts," MEMRI, No. 642, January 13, 2004.
2   "Salafist Group for Call and Combat (GSPC)," *Patterns of Global Terrorism 2001*, (Washington, DC: United States Department of State, 2002). http://www.state.gov/s/ct/rls/pgtrpt/2001/html/10252.htm - gspc
3   "Middle East Overview," *Patterns of Global Terrorism 2001*, (Washington, DC: United States Department of State, 2002). http://www.state.gov/s/ct/rls/pgtrpt/2001/html/10247.htm

4   "Interview with Algerian Terror Leader..." Jan. 13, 2004.

5   "Interview with Algerian Terror Leader..." Jan. 13, 2004.

6   "Salafist Group for Call and Combat (GSPC)," *Patterns of Global Terrorism 2001*, (Washington, DC: United States Department of State, 2002). http://www.state.gov/s/ct/rls/pgtrpt/2001/html/10252.htm - gspc; Also see Andreu Manresa, "Algiers Accuses the Saudi Millionaire Bin Laden of Paying the GIA Terrorists," *El Pais* (Madrid), October 8, 1998.

7   Algerians claim that one million people were killed during the war of independence, though official estimates indicate that the death toll was between 300,000 and 500,000. See Avraham Sela (ed.)"Algeria," *Political Encyclopedia of the Middle East*. (NY: Continuum, 1999), p. 28.

8   Luis Martinez, *The Algerian Civil War: 1990-1998*, (NY: Columbia University Press, 2000), p. 2.

9   John P. Entelis, "Islam, Democracy, and the State: The Reemergence of Authoritarian Politics in Algeria," *Islamism and Secularism in North Africa*, John Reudy, ed., (NY: St. Martin's Press, 1994), p. 225. Also see: Cathie Lloyd, "Multi-Causal Conflict in Algeria: National Identity, Inequality and Political Islam," QEH Working Paper, No. 104, April 2003, p. 6.

10   Hugh Roberts, *The Battlefield, Algeria 1988-2002: Studies in A Broken Polity*, (London: Verso, 2003), p. 20. Also see: Avraham Sela, ed., "Algeria," *Political Encyclopedia of the Middle East*. (NY: Continuum, 1999), p. 30.

11   Hugh Roberts, pp. 20-21.

12   Paul Schemm, "Algeria's Return to its Past: Can the FIS Break the Vicious Cycle of History?" *Middle East Insight*, Vol. 11, no. 2 (1995), p. 37.

13   Edgar O'Ballance, *Islamic Fundamentalist Terrorism, 1979-1995: The Iranian Connection*. (NY: NYU Press, 1997) p. 187; and Mohammed Mohaddessin, *Islamic Fundamentalism: The New Global Threat*, (Washington, DC: Seven Locks Press, 1993), p. 88.

14   Luis Martinez, p. 57.

15   "Algeria: A Decade of Events," (in Arabic), May 25, 2002. http://www.aljazeera.net/in-depth/aljeria-election/2002/5/5-25-1.htm

16   Cathie Lloyd, "Multi-Causal Conflict in Algeria: National Identity, Inequality and Political Islam," QEH Working Paper, No. 104, April 2003, p. 10.

17   Hugh Roberts, pp. 70-71.

18   Paul Schemm, p. 38.

19   John P. Entelis, p. 243

20   John P. Entelis, p. 219.

21   Cathie Lloyd, p. 14.

22   Hugh Roberts, p. 76.

23   Luis Martinez, p. 69.

24   John P. Entelis, p. 243.

25   Abu Hamza al-Masri, *The Khawaarij and Jihaad*, (London: Finsbury Park Mosque, 2000), p. 150.

26   Simon Reeve, p. 3.

27 For more on this process, see: Osman Tasgart, "Report on Bin Laden's Sleeper Networks in Europe," *Al-Majallah*, November 4, 2001 (FBIS).

28 Mona Yacoubian, "Algeria's Struggle for Democracy," Occasional Paper Series No. 3, Council on Foreign Relations, 1997, p.25.

29 Alistair Horne, "The Algerian Connection: What it Means and What it has Done," *National Review*, February 10, 2003.

30 Youssef M. Ibrahim, "Algeria is Seen Edging Toward Breakup," *New York Times*, April 4, 1994.

31 Luis Martinez, p.94.

32 Quintan Wiktorowicz, "The GIA and the GSPC in Algeria." *In the Service of al-Qaeda: Radical Islamic Movements*, Magnus Ranstorp, ed. (NY: Hurst Publishers and New York University Press) forthcoming.

33 "Civil Concord: A Peace Initiative Wasted," International Crisis Group Africa Report, No. 31, July 9, 2001. Also see: Cathie Lloyd, p. 19.

34 Abu Hamza al-Masri, p. 157.

35 Paul Harris, "Algeria Faces the Challenges of Peace," *Jane's Intelligence Review*, Vol. 12, No.3 (March 2000), p. 47.

36 Mona Yacoubian, "Algeria's Struggle for Democracy," Occasional Paper Series No. 3, Council on Foreign Relations, 1997, p.7.

37 Paul Harris, p. 48.

38 John Phillips, "Assassins Pierce Heart of Algeria," *Sunday Times* (London), December 1, 1996.

39 Scott Peterson, "Algeria's Real War: Ending the Cycle of Violence," *Christian Science Monitor*, June 24, 1997.

40 "The Algerian Crisis: Not Over Yet," International Crisis Group, No. 24, October 20, 2000, p. 2.

41 "Violence in Algeria Since July 2002," (Maps based on available news reports), http://www.algeriainterface.com/new/rubriques/english/violence/pages/sin2002. htm. Also see Michael Knights and Jonathan Schanzer "Algeria's GSPC: Dichotomy and Anomaly," Forthcoming, completed December 2003.

42 Florence Beauge, "Armed Islamists in Algeria have Reorganized into Three Groups," *Le Monde* (Paris), October 31, 2002. (FBIS)

43 "Violence in Algeria..." Also see Michael Knights and Jonathan Schanzer, forthcoming, compl. Dec. 2003.

44 "Violence in Algeria ..."

45 Jean-Michel Salgon, "Le Groupe Salafite Pour la Predication et le Combat (GSPC),"*Le Cahiers de L'Orient*, No. 62, 2nd trimester 2001, p.68.

46 Michael Knights and Jonathan Schanzer, forthcoming, compl. Dec. 2003.

47 Author's interview with Ferhat Mehenni, Washington, DC. November 30, 2003. See also: Roger Kaplan, "Democracy in Algeria: Singer-Activist Ferhat Mehenni's Campaign for Liberal Self-Government," *Weekly Standard*, Vol.8, No. 9. June 16, 2003.

48 Author's interview with Ferhat Mehenni, June 16, 2003.

49 Azzedine Layachi, "Algeria: Flooding and Muddied State-Society Relations," MERIP Press Information Note 79, December 11, 2001.

www.reliefweb.int/w/rwb.nsf/0/eab7223dd78775ca85256b20006c87a3?OpenDocument
50 Marc Pondaven, "Extremist violence in Algeria recedes in 2003," Middle East Online, December 19, 2003.http://www.middle-east-nline.com/english/?id=8233
51 Quintan Wiktorowicz, forthcoming.
52 See USA vs. Usama bin Laden, Trial Transcript, Day 2, http://cryptome2.org/usa-v-ubl-02.htm
53 Giles Keppel, *Jihad: The Trail of Political Islam*, (Cambridge, MA: Belknap Press of Harvard University, 2002), p. 263.
54 Osman Tasgart, "Report on Bin Laden's Sleeper Networks in Europe," *Al-Majallah*, November 4, 2001 (FBIS). Also see: Jason Burke, *Al-Qaeda: Casting a Shadow of Terror*, (NY: I.B. Taurus, 2003), p.196.
55 Susan Sachs, "An Investigation in Egypt Illustrates Al Qaeda's Web," *New York Times*, November 21, 2001.
56 Jason Burke, *Al-Qaeda: Casting a Shadow of Terror*, (NY: I.B. Taurus, 2003), p.185.
57 Abu Hamza al-Masri, *The Khawaarij and Jihaad*, (London: Finsbury Park Mosque, 2000), p. 159.
58 Abu Hamza al-Masri, pp. 169-170.
59 Giles Keppel, pp. 270-271.
60 Osman Tasgart, Nov. 4, 2001.
61 Farid Aichoune, "GSPC: Les Meandres de la Piste Terroriste," *Le Nouvel Observateur* (France), May 8, 2003.
62 "Bin Laden Held to be Behind an Armed Algerian Islamic Movement," AFP, February 15, 2002.
63 Quintan Wiktorowicz, forthcoming.
64 Jean-Michel Salgon, p. 55.
65 Simon Reeve, p. 209.
66 Quintan Wiktorowicz, "Centrifugal Tendencies in the Algerian Civil War," *Arab Studies Quarterly*, Volume 23, Number 3, Summer 2001, p.77. Also see: Pascal Ceaux, "Intelligence Note Describes Breakthrough of Fundamentalist Movement in Seine-Saint-Denis, *LeMonde* (Paris), January 25, 2002 – citing El-Khabir of September 15, 2001.
67 Osman Tasgart, p. 55.
68 "Algeria: Hattab Faction Announces Split from GIA," *Ash-Sharq al-Awsat*, September 17, 1998 (FBIS). Also see: Jean-Michel Salgon, p. 53.
69 Paul Harris, p. 47.
70 Simon Reeve, "The Worldwide Net: is bombing effective against terror-ism?" *The Ecologist*, November 22, 2001, http://www.theecologist.org/archive_article.html?article=256&category=71 . Also see "GSPC," *Dictionnaire Mondial de L'Islamisme*. (France: Plon, 2002), p. 219. Algeria's ambassador the U.S., by contrast, claimed in January 2004 that the GSPC had been reduced in Algeria to some 250 fighters. (2004 Ambassador's Forum, January 7, 2004, Washington, DC).
71 Courtney C. Walsh, "Italian Police Explore Al Qaeda Links to Cyanide Plot," *Christian Science Monitor*, March 7, 2002.

72   Florence Beauge, "Armed Islamists in Algeria have Reorganized into Three Groups," *Le Monde*, October 31, 2003. (FBIS).

73 Michael Knights, "Algeria's Security Situation Declines Precipitously," *Defense & Foreign Affairs' Strategic Policy*, January/February 2003.

74 Jean-Michel Salgon, p. 57. Also see "GSPC," *Dictionnaire...* p. 218.

75   "The Algerian Crisis: Not Over Yet," International Crisis Group, No. 24, October 20, 2000, p.2.

76   Maria Ressa, *Seeds of Terror: An Eyewitness Account of al-Qaeda's Newest Center of Operations in Southeast Asia*, (NY: Free Press, 2003), p.133.

77 Maria Ressa, pp. 132-133.

78 "GSPC," *Dictionnaire Mondial de L'Islamisme. France: Plon, 2002*, p. 221.

79 Rohan Gunaratna, "The Post-Madrid Face of Al Qaeda," *Washington Quarterly*, Summer 2004, p.96.

80 Therese Delpech, "International Terrorism and Europe," Institute for Security Studies (European Union), Chaillot Papers, No. 56, December 2002, p. 8.

81 Therese Delpech, p. 8.

82 "Algerian Appeals Paris Bomb Sentence," *Ash-Sharq al-Awsat*, November 5, 2003.

83 Rohan Gunaratna, "Terror From the Sky," *Janes Intelligence Review*, September 24, 2001. http://www.janes.com/security/international_security/news/jir/jir010924_1_n.shtml

84 Anonymous, *Through Our Enemies' Eyes...* p. 139.

85 Cathie Lloyd, p. 18.

86 Anonymous, *Through Our Enemies' Eyes...* pp. 140-141.

87 Osman Tasgart, Nov. 4, 2001.

88 Jean-Michel Salgon, p. 55.

89 Jean-Michel Salgon, p. 57.

90 Paul Gallagher, "Algerian Militants the Main Terror Threat to Britain, Experts Warn," *The Scotsman*, January 16, 2003.

91 Therese Delpech, p. 20.

92 Osman Tasgart, Nov. 4, 2001 [FBIS].

93   "Six Algerians Allegedly Linked to Bin Laden Arrested in Spain," *Xinhua* (Beijing), September 27, 2001 [FBIS].

94 Jason Burke, p. 197.

95   Author's phone interview with Reda Hassaine in London, October 1, 2003; Author's interview with French official, Washington, DC, October 2, 2003.

96 Paul Gallagher, "Algerian Militants the Main Terror Threat to Britain, Experts Warn," *The Scotsman*, January 16, 2003.

97 Author's phone interview with Reda Hassaine in London, October 1, 2003.

98   CIA Document, "Terrorism: Reported Planning by an Australian-based al-Qa'ida Associate to Attack the U.S. Embassy in Venezuela and U.S. Interests in the Philippines; Presence of al-Qa'ida Members in Australia." Dated "Mid-June 2002."

99 Author's phone interview/Reda Hassaine, Oct. 1, 2003.

100   David Leppard, "MI5 Knew for Years of London Mosque's Role," *Sunday Times* (London), November 25, 2001. See also Charles Bremner and Daniel McGrory, "Bin Laden Cell Plotted French Poison Attack," *The Times* (London), November 30, 2001.

101   Daniel Benjamin and Steven Simon, p. 214.
102   Daniel McGrory, "Clerics Aid Secret Fight Against Islam Terror Gangs," *The Times* (London), January 26, 2004.
103   Bruce Crumley, "Uncle Osama Wants You: A journalist infiltrates a radical network in Paris, and gets a rare glimpse of a terror recruiter in action," *Time*, http://www.time.com/time/europe/magazine/2003/0324/war/recruit.html.
104   Therese Delpech, p. 54.
105   "Middle East Overview," *Patterns of Global Terrorism, 2000*, http://www.state.gov/s/ct/rls/pgtrpt/2000/2438.htm
106   "Islamic Extremist Threat Forces Cancellation of Two Stages of Dakar Rally," AP, January 29, 2004.
107   Carsten Hauptmeier, "Al-Qaeda Trial Underway in Germany," AFP, April 17, 2002.
108   "Islamic Extremist Threat ..." Jan. 29, 2004.
109   Craig S. Smith, "Terror Suspect Said to be Held by Algeria," *New York Times*, June 5, 2004.
110   "French Intelligence Note Outlines Islamic Fundamentalists' Activities," *LeMonde*, January 25, 2002 [FBIS].
111   Jason Burke, p. 197.
112   "Italy Arrests Two People Who Funded the Algerian GSPC," *Ash-Sharq al-Awsat*, October 30, 2003.
113   "Moroccan is Convicted on Terrorism Charges, Another Defendant is Cleared," AP, January 22, 2004.
114   "Moroccan is Convicted..." Jan. 22, 2004.
115   Italian Court Brief Regarding the Arrests of: El Ayashi Radi Abd El Samie Abou El Yazid, Ciise Maxamed Cabdullah, Mohammed Tahir Hammid and Mohamed Amin Mostafa, March 31, 2003.
116   "U.S. Designates Additional Members of Italian Al Qaida Cell," U.S. Treasury Press Release, June 24, 2004, http://www.treas.gov/press/releases/js1739.htm.
117   "Suspected Algerian Extremists Held in the Netherlands," AFP, April 24, 2002.
118   "War on Terrorism," United States European Command, February 14, 2002, http://www.eucom.mil/Directorates/ECPA/News/index.htm?http://www.eucom.mil/directorates/ecpa/news/CBA/CBA.htm&2
119   David Crawford, "Prosecution Suffers Blow in Dutch al-Qaeda Trial," *Wall Street Journal*, May 21, 2003.
120   Rohan Gunaratna, *Inside Al-Qaeda...*, p. 128.
121   "Anti-terror Campaign Sparks Biggest Probe Ever," AFP, October 1, 2001. Also see "GSPC," Dictionnaire... p. 221.
122   "Six Algerians Allegedly Linked to Bin Laden Arrested in Spain," *Xinhua* (Beijing), September 27, 2001 (FBIS).
123   Marie-Claude Decamps, "Spain, Logistic Base," *LeMonde*, March 12, 2002 [FBIS].
124   Author's interview with three U.S. government officials, Washington, D.C. June 23, 2004.
125   "European Hostages' Mediator Back in Mali Capital from Desert Talks," AFP, August 6, 2003.
126   "Algeria Gives Germany Names of Tourists' Suspected Kidnappers:

Paper," AFP, September 24, 2003.

127 "17 European Tourists Freed from al-Qaeda Linked Group in Algeria," AFP, May 14, 2003.

128 Paul de Bendern, "Sources: Last 15 European Tourists Freed in Algeria," Reuters, May 19, 2003.

129 "Videotape Shows Desert hostages Now in Mali-Paper," Reuters, July 30, 2003.

130 Kate Connolly, Germany accused of buying hostages' release," *London Daily Telegraph*, August 20, 2003.
http://www.telegraph.co.uk/news/main.jhtml?xml=/news/2003/08/20/wmali20.xml&sSheet=/news/2003/08/20/ixworld.html

131 Michael Radu, "Hostages, Terrorism and the West," Foreign Policy Research Institute E-Notes, August 27, 2003.

132 "Libya mediated Mali hostage release," Al-Jazeera.net. August 19, 2003.
http://english.aljazeera.net/NR/exeres/ECB15EC7-F193-421B-8D1D-FF3162038EA7.htm

133 "Libyan Ransom Raises Terror Fears," *The Australian*, August 29, 2000.

134 Author's interview with Algerian official, October 1, 2003. Author's interview with French official, October 2, 2003.

135 "GSPC," *Dictionnaire...* p. 219.

136 "Al-Qaeda-linked Group in Algeria Replaces Founder: Reports," AFP, October 12, 2003.

137 "Hattab Still Head of Biggest Algerian Extremist Group: Report," AFP, October 16, 2003.

138 "Algerian Islamic Extremist Group Pledges Allegiance to al-Qaeda," AFP, October 22, 2003.

139 "Designation of Dhamat Houmet Daawa Salafia Under Executive Order 13224," U.S. Treasury Press Release, October 20, 2003.
http://www.state.gov/r/pa/prs/ps/2003/25413.htm

140 "U.S. Designated Three Individuals and One Organization Involved in Terrorism in Algeria," U.S. Treasury Press Release, October 24, 2003.
http://www.treas.gov/press/releases/js944.htm

141 The U.S. Treasury posted this listing on December 5, 2003.
http://www.ustreas.gov/offices/eotffc/ofac/sanctions/terror.txt

142 The U.S. Treasury posted this listing on April 30, 2004.
http://www.treas.gov/offices/eotffc/ofac/bulletin.txt

143 "US Official Pledges Aid to Algeria," AP, October 27, 2003.

144 "Press Briefing with Algerian Foreign Minister Abdelaziz Belkhadem," December 3, 2003. www.state.gov/secretary/rm/2003/26873.htm

145 Damien Mcelroy, "US Extends the War on Islamic Terror to the Sahara Desert," *Telegraph* (UK), June 6, 2004.

146 Craig S. Smith, "U.S. Training African Forces to Uproot Terrorists," *New York Times*, May 11, 2004.

147 Craig S. Smith, "Terror Suspect Said to be Held by Algeria," *New York Times*, June 5, 2004.

148   Nick Tattersall, "U.S. Trained Malian Troops Ready for Desert Battle," Reuters, March 18, 2004.

149   Author's interview with three U.S. government officials, Washington, D.C. June 23, 2004.

150   Craig S. Smith, "Militant Slain in Algeria; Ties to Qaeda are Reported," *New York Times*, June 21, 2004.

151   "Four Killed by Extremists in Eastern Algeria: Security Forces," AFP, June 19, 2003; and "Twelve Dead, Including Three Children, In More Algeria Unrest," AFP, June 22, 2003.

152   "Algeria captures Sahara terrorists," Deutche Presse-Agentur, September 23, 2003.

153   "Algerian Army Kills 150 Islamists in Search Operation: Press," AFP, September 27, 2003.

154   Muhammad Muqaddam, "Algeria: Reports of Arresting "The Emir of the GIA," *al-Hayat*, November 20, 2003.

155   "Founder of Biggest Muslim Group Executed-Report," *Jordan Times* (AFP), May12, 2004.

156   "Algerian Leader, Hassan Hattab, Still Alive: Report," AFP, May 24, 2004.

157   Cathie Lloyd, p. 26.

158   "U.S.-Algerian Relations, Past and Future," Statement by Ambassador Idriss Jazairy, Middle East Institute, Washington, DC, May 6, 2003.

159   "Press Briefing with Algerian Foreign Minister Abdelaziz Belkhadem," December 3, 2003. www.state.gov/secretary/rm/2003/26873.htm

160   "The Algerian Crisis: Not Over Yet," International Crisis Group, No. 24, October 20, 2000, p. 4.

161   Brian Love, "Libyan Agents Discover Camp Linked to al-Qaeda," AFP, July 5, 2004.

Chapter Six: Northern Iraq

Prior to the U.S.-led war in spring 2003, Iraq could never have been characterized as a state with weak central authority. Most of Iraq suffered under the iron grip of Saddam Husayn, although a small enclave the size of Vermont, home to some four million Kurds, enjoyed more than a decade of freedom from Saddam's brutality, protected by a safe-haven and no-fly zone.

The Kurdish area of northern Iraq is part of a larger Kurdish region that spans parts of Turkey, Syria and Iran, making up some 24 million people.[1] This swath of land has never been unified and is a mélange of tribes, ethnicities and languages, similar to the Caucasus.[2] Iraqi Kurds have maintained a fierce sense of independence based on language and culture, even during the tumultuous years of Arab nationalism. Depending on political contingencies, Iraq's Kurds have wavered between demands for autonomy and outright independence. Attempts to negotiate an autonomy accord in 1970 failed over disputes concerning the status of oil-rich Kirkuk and the Baathist government's refusal to implement the deal. Internecine violence, coupled with regional interference, undermined Kurdish cohesion, and the rugged mountains of northern Iraq became a semi-independent area of relatively weak central authority.

In the aftermath of the 1991 Gulf War, the Iraqi Kurds successfully united, albeit loosely, to create a semi-autonomous region they called Kurdistan.[3] But Northern Iraq lacked any overarching central control, and opposing political factions held power in small enclaves. They coordinated on some levels, including education, but not on others, such as finance and security. Differences between Patriotic Union of Kurdistan (PUK) leader Jalal Talabani and Kurdistan Democratic Party (KDP) leader Masud Barzani erupted in civil war between 1994 and 1997. The struggle, accompanied by regional maneuvering, weakened the

Kurdish political leadership's authority, especially in the rugged mountains along the Iranian and Turkish borders. Islamists quickly filled the vacuum. In September 2001, an al-Qaeda affiliate group, serving as an umbrella for several local Islamist organizations, established a base in the mountainous terrain on the Iranian border and began attacking the general Kurdish population.

Ansar al-Islam, created just prior to the al-Qaeda attacks on America in fall 2001, was disrupted two years later by U.S. Special Forces and the Kurdish peshmerga[4] militia in the war that toppled Saddam. But Ansar al-Islam soon reconstituted after the 2003 Iraq war, and is now suspected of involvement in a number of deadly attacks against American soldiers patrolling the Sunni triangle (an area between the cities of Baghdad, Tikrit and Ramadi) and elsewhere throughout post-war Iraq. It is also now believed to be one of the corner stones of Tawhid w'al-Jihad, the terrorist group headed by Abu Musab az-Zarqawi.

Under British Rule

Modern Iraq was officially created in 1920 after Britain ousted the Ottoman Empire in 1918. Almost immediately after the British took control of Iraq, a Kurdish nationalist movement "expressed the refusal of the Kurds to being dominated...or to be included in an Arab state."[5] That movement was suppressed; the British did not view the Kurds as a nation worthy of independence.

The League of Nations sent a commission of inquiry into northern Iraq (the former Ottoman governorate of Mosul) in 1925 to determine whether the area should fall under Turkish or British control. The commission recognized the existence of a separate Kurdish identity there, but elected to keep the area as part of Iraq, denying Kurdish nationalist aspirations. The Iraqi Kurds were furious with the subsequent Anglo-Iraqi treaty of 1930, which made no mention of their rights.

After the British

The Kingdom of Iraq was founded in 1932. By then, however, Kurds had already been agitating for autonomy. Among the major issues was Kurdish discontent with the new Iraqi authority, resulting from taxation and other forms of authority rarely imposed upon Kurds under Ottoman rule. In the 1940s, Mullah Mustafa Barzani capitalized on growing Kurdish nationalism, forming the KDP with support from communist groups in Iran.[6] With foreign aid, the Kurdish movement took up arms in the mid-1940s. This would become a trend; over the years, Iraqi Kurdish groups often found support from outside parties. Soviet encouragement in 1946 prompted Kurds to establish an independent republic in Mahabad, Iran, but that rebellion was soon crushed by Tehran, with support from outside Kurdish factions.

A bloody 1958 coup d'etat overthrew the monarchy, and the putsch leaders declared Iraq a republic. General Abd al-Karim Qasim initially recognized Iraq as the homeland of both Arabs and Kurds. Relations with the Kurds, however, soon soured again. In 1961, Kurdish secessionists renewed their campaign of agitation. As a result, the government banned Kurdish newspapers and imposed other restrictions. Meanwhile, inside the Kurdish region, internal cohesion began to unravel, and clashes between rival clans increased.[7]

Fighting briefly subsided when Qasim was deposed in 1962, but resumed the following year. The army responded by invading a number of Kurdish towns, resulting in hundreds of deaths. During one attack, some 40,000 Kurds were expelled from the Kirkuk area.[8] A ceasefire agreement was reached in 1963, but was breached in 1965. Similar to the foreign support of the 1940s, it was Iranian and even Israeli aid that allowed the Kurdish peshmerga to fight the Iraqi military through 1966.[9]

Baathist Iraq

The Baath party, which seized power in 1968, appeared initially tolerant of the Kurds, appointing two as ministers. However, the KDP launched another round of violence against the regime in 1969, attacking Kirkuk oil installations. In retaliation, the Baathists destroyed approximately 300 Kurdish villages.

In 1970, Baghdad agreed to Kurdish autonomy. The Kurds were also promised a certain degree of representation in Baghdad. When these goals were not realized, the Kurds again took up arms in 1974. The Iraqi military launched a brutal counter-offensive designed to "Baathize" northern Iraq. The Kurds found support from Iran to resist the Baathists.

In early 1975, however, Iran and Iraq reached a surprise agreement on these disputed borders. Putting more of a premium on relative peace with Iraq than Kurdish support, Iran abruptly pulled its funding. Under the terms of the Algiers Agreement, negotiated by U.S. Secretary of State Henry Kissinger, Iraq agreed to share with Iran the disputed Shatt al-Arab, an estuary of the Tigris and Euphrates Rivers, while the Shah of Iran pledged to cut support for the Kurdish rebellion.[10] The Kurds had become a bargaining chip for more powerful parties.

The Iranian agreement left the Kurds in utter disarray. Political turmoil led indirectly to the creation of the Patriotic Union of Kurdistan (PUK) in 1976, formed with assistance from Damascus, which became the KDP's foremost rival. By 1978, the two factions feuded in both political and provincial conflicts. Their bitter rivalry, a Middle Eastern version of the Hatfields vs. the McCoys, can still be seen today on a more peaceful level; the two political factions compete rigorously for the allegiance of Iraqi Kurds.

Saddam and the Kurds

Iraqi strongman Saddam Husayn formally assumed the presidency of Iraq in 1979, although he had been a top power broker behind the scenes for almost a decade. The eruption of the Iran-Iraq war in 1980 saved the Kurds from an immediate showdown with the brutal despot. During the war, however, some Kurds assisted the Iranians against Saddam's regime.

In 1985, Iraqi forces destroyed some 200 Kurdish villages, expelling more than 50,000 Kurdish refugees.[11] Faced with a common enemy in the Iraqi regime, the PUK and KDP began cooperating, and joined forces with Iran. Cooperation continued through 1988, when the Kurds helped Iran capture the town of Hajji Umran. In response, Saddam deployed chemical weapons against the Kurdish town of Halabja. When the Iran-Iraq War ended, Husayn ordered massive strikes on Kurdish villages, expelling an estimated 65,000 to Turkey.[12] In the notorious *Anfal* campaign, Iraqi forces ravaged some 4,000 Kurdish villages,[13] killed more than 5,000 civilians with chemical weapons, and deported tens of thousands of Kurds in one of the worst instances of ethnic cleansing in recent decades.[14] By the end, 182,000 men, women, and children were killed or reported missing.[15]

After the Gulf War

After the 1991 Gulf War, encouraged by President George H.W. Bush's February 15 call to overthrow Saddam, the Kurds launched an offensive against the regime while Saddam's forces were tied up along the southern border with Kuwait. The Kurds made advances in March 1991, conquering the main urban centers of Irbil and Sulaymaniyya, and even capturing Kirkuk briefly.[16] These gains were transient; the Iraqi military responded with deadly attacks from helicopter gunships, driving more than one million Kurds to the Iranian and Turkish borders.

Realizing its responsibility for this tragedy, the U.S. forced

Husayn's troops out of northern Iraq. At the prompting of Turkish President Turgat Ozal, whose government was facing a humanitarian crisis, the U.S., Britain and France created a safe haven, protected by allied aircraft, known as the Northern no-fly zone, which was a small patch of Iraqi territory north of the 36th parallel. This territory expanded to encompass 3,600 square miles by the start of the 2003 Iraq war.

Within this growing no-fly zone, the Kurds set about creating a mini-state within Iraq. In April 1991, the Kurdish factions reached an "agreement of principle on the status of Iraqi Kurdistan."[17] The subsequent 1992 elections yielded a tie between the KDP and PUK. The parties struck a power-sharing arrangement, but years of fighting had taken their toll. Fierce competition between the parties yielded to open war in 1994, leaving some 2,000 dead before the U.S. mediated a ceasefire in 1995. Fighting resumed in 1996, prompting the Iraqi army to deploy thousands of troops. They captured Irbil and handed it to the KDP, leading to the creation of two separate Kurdish enclaves. Since then, strong fences have made for peaceful coexistence between the PUK and KDP. In 2002, in a move toward national unity, the two factions agreed to reconvene their parliament, the Kurdistan Regional Assembly.

The Origins of Ansar al-Islam

The roots of Ansar al-Islam date back to the 1980s. The group is an amalgam of several Islamist groups in Kurdish Iraq. In the 1980s, several Kurdish Islamist factions established ties to the precursors of al-Qaeda in Afghanistan. Majmuddin Freraj Ahmed, now known as Mullah Krekar, was the leader of one of these groups. He would eventually become the spiritual leader of Ansar al-Islam. Ties between Krekar and the lieutenants of al-Qaeda continued after he returned from Afghanistan to Iraq in 1991, as did the relationship between al-Qaeda and other Kurdish Islamist groups.[18] Those ties were strengthened in the mid-1990s, when the

Kurds of northern Iraq suffered from an acute economic crisis. Wahhabi (strict Islamic orthodox) outreach groups such as the International Islamic Relief Organization soon set up shop in northern Iraq to distribute aid while preaching a more ascetic version of Islam.[19]

Throughout the 1990s, the Islamist movement in Northern Iraq was primarily represented by the Islamic Movement of Kurdistan (IMK), which captured some six percent of the vote in the 1991 Kurdish elections.[20] Within the IMK, there were several competing factions, including Hamas, Tawhid, the Second Soran Unit, and the Islamic Unity Movement. These Islamist groups represented a spectrum of ideologies, from relatively benign to radical. By the late 1990s, some of the more militant groups of northern Iraq had established branches in Afghanistan to assist al-Qaeda and the Taliban.[21] In the spring of 2001, leaders from two Kurdish factions visited the al-Qaeda leadership in Afghanistan.[22] Reportedly, they met with a representative of Osama bin Laden who was seeking to create a base for al-Qaeda in northern Iraq.[23] These groups were the foundation of Ansar al-Islam, which announced its formation just days before the September 11 attack. Al-Qaeda likely realized that Afghanistan would be targeted soon after the attacks of September 11, 2001. Perhaps they chose northern Iraq because it was weakly governed.

A document found in Kabul after the U.S. invasion described Ansar al-Islam's platform. The authors vowed to "expel those Jews and Christians from Kurdistan and join the way of Jihad, [and] rule every piece of land... with the Islamic Shari'a rule."[24] The *Los Angeles Times*, based on interviews with an Ansar prisoner, corroborates Ansar's goals of establishing a Taliban-style regime in northern Iraq:

> [In October 2000, Kurdish Islamist leaders] sent a guerrilla with the alias Mala Namo and two bodyguards into Iran and then on to bin Laden's camps...When teams began returning

from the Afghan camps in 2001... they carried a message
from bin Laden that Kurdish Islamic cells should unite. By that
time, a number of al-Qaeda operatives had left Afghanistan
and moved to northern Iraq... militant leaders in Kurdistan
were replicating al-Qaeda type camps on military training,
terrorism and suicide bombers.[25]

Ansar al-Islam operated in fortified mountain positions
along the Iran-Iraq border known as "Little Tora Bora" (after the
stronghold in Afghanistan).[26] U.S. Secretary of State Colin Powell,
in a February 5, 2003 statement to the United Nations Security
Council, noted that the organization established a "poison and
explosive training center camp....in northeastern Iraq." [27]

According to several reports, the camp was established
with $300,000 to $600,000 in al-Qaeda seed money.[28] At least three
prominent media sources indicate that the group received money
from Abu Qatada, a key cleric in the al-Qaeda network based in
London.[29] Mullah Krekar, spiritual leader of Ansar al-Islam, also
admitted his ties to Osama bin Laden, dating back to a meeting the
two attended "along with seven Saudi VIPs" in 1988.[30] A
congressional report also asserts that he studied under Abdullah
Azzam, bin Laden's spiritual mentor and a co-founder of al-Qaeda.[31]

Ansar al-Islam recruited around the world. According to
Italian court documents, an area of focus is northern Italy,
specifically in Milan's Mosque of Via Quaranta.[32] Wiretapped
conversations with an imam from Cremona, Italy indicate that
Syria served as a hub for recruits and that Saudi Arabia provided
financing.[33] Other Italian wiretaps indicate that funding came from
Austria, Jordan, Iraq, and Eritrea.[34] Iraq scholar Michael Rubin
agrees that some funds likely came from Saudi Arabia.[35]

Out of the estimated 650 fighters in Ansar al-Islam, Kurdish
sources assessed the foreign fighter element to be about 120,[36]
including Kurdish, Iraqi, Lebanese, Jordanian, Moroccan, Syrian,
Palestinian, and Afghan fighters trained in a wide array of

guerrilla tactics.[37] They initially came to the Biara and Tawella areas of northern Iraq in groups of three or four with the aid of smugglers. On several occasions, according to Kurdish intelligence, Iranians helped to smuggle these militants into Iraq.[38] By summer of 2002, Kurdish intelligence had identified at least 31 of Ansar al-Islam's top Arab leaders.[39]

Armed with heavy machine guns, mortars, and anti-aircraft weaponry, the group sought to disrupt civil society and create a Taliban-like regime. The group banned music, alcohol, photographs, and advertising in the territory they controlled. Girls were prevented from studying, and men were forced to grow beards and pray five times daily. In one instance, a car belonging to the aid organization Qandil was fired upon because a woman in the vehicle was not wearing a veil.[40]

Ansar on the Offensive

Ansar al-Islam made headlines in September 2001 when it ambushed, killed, and mutilated 42 PUK fighters. The Kurds realized that they were the targets of a new jihadi war and quickly established a conventional defensive front. A wave of violence erupted in 2002, beginning with politically motivated attacks. That spring, Ansar al-Islam attempted to murder Barham Salih, a PUK leader. Five bodyguards and two attackers were killed in the ensuing gunfight.[41]

Ansar began to use cruder tactics designed simply to inflict as much damage as possible. In June, the group bombed a restaurant, injuring scores and killing a child.[42] In July, Ansar killed nine PUK fighters.[43] In a move reminiscent of the Taliban, the group destroyed Sufi shrines.[44] In December 2002, Ansar al-Islam launched a surprise attack after the PUK sent 1,500 fighters home to celebrate the end of Ramadan.[45] According to Ansar al-Islam's website, the group killed 103 PUK members and wounded 117.[46] Gruesome pictures of the victims were long available on the internet.[47]

In December 2002, Jordan announced that Jordanian al-Qaeda operative Ahmad Fadel al-Khalayla, more commonly known as Abu Musab az-Zarqawi, had sought refuge with Ansar al-Islam.[48] He was reportedly injured during the U.S.-led campaign against the Taliban regime of Afghanistan in 2001, but had escaped to run a terrorist training camp in northern Iraq.[49] At that point, az-Zarqawi led a 116-person global al-Qaeda network.[50] He was also the operational leader of a German al-Qaeda cell known as al-Tawhid.[51] In his capacity as an al-Qaeda leader in Iraq, az-Zarqawi ordered both the attempt on Salih in spring 2002 and the murder of USAID officer Laurence Foley in Amman in October 2002. As war drew near, he sought medical attention in Baghdad for wounds he suffered in Afghanistan,[52] where Saddam allowed him to convalesce for eight months.[53] Az-Zarqawi's other possible ties to terrorist attacks include the November 2003 bombings in Istanbul and the May 2003 attacks in Casablanca. By 2004, he was the most wanted terrorist in Iraq. The U.S. placed a $25 million bounty on his head.

WMD, Iran, and Saddam?

By early 2003, more than 30 Ansar al-Islam militants (including 15 to 20 Arab fighters)[54] were incarcerated in the PUK's capital of Sulaymaniyya. One *New York Times* journalist reported that, "critical information about this network emerged from interrogations of captured cell members."[55] Based on that report and other intelligence, information was gleaned about Ansar al-Islam's chemical weapons facilities.

Specifically, it was reported that cyanide gas and the poison ricin were among the chemicals tested for future use by Ansar al-Islam.[56] *The Washington Post* also reported that Ansar al-Islam smuggled VX nerve gas through Turkey in the fall of 2001.[57] PUK Prime Minister Barham Salih cited "clear evidence" of animal testing.[58] Other Kurdish leaders said they had "eyewitness accounts, prisoners' confessions, and seized evidence" to support this.[59]

Bush administration and PUK officials also claimed that Ansar al-Islam had worked directly with Saddam. This assertion has since been the subject of considerable debate. Indeed, the reports that support the argument are still inconclusive, and many within the U.S. intelligence committee doubt the veracity of these claims. The *New Yorker*, for instance, indicated that Saddam's regime helped smuggle weapons from U.S.-occupied Afghanistan.[60] Kurdish explosives experts also claimed that TNT seized from Ansar al-Islam was produced by the Iraqi military, and that truck-loads of arms arrived from areas controlled by Saddam on several occasions.[61] The *Christian Science Monitor* further reported that Saddam used, "smugglers and middlemen to provide dirt-cheap weapons to Ansar," and would then cut off future supplies and demand concessions. Allegedly, Ansar was one of the biggest buyers of weapons from Baghdad.[62]

Another link was said to be a man named Saadun Mahmud Abd al-Latif al-Aani, or Abu Wael, reportedly an Iraqi operative on al-Qaeda's payroll.[63] Kurdish intelligence also claims that a man named Saad Fawzi Hatam al-Ubaidi, or Abu Zuhair was, "the direct liaison with the Iraqi intelligence 'al-Mukhabarat'..."[64] Kurdish intelligence further alleged an "on-going clandestine connection" between Ansar al-Islam and Saddam's Iraq in the months leading up to the war. They claimed that on April 12, 2002, the mukhabarat "transferred a number of Arabs from their territory to Arbil and then with the help of Islamists transferred them to Biyara and Khormal."[65] The PUK also alleges that Ansar al-Islam sent Islamist women, who are often not screened as carefully as men, to Baghdad in order to exchange information with mukhabarat officials.[66]

While the ties to Saddam where not definitively established, it was known that Iran played a significant role in supporting Ansar al-Islam. Iran allowed the group to operate along its borders with Iraq. Kurds further allege that Iran provided logistical support by allowing for the flow of goods and weapons, and providing a safe area beyond the front lines.[67]

There were other links, too. Krekar spent many years in Iran, and was arrested in Amsterdam after a flight from Tehran. The Turkish *Milliyet* also notes that Ansar al-Islam checked cars going into Iran, indicating coordination with the Islamic Republic.[68] Recent reports further indicate that Tehran attempted to manipulate the group by flooding "the Ansar area with extremely cheap food supplies, then stopped them abruptly, to squeeze concessions out of Ansar."[69]

After Powell's U.N. speech on February 5, 2003, Ansar allowed a small group of reporters to visit their enclave, "where Ansar was believed to be developing Ricin."[70] However, neither Powell's claims nor the militants' denials could be verified in the days that followed. The journalists were given access to only some parts of the enclave. One area, which was vaguely defined as a media center, was "surrounded by barbed wire fence with a skull and crossbones on it... it could well have been used earlier for something like a weapons depot," said BBC correspondent Robin Benselow. Benselow further adds that the journalists did not see much of the enclave during their tour.[71] In other words, weapons of mass destruction could have been hidden in the areas that the journalists did not see.

On February 8, 2003, the group claimed responsibility for the assassination of Kurdish leader Shawkat Hajji Mushir.[72] Later that month, a man thought to belong to Ansar al-Islam detonated a suicide bomb near a Kurdish enclave checkpoint. The bomb, packed with metal shards, marked the first use of suicide bombings by the group.

By February 20, 2003, the U.S. government named Ansar al-Islam a Specially Designated Terrorist Group.[73] With war threatening in Iraq, Ansar al-Islam prepared for a combined U.S.-Kurdish assault. One Kurdish official noted, "Nervousness had set into the group. They immediately began relocating their forces, retreating to the more mountainous areas of Hawar-Barza, and digging themselves into the caves and higher mountain peaks."[74]

The U.S. Invasion

On March 23, 2003, PUK fighters attacked Ansar al-Islam's 16-village stronghold, backed by U.S. unmanned aerial vehicles and aircraft strikes. Cruise missiles destroyed much of the enclave. Deserters left behind artillery, machine guns, mortars and Katyusha rockets. Two days later, Ansar made a desperation attack on PUK forces near Halabja, but were repelled. Dozens of their forces were wounded or killed.[75] The group retaliated with a suicide operation, killing an Australian journalist. Within eight days, however, the entire Ansar enclave was decimated. At least 253 Ansar al-Islam fighters were killed in the fighting. According to Krekar, 28 planes and 108 rockets destroyed the compound.[76] The PUK also took eight fighters into custody, including Jordanians, Syrians, Tunisians, and one Palestinian who stated that he came to Iraq to "kill Americans." Interestingly, many captured Arab fighters held passports with Iraqi visas, signaling that the former regime had approved their presence.[77]

Combing through the debris, coalition officials found multiple intelligence leads, including a list of suspected militants living in the U.S. Evidence also showed that specific meetings took place between Ansar and al-Qaeda activists.[78] German media reported that a three-volume manual was found describing chemical and biological experiments, including the use of ricin and cyanide.[79] Bomb vests and four bomb-laden cars were also found in the Ansar stronghold.[80] No weapons of mass destruction, however, were discovered.

After the U.S. began its March 23 assault on Ansar positions, wounded fighters sought Iran's assistance. However, one Kurdish official noted, "they went inside one kilometer, but the

Iranians made them go back."[81] On March 30, dozens more fighters escaped to Iran. On that occasion, Tehran detained them as prisoners.

Hamid-Reza Asefi, a spokesman for Iran's foreign ministry, "rejected as a sheer lie the report broadcast by a television station to the effect that Iran was assisting the Ansar al-Islam group."[82] Some Iranian dissidents, however, claim that the al-Quds forces of the Revolutionary Guards were actively aiding Ansar militants to cross the border.[83]

Throughout the summer following the war, it became clear that Ansar militants and other al-Qaeda fighters had sought refuge in Iran. Washington and Tehran were reportedly negotiating the extradition to their home countries. Among those sought by the U.S. was Abu Wael.[84] In October, Iran announced that it had deported some al-Qaeda suspects, but would not extradite any to the U.S.[85] By the following year, reports emerged that dozens of Ansar al-Islam militants had found refuge in Iranian towns such as Mariwan, Ravanshar, and Jebel Shiram.[86]

Post-War Ansar

Despite the extensive U.S.-led attack, it was estimated that some 300 to 350 members escaped the Ansar compound, indicating that the group was not entirely defeated.[87] In June, Ansar al-Islam issued a call for volunteers to fight U.S. forces in Iraq. In a statement sent to the *ash-Sharq al-Awsat* newspaper, Abdullah ash-Shafi' boasted that his group had already destroyed ten U.S. tanks.[88] This, of course, was wishful thinking on the part of ash-Shafi'.

In July 2003, as U.S. soldiers came under daily attack by guerrilla forces, General Richard B. Meyers, Chairman of the Joint Chiefs of Staff, expressed concern over the re-emergence of Ansar. "The one thing we knew going into the war in Iraq is that the group Ansar al-Islam was operating in northeastern Iraq, it has ties to al-Qaeda," he said. "That group is still active in Iraq."[89]

When a car bomb rocked the Jordanian embassy in Iraq on

August 7, 2003 and killed at least 14 people, Ansar al-Islam was among the first suspected culprits. An *al-Hayat* article on the same day cited concerns that Islamic militants from Pakistan had infiltrated northern Iraq with the help of bin Laden. "It was suspected that the Ansar al-Islam group was in connection with the Islamists in Falluja, Tikrit, Bayali and Baghdad" where attacks against Americans were taking place.[90] Washington expressed fears that Ansar operatives might number in the hundreds.[91]

Several days later, the PUK reported that its forces had captured Ansar fighters among a group of 50 people caught infiltrating northern Iraq via Iran from Afghanistan.[92] Among them were five Iraqis, a Palestinian, and a Tunisian.[93]

Although the U.S. military battled a number of terrorist groups in the summer of 2003, Ansar was thought to be the most dangerous. Among the groups that were active in Iraq, it had access to international terror networks, training in a host of military tactics, as well as foreign fighters with combat experience. Administration officials expressed fears that safe houses and other logistical operations in Iraq were being run by Ansar al-Islam.[94]

On August 13, several gunmen attacked U.S. troops in Baghdad and then fled the scene, but not before dropping leaflets in Arabic stating "Death to the Collaborators of America – al-Qaeda." It was not known if they represented Ansar al-Islam; the threat may have been a reference to the August 7 Jordanian embassy bombing, or even to the forthcoming bombing, claimed by al-Qaeda, at the U.N. compound in Baghdad. In that attack on August 19, a suicide bomber drove a truck full of explosives into the United Nations compound in Iraq, sparking an explosion that killed 17 and wounded more than 100 people. While three previously unknown groups claimed responsibility for the attack, including one that professed to be part of al-Qaeda, the *New York Times* noted that "the immediate focus of attention was Ansar al-Islam, a militant Islamic group that American officials believe has been plotting attacks against Western targets in Baghdad."[95] Subsequent reports indicate that at least one Ansar recruit from Italy was involved in the U.N. attack. Another recruit was implicated in a rocket attack on the al-Rashid hotel in October.[96]

More Alleged Saddam-al-Qaeda Ties[97]

In January 2004, the Washington Institute for Near East Policy sent a delegation of five analysts to Iraq. This author was among the analysts, sent with the charge of learning new details about Ansar al-Islam. During interviews in Sulaymaniyya on January 28, two prisoners from Ansar al-Islam claimed that there was an established relationship between Saddam and al-Qaeda. At the time of writing, these ties were still the subject of a heated debate. The prevailing wisdom is that high-level ties never existed, casting doubt upon the Bush administration's rationale for the 2003 Iraq war. Nonetheless, the prisoners insisted that there was a relationship.

Of particular interest was a prisoner named Abd ar-Rahman ash-Shamari, a former member of Saddam Husayn's mukhabarat, who admitted to being involved in Ansar al-Islam operations. While the veracity of his statements cannot be ascertained, ash-Shamari's statements are worth recounting. He flatly admitted that his division of the mukhabarat provided weapons to Ansar, "mostly mortar rounds." In addition to weapons, ash-Shamari said, the mukhabarat also helped finance the group. "On one occasion we gave them ten million Swiss dinars [$700,000]," ash-Shamari said, referring to the pre-1990 Iraqi currency. On other occasions, the mukhabarat provided more than that. The assistance, he added, was furnished "every month or two months."

Upon viewing a photo of the infamous Abu Wael, ash-Shamari said that he not only recognized the man, but that he had worked for him. He stated that Abu Wael's full name is Colonel Saadan Mahmoud Abd al-Latif al-Aani, and that he was the leader of a special intelligence directorate in the mukhabarat. That section provided financial and provisional assistance to Ansar al Islam at the behest of Saddam Husayn, whom Abu Wael had met "four or five times." Ash-Shamari added that "Abu Wael's wife is Izzat ad-Douri's cousin," making him a part of Saddam's inner circle. Ad-Douri, of course, was the deputy chairman of Saddam's Revolutionary Command Council, a high-ranking official in Iraq's armed forces, and Saddam's right hand man.

Ash-Shamari claimed that the links between Saddam's regime and the al-Qaeda network went beyond Ansar al-Islam. He explained that Saddam actually ordered Abu Wael to recruit foreign fighters to join Ansar. Ash-Shamari estimated that some 150 militants were imported from al-Qaeda cells in Jordan, Turkey, Syria, Yemen, Egypt, and Lebanon in the late 1990s.

"The man we worked with [in Lebanon] was named Abu Aisha," ash-Shamari said. He was likely referring to Bassam Kanj, alias Abu Aisha, who was a little-known militant of the Dinniyeh Group, a faction of the Lebanese al-Qaeda affiliate Asbat al-Ansar. Kanj was killed in a January 2000 battle with Lebanese forces.

Ash-Shamari said that there was also contact with the Egyptian "Gamaat al-Jihad," as well as the GSPC. He spoke of Abu Wael's links with Turkey's "Jamaa al-Khilafa" – likely the group also known as the "Union of Islamic Communities" (UIC) or the "Organization of Caliphate State." This group was established in 1983 by Cemalettin Kaplan, who reportedly met with bin Laden in Afghanistan in 1997, and later sent his fighters there for training. Three years before 9/11, the UIC plotted to crash a plane into Ankara's *Anitkabir* Mausoleum (where Ataturk is buried) on a day when hundreds of Turkish officials were present. According to ash-Shamari, Abu Wael also sent money to the aforementioned al-Qaeda affiliates, and to other groups that "worked against the United States." All of them, he added, visited Abu Wael in Iraq and were provided with Iraqi visas.

Ash-Shamari claimed that recruiting foreign fighters to

train in Iraq was part of his job in the mukhabarat. The fighters trained in Salman Pak, a facility reportedly located about 20 miles southeast of Baghdad. Ash-Shamari also claimed to have personal knowledge of 500 fighters who went through Salman Pak beginning in the late 1990s; they trained in "urban combat, explosives, and car bombs." His account matches a White House background paper on Iraq dated September 12, 2002, which described the "highly secret terrorist training facility in Iraq known as Salman Pak, where both Iraqis and non-Iraqi Arabs receive training on hijacking planes and trains, planting explosives in cities, sabotage, and assassinations."[98]

The plan for a post-war insurgency came directly from the top Iraqi leadership, ash-Shamari claimed. "If the U.S. was to hit [the Ansar base], the fighters were directed to go to Ramadi, Tikrit, Mosul... Faluja and other places," he said. The new, relocated group was to be named Jund ash-Sham, and would deal mainly in explosives. He believed that az-Zarqawi and Abu Wael were responsible for some of the attacks against U.S. soldiers in central Iraq. "Their directives were to hit America and American interests," he said. At the time of writing, these reports were still under investigation.

Some Small Breaks?

On October 14, 2003, U.S. officials announced the capture of Aso Hawleri, also known as Asad Muhammed Hasan, believed to be the third-ranking official in Ansar al-Islam. Hawleri began his jihadi career as a leader of the Second Soran Unit, one of the original Kurdish Islamist groups that joined forces to create Ansar al-Islam.[99]

Later that month, Izzat ad-Douri, who ranked number six among the most wanted former Baathist officials, was fingered as an instigator of the campaign of violence against Americans in Iraq by two captured members of Ansar al-Islam.[100] While the report lent credibility to the oft-challenged U.S. assertion that Saddam and his regime were closely tied to terrorists, subsequent reports indicated that ad-Douri could not have played a major role in coordinating attacks, since he was struggling for his life in a battle with leukemia.[101] Few analysts disputed that ad-Douri was ill. Whether he was capable of coordinating attacks in his ailing condition, however, was still not verified as the U.S. continued to come under guerrilla fire throughout the fall.

In late November, Italian and German security forces arrested at least three suspects accused of recruiting European Islamists to go to Iraq for training. Among those arrested was Moroccan-born Kamal Morchidi, who played a part in the pre-war Ansar camp. Morchidi reportedly participated in the October attack against the al-Rashid hotel in Baghdad while Deputy Defense Secretary Paul Wolfowitz was there.[102] German intelligence also apprehended a 32-year-old operative in Amsterdam who was attempting to fly to Turkey. It was estimated that more than 100 other Ansar operatives were active there in 2004.[103] Reports also emerged in January 2004 that Germany was holding an Algerian linked to Ansar while courts waited to rule on an Italian request for his extradition. The suspect had been linked to other militants arrested in Milan.[104]

Quagmire?

While the capture of Hawleri was good news, the long-term prognosis in Iraq appeared increasingly bleak. U.S. force stationed throughout Iraq were increasingly bogged down in guerrilla warfare, with attacks on American troops surging at one point to about 33 per day.[105] While prevailing U.S. government wisdom was that the attacks were primarily carried out by former Baathists, the situation appeared to be more complicated.

A *Newsweek* report, corroborated by U.S. officials, indicated that, "Ansar fighters are joining forces with Baathists and members of al-Qaeda. In one such case, a suspected al-Qaeda operative was caught with 11 surface-to-air missiles in Ar-Ramadi, west of Baghdad. He told investigators he had trained with Ansar members to use the weapons against Americans."[106]

It appeared that Ansar, despite the small numbers of foreign fighters on the ground in Iraq (estimated at 1,000 in July 2004), had become a microcosm of the larger al-Qaeda network. Each "fighting force [was] said to be reorganized into small units of 10 to 15 members, each headed by an 'emir.'"[107] In other words, Ansar's previously hierarchal units had become self-sufficient cells. In some cases, they were dormant, not unlike some of the cells discovered in Europe and America. Indeed, the fighters coming into Iraq from Iran were "told only where to go for further instructions, usually a shop or house near the border where they would be sent on to another meeting place."[108] Clearly, the group learned how to adapt to U.S. counterterrorism. Moreover, it spawned another radical outgrowth known as Ansar as-Sunna, which espouses a wider struggle, involving more actors from around the Arab world, between Islamists and U.S. forces in Iraq.[109]

A Missed Opportunity

In May 2003, just after the official end of hostilities, a Kurdish spokesman reported that Ansar was trying to "regroup in the mountainous Iraqi-Iranian border region," and that "a number of Ansar members are trying to join another Islamic group" in the region.[110] By December, reports emerged that Ansar cells were operating in Kirkuk, Mosul, Samarra and Haweja.[111] The network also appears to be heavily armed. One small arrest that month yielded two rocket-propelled grenade launchers and 11 rounds, regular grenades, a pair of Kalashnikov rifles, 1,100 rounds of ammunition, and some $30,000 in U.S. currency.[112] One can only wonder what larger arrests would yield.

Tellingly, after the Iraq war, one PUK spokesman lamented, "if the strikes had occurred one year [before], we would have completely destroyed Ansar. They were half expecting the strikes, which gave them plenty of time to disperse, or for their leaders to relocate."[113] Another official noted that if the group had developed chemical weapons, it had ample time to move them before the strikes, and could therefore conceivably still carry out a future chemical attack. In the meantime, the group has wrought increased conventional damage. As one journalist noted, "few fighters are as qualified to carry out the recent spate of suicide-bomb attacks in Iraq as the men trained in Ansar's camps."[114]

Kurdish officials feared that sleeper cells waited to be activated in the Kurdish enclave. Two wartime operations appeared to support these suspicions: the March 22, 2004, suicide bombing carried out by a Saudi, killing an Australian cameraman at a checkpoint near Halabja,[115] and the attempted suicide car-bombing on March 27, which was thwarted when security personnel shot the assailant before he reached the Zamaki checkpoint.[116] Ansar's website, during the war and after, featured a "Letter from the Emir of Ansar al-Islam, Abu Abdullah ash-Shafi' to the Muslims of Kurdistan and Iraq and the World" threatening that "300 jihad martyrs renewed their pledge to Allah, the strong and the sublime, in order to be suicide bombers in the victory of Allah's religion."[117] U.S. officials later revealed that some Ansar fighters were given mock funerals to prepare themselves for a fiery death.[118]

A Growing Global Threat

Reports from Europe and other parts of the Middle East now indicate that Ansar al-Islam is a growing global threat. Italy, for instance, has become a hotbed of activity for Ansar. *Ash-Sharq al-Awsat* reports that two Tunisians were arrested in Italy for ties to Ansar al-Islam.[119] Further, several Ansar fighters were found in Iraq with five Italian passports in their possession.[120] By October 2003, Italian military police learned that Ansar al-Islam had established a network in the "Milan-Varese-Cremona triangle [that] funneled money to Ansar and al-Qaeda operatives abroad and served as a recruitment base for both organizations."[121] By the following month, the U.S. government designated 15 people as terrorists for their involvement in al-Qaeda cells that recruited trainees for Iraqi military camps, while also providing logistical and financial assistance to militants throughout Europe. It was not clear how many of these al-Qaeda personnel were connected to Ansar al-Islam.[122]

Other information that merely indicates global ties to Ansar al-Islam is quite daunting. The fact that Lebanese, Jordanian, Moroccan, Syrian, Palestinian, and Afghan fighters have all fought among the ranks of Ansar suggests that there was at least some recruiting infrastructure to bring them to northern Iraq. That Abu-Imad al-Masri, a former leader of the Egyptian al-Gamaa, is an official in the Milan mosque where Ansar al-Islam frequently recruited illustrates possible links between al-Gamaa and Ansar.[123] If German authorities were correct in their estimate that 100 Ansar militants were active within their borders, then Germany has also become an important hub for the group.[124] In addition, Italy, Norway, and Spain claimed that Ansar maintains a presence on their soil.[125] Further, if the group did receive funds from Abu Qatada in London, as *Le Monde* reported, then Ansar al-Islam also has a presence there. If Syria is a staging ground for Ansar fighters, as Italian wiretaps revealed, then the U.S. can add one more name to the long list of terrorist organizations operating with covert encouragement from Damascus. If Turkish officials are correct, then Ansar may have been linked to the blasts that rocked Istanbul in November 2003.[126] And finally, if some funding for the group came from Saudi Arabia, then one can deduce that the state-financed Wahhabi infrastructure supports this group.[127]

Unfortunately, definitive answers to many of these questions remain elusive. Ansar al-Islam is a relatively new terrorist group, which means that information about it is still emerging.

What is known is that Washington views the group, which was once a small rag-tag cluster of fighters in the northeast mountains of Iraq, as a top "organized terrorist adversary."[128] Moreover, the global reach of this al-Qaeda affiliate continues to expand, making Ansar al-Islam a more serious threat among al-Qaeda affiliates in the Middle East and beyond.

Notes

1 Michael Rubin, "Are Kurds a Pariah Minority?" *Social Research*, Spring 2003. www.findarticles.com/cf_dls/m2267/1_70/102140955/print.jhtml
2 Ofra Bengio, "Iraqi Kurds: Hour of Power?" *Middle East Quarterly*, Volume 10, Number 3, Summer 2003, p. 39.
3 In Iran, there is also a province known as Kurdistan. In Iraq, the term defines the area comprising Dohuk, Iribil and Sulaymaniyya, which was found by the 1957 census to have a Kurdish majority (See Rubin, *Social Research*, Spring 2003).
4 Literally, "Those who face death."

5   Gerard Chaliand, *The Kurdish Tragedy*, (London: Zed Books, 1994), p. 51.
6   Ofra Bengio, "Iraqi Kurds: Hour of Power?" *Middle East Quarterly*, Volume 10, Number 3, Summer 2003, p. 40.
7   Gerard Chaliand, p. 57.
8   Gerard Chaliand, p. 58.
9   David McDowall, *A Modern History of the Kurds*, (NY: I.B. Taurus, 1996), p.320.
10 Michael Rubin, "Kurdistan Dispatch: Bomb Shelter," *The New Republic*, June 17, 2002.
11 Michael Rubin, *Social Research*, Spring 2003.
12 Peter Galbraith, "The Wild Card in a Post-Saddam Iraq," *Boston Globe*, December 15, 2002. That article can be found at http://www.krg.org/docs/articles/galbraith-dec-2002.asp
13 Peter Galbraith, Dec. 15, 2002.
14 "The Kurdish Regional Government: The Story of Rehabilitating Iraq," (Kurdistan Regional Government – Winter 2002).
15 Michael Rubin, *Social Research*, Spring 2003.
16 Gerard Chaliand, p. 1.
17 Gerard Chaliand, p. 3.
18 Jason Burke, *Al-Qaeda: Casting a Shadow of Terror*, (NY: I.B. Taurus, 2003), p. 201.
19 Jason Burke, p. 201.
20 Michael Rubin, "The Islamist Threat in Iraqi Kurdistan," *Middle East Intelligence Bulletin*, December 2001.
21 Jason Burke, p. 203.
22 Jason Burke, p. 14.
23 C. J. Chivers," Kurds Face a Second Enemy: Islamic Fighters on Iraq Flank," *New York Times*, January 13, 2002; Author's interview with Barham Salih, Washington, DC. January 10, 2002; Robin Wright, "Wanted Iraqi May Be Al-Qaeda Link," *Los Angeles Times*, December 9, 2002.
24 "Memorandum From 'Iraqi Kurdistan Islamic Brigade' Found in Al Qaeda Guest House in Kabul," *Kurdistan Observer*, January 14, 2002.
25 Jeffrey Fleishman, "Hinting at Hussein's Links to Al Qaeda," *Los Angeles Times*, February 5, 2003.
26 Jeffery Goldberg, "The Great Terror," *The New Yorker*, March 25, 2002.
27 Colin Powell, Remarks to the United Nations Security Council, February 5, 2003. http://www.state.gov/secretary/rm/2003/17300.htm
28 Dave Eberhart, "Iraqi Terrorist Detail Ties to Bin Laden," NewsMax, March 18, 2002, and Catherine Taylor, "Taliban-Style Group Grows in Iraq," *Christian Science Monitor*, March 15, 2002.
29 Tim Judah, "London Arrest is Boost for Iraqi Kurd Nationalists," *Jerusalem Report*, November 18, 2002; Scott Peterson, "Iraqi Funds, Training Fuel Islamic Terror Group," *Christian Science Monitor*, April 2, 2002; and Jego Marie, "L'Islam Radical S'est Implante Dans L'est du Kurdistan Irakien," *Le Monde*, November 13, 2002.
30 "Ansar al-Islam's Krekar Cited on 1988 Meeting with Bin Laden in Pakistan," *Ash-Sharq al-Awsat*, March 1, 2003 (FBIS). Also see "I Met Bin Laden," *Newsweek*, October 13, 2003, p. 41.

31   Kenneth Katzman, "Iraq: U.S. Regime Change Efforts and Post-Saddam Governance," CRS Report for Congress, November 18, 2003, p. 5.

32   Italian Court Brief Regarding the Arrests of: El Ayashi Radi Abd El Samie Abou El Yazid, Ciise Maxamed Cabdullah, Mohammed Tahir Hammid and Mohamed Amin Mostafa, March 31, 2003.

33   Sebastian Rotella, "A Road to Ansar Began in Italy: Wiretaps are said to show how al-Qaeda sought to create in Northern Iraq a substitute for training camps in Afghanistan," *Los Angeles Times*, April 28, 2003. Also see Daniel Williams, "Italy Targeted by Recruiters for Terrorists; Attacks Tied to New Alliance," *Washington Post,* December 17, 2003.

34   Italian Court Brief Regarding the Arrests of: El Ayashi Radi Abd El Samie Abou El Yazid, Ciise Maxamed Cabdullah, Mohammed Tahir Hammid and Mohamed Amin Mostafa, March 31, 2003.

35   Michael Rubin, *Middle East Intelligence Bulletin*, December 2001.

36   Author's interview with Barham Salih, Washington, DC. January 10, 2003.

37   Catherine Taylor, "Taliban-Style Group Grows in Iraq," *Christian Science Monitor*, March 15, 2002; and author's interview with Barham Salih, Washington, DC. January 10, 2003.

38   "Links Between Ansar al-Islam with Al-Qaeda and Iraq," PUK Information Department, July 30, 2002.

39   "Links Between Ansar al-Islam..." Jul. 30, 2002.

40   Author's interview with official at Department of Defense, December 11, 2003.

41   Scott Peterson, "US vs. Iraq: Saddam May Have Fired the First Shot," *Christian Science Monitor*, April 9, 2002.

42   "PUK Forces Reportedly Repulse a Major Attack by Ansar al-Islam Forces," *Iraqi Kurdistan Dispatch*, July 5, 2002. http://www.ikurd.info/news-05jul-p1.htm

43   Daniel Williams, "Islamic Militants Harassing Iraqi Kurds; Group in North Iraq Backed by Iran and Bolstered by al-Qaeda, Opposition Leaders Say," *Washington Post*, Sept 5, 2002.

44   "Kurdish Leader Calls for the Elimination of Ladenite Ansar Al-Islam," Kurdistan Newsline, July 23, 2002, http://www.puk.org/web/htm/news/knwsline/nws/kurdlead.html.

45   "Talbani's Forces Restore Their Positions from Ansar al-Islam in Armed Clashes that Resulted in the Death of 35 from Both Sides," *ash-Sharq al-Awsat*, December 6, 2002.

46   "Militant Group Puts Battle on the Web," AP, December 15, 2002.

47   See http://www.nawend.com/ansarislam.htm. (This site has since been shut down.)

48   "Al-Qaeda Man Behind Murder of US Diplomat Hiding in Northern Iraq: Jordan," AFP, December 18, 2002, and C. J. Chivers, "Kurds Face a Second Enemy: Islamic Fighters on Iraq Flank," *New York Times*, January 13, 2003.

49   Bill Gertz, "September 11 Report Alludes to Iraq-al Qaeda Meeting," *Washington Times*, July 30, 2003.

50   Matthew Levitt, "Placing Iraq and Zarqawi in the Terror Web," Policywatch. no. 710, Washington Institute for Near East Policy, February 13, 2003.

51   "Treasury Designates Six Al-Qaida Terrorists," U.S. Treasury Press Release, September 24, 2003.

52   Patrick E. Tyler, "Intelligence Break let Powell Link Iraq and Qaeda,"

International Herald Tribune, February 7, 2003.
53   Colin Powell, Remarks to the United Nations Security Council, February 5, 2003. http://www.state.gov/secretary/rm/2003/17300.htm
54   Author's interview/Barham Salih, Jan. 10, 2003.
55   Patrick E. Tyler, "Intelligence Break let Powell Link Iraq and Qaeda," *International Herald Tribune*, February 7, 2003.
56   Ismail Zayir, "Ansar al-Islam Group Accuses Talabani of Spreading Rumors about its Cooperation with al-Qaeda," *al-Hayat* (London), August 22, 2002; and Robin Wright, "Wanted Iraqi May Be Al-Qaeda Link," *Los Angeles Times*, Dec 9, 2002.
57   Bart Gellman, "U.S. Suspects Al Qaeda Got Nerve Agent From Iraqis; Analysts: Chemical May Be VX, And Was Smuggled Via Turkey," *Washington Post*, December 12, 2002.
58   Author's interview/Barham Salih, Jan. 10, 2003.
59   Author's interview with official PUK representative in Washington, March 2003.
60   Jeffery Goldberg, "The Great Terror," *The New Yorker*, March 25, 2002.
61   "Links Between Ansar al-Islam with Al-Qaeda and Iraq," PUK Information Department, July 30, 2002; and Michael Howard, "Militant Kurds Training al-Qaida Fighters," *The Guardian*, August 23, 2002.
62   Scott Peterson, "The Rise and Fall of Ansar al-Islam," *Christian Science Monitor*, October 16, 2003. www.csmonitor.com/2003/1016/p12s01-woiq.html
63   "Ansar al-Islam," Iraq News Wire, No.8, Part II, MEMRI, September 1, 2002; Scott Peterson, "Iraqi Funds, Training Fuel Islamic Terror Group," *Christian Science Monitor*, April 2, 2002. Also see Robin Wright, "Wanted Iraqi May Be Al-Qaeda Link," *Los Angeles Times*, Dec. 9, 2002 and "Links Between Ansar al-Islam with Al-Qaeda and Iraq," PUK Information Department, July 30, 2002.
64   "Links Between Ansar al-Islam…" Jul. 30, 2002.
65   "Links Between Ansar al-Islam…" Jul. 30, 2002.
66   "Links Between Ansar al-Islam…" Jul. 30, 2002.
67   "Islamic Militants Harassing Iraqi Kurds; Group in North Iraq Backed by Iran and Bolstered by al-Qaeda, Opposition Leaders Say," *Washington Post,* Sept 5, 2002.
68   Namik Durukan, "Al-Qaida of Northern Iraq, Ansar al-Islam Says Confidently: If America Hits, Jihad Will Begin," *Milliyet* (Turkish), January 7, 2003.
69   Scott Peterson, "The Rise and Fall of Ansar al-Islam," *Christian Science Monitor*, October 16, 2003. www.csmonitor.com/2003/1016/p12s01-woiq.html
70   Author's interview with PUK official, Washington, DC. April 1, 2003.
71   Author's phone interview with Robin Benselow, June 29, 2004.
72   C.J. Chivers, "Kurdish Leader is Assassinated in Militant Raid," *New York Times*, February 10, 2003.
73   "Ansar al-Islam Named to SDGT List," U.S. Treasury Press Release, February 20, 2003.
74   Author's interview/PUK official, Apr. 1, 2003.
75   "USWAR/Ansar al-Islam Attacks PUK Positions," IRNA, March 26, 2003.
76   William Stoichevski, "Former Leader of Kurdish Guerrilla Group Says Ansar al-Islam Unlikely Responsible for Attacks on Americans in Iraq," AP, August 12, 2003.
77   Author's interview/PUK official, Apr. 1, 2003.

78   "Raid Finds al-Qaida Tie to Iraq Militants," AP, March 31, 2003.

79   "Terror Handbook Found at Ansar al-Islam Camp: Report," AFP, April 9, 2003.

80   "Islamic Militant Group is Spreading Across Iraq," *Los Angeles Times*, September 3, 2003.

81   Karl Vick, "Iran Turns Away Militant Group: Halt in Aid to Kurdish Faction Comes After Missile Attacks," *Washington Post*, March 25, 2003.

82   "Iran: FM Spokesman Rejects Allegations of Assisting Ansar al-Islam," IRNA, March 24, 2003.

83   Reports from Iranian dissidents, January 2004.

84   Eli J. Lake, "US Negotiates Trade Terror Suspects," UPI, May 9, 2003.

85   Chris Brummitt, "Iran: We've Deported al-Qaida Suspects,"AP, October 17, 2003.

86   Author's conversations with CPA official, March 11, 2004, Ansar al-Islam prisoners in Sulaymaniyya, January 2004, and American journalist in Baghdad, April 27, 2004.

87   Neil Macfarquhar, "Iraq Drawing a New Tide of Islamic Militants," *New York Times*, August 13, 2003.

88   Muhammed ash-Shafi'i, "Ansar al-Islam Group Threatens to Fight Americans, Seculars in Iraq," *Ash-Sharq al-Awsat*, June 13, 2003 (FBIS).

89   Mike Patterson, "Iraq Operations Providing Intelligence on al-Qaeda: Myers," AFP, July 30, 2003

90   "Hunting Islamists in Northern Iraq Coming From Pakistan with Support from Bin Laden," *al-Hayat*, August 7, 2003.

91   Ned Parker, "Ansar al-Islam, The Vanguard of Radical Islam in Iraq," AFP, August 14, 2003.

92   "Kurdish Party Says it Captures Iraqi Islamists," Reuters, August 12, 2003.

93   Neil Macfarquhar, "Iraq Drawing a New Tide of Islamic Militants," *New York Times*, August 13, 2003.

94   Neil Macfarquhar, Aug. 13, 2003.

95   Dexter Filkins and Richard A. Oppel, Jr. "Huge Suicide Blast Demolishes U.N. Headquarters in Baghdad; Top Aid Officials Among 17 Dead," *New York Times*, August 20, 2003.

96   Daniel Williams, "Italy Targeted by Recruiters for Terrorists; Attacks Tied to New Alliance," *Washington Post*, December 17, 2003.

97   For the full version of this account, see: Jonathan Schanzer, "Saddam's Ambassador to al Qaeda: An Iraqi prisoner details Saddam's links to Osama bin Laden's terror network," *The Weekly Standard*, March 1, 2004.

98   http://www.state.gov/p/nea/rls/13456.htm

99   "US Forces Capture Senior Ansar al-Islam Leader: Defense Official," AFP, October 14, 2003. Also see "Arresting the Third Person from Ansar al-Islam," *ash-Sharq al-Awsat*, October 15, 2003.

100   Matt Kelley, "Saddam Confidant Linked to al-Qaida Group," AP, October 30, 2003.

101   Paul Martin, "Suspect in Attacks Said to be Very Ill," *Washington Times*, October 31, 2003.

102   Sebastian Rotella, "3 Terror Network Suspects Arrested," *Los Angeles Times*, November 29, 2003. Also see Desmond Butler and Don Van Natta, Jr.,

"Trail of Anti-U.S. Fighters Said to Cross Europe to Iraq," *New York Times*, December 6, 2003.

103   "Dutch Police Detain Suspected Iraqi Radical Wanted in Germany," AFP, December 8, 2003.

104   "Algerian Terror Suspect Held in Germany Pending Extradition," AP, January 7, 2004.

105   Matt Kelley, October 30, 2003.

106   Babak Defghanpisheh, "Inside Al Ansar: Jailed Militants Tell Newsweek how their Group has Adapted to Fight U.S. Occupation," *Newsweek*, October 13, 2003, p.41.

107   Babak Defghanpisheh, p. 41.

108   Babak Defghanpisheh, p. 41.

109   For more, see: Michael Rubin, "Ansar al-Sunna: Iraq's New Terrorist Threat," *Middle East Intelligence Bulletin*, Vol.6, No. 5, May 2004.

110   Author's interview with Kurdish spokesman, Washington, DC. May 20, 2003.

111   Brian Bennet and Michael Ware, "Life Behind Enemy Lines," *Time Magazine*, December 15, 2003.

112   "US Troops Kill Three in Battle with Ansar al-Islam," AFP, January 1, 2004.

113   Author's interview/PUK official, Apr. 1, 2003.

114   Brian Bennet and Michael Ware, "Life Behind Enemy Lines," *Time Magazine*, December 15, 2003.

115   "Ansar Al-Islam Suicide Bomber was from Saudi Arabia," Kurdish Media News, March 25, 2003. http://www.kurdmedia.com/news.asp?id=3635

116   Author's interview/PUK official, Apr. 1, 2003.

117   http://www.nawend.com/ansarislam.htm (This site has since been shut down.)

118   Brian Bennet and Michael Ware, Dec. 15, 2003.

119   "Arrest of Two Tunisians in the 'Italian Cell' for their Relations with the Ansar al-Islam Group," *Ash-Sharq al-Awsat*, April 3, 2003.

120   Neil Macfarquhar, "Iraq Drawing a New Tide of Islamic Militants," *New York Times*, August 13, 2003.

121   "Ansar al-Islam's European Base," AFPC email update, October 31, 2003.

122   "U.S. Freezes Assets of 15 in Italy," CNN.com, November 12, 2003. http://edition.cnn.com/2003/US/11/12/terror.list/

123   "Milan-Based Islamist on 'Abduction' of his Deputies, Denies Links to al-Qaeda," *Ash-Sharq al-Awsat*, June 19, 2003. (FBIS).

124   Asaf Moghadam and Matthew Levitt, "Radical Islamist Groups in Germany: A Lesson in Prosecuting Terror in Court," Policywatch #834, Washington Institute for Near East Policy, February 19, 2004.

125   Daniel Williams, "Italy Targeted by Recruiters for Terrorists; Attacks Tied to New Alliance," *Washington Post*, December 17, 2003.

126   Andrew Purvis and Pelin Turgut, "Al-Qaeda's Tracks?" *Time*, December 8, 2003.

127   Michael Rubin, *Middle East Intelligence Bulletin*, December 2001.

128   Robert Burns, "Iraq Group Said Main Threat to U.S. Forces," AP, October 23, 2003.

Chapter Seven: Implications

A l-Qaeda and its network of affiliates clearly do not pose a new threat. From Lebanon and Yemen to Egypt, Iraq and Algeria, the dangerous role of affiliates has been expanding for a decade or more. While the attacks of September 11 were a shock to Americans, they fit a long-established pattern of attacks in Middle East states, European nations, and other countries around the world.

As Washington readies itself to combat the al-Qaeda phenomenon in the years to come, it can learn a great deal from the activities of the network's smaller affiliate groups in years past. Armed with information about how these groups operate, the gray areas in which they hide, the tactics they employ, and the ideologies they espouse, decision makers may be better prepared to craft sensible counterterrorism policies that are geared on a practical level to defeat the forces of militant Islam worldwide.

More Focus Needed on Affiliate Groups

As Washington prepares for the next phase of the war on terror, affiliate groups, the building blocks for the al-Qaeda network, deserve more attention. The affiliates' potential to become logistical centers for the global terror network makes them particularly dangerous. As discussed in Chapter Six, the Iraqi Ansar al-Islam served as a logistics center for Abu Musab az-Zarqawi's growing terror network before the Iraq war. By July 2004, he arguably controlled the most active terrorist network in Iraq, possibly even worldwide. Further, the chapter on the GSPC demonstrated how Algeria's al-Qaeda affiliate expanded beyond its home turf, establishing operational and logistical support in Belgium, England, France, Italy, the Netherlands, and Spain.

Affiliates are also dangerous in that they are essentially pools of seasoned fighters with experience on one or more of al-Qaeda's battlefields. Every al-Qaeda affiliate discussed in this book grew stronger in their home countries after their fighters received hands-on training in Afghanistan between 1979 and 1989. Al-Gamaa al-Islamiyya, al-Jihad, Asbat al-Ansar, the IAA, the GIA, the GSPC, and Ansar al-Islam all drew veteran fighters from al-Qaeda's fronts in Bosnia, Chechnya, or the Philippines.

Looking ahead, Ansar al-Islam and the Zarqawi network could play a similar role in training future jihadis through the guerrilla war in post-Saddam Iraq. Indeed, a number of the militants fighting in Iraq come from al-Qaeda affiliates. U.S. forces in Iraq killed at least two Palestinian guerrillas hailing from Asbat al-Ansar's base of Ein al-Hilweh.[1] Kurdish sources report that GSPC fighters have been spotted in Iraq, and several additional GSPC operatives may have been dispatched to Iraq by the al-Qaeda leadership.[2] As U.S. forces fend off the insurgency in Iraq, "reservists" from the smaller affiliates help to reinforce the Ansar cadre. When they return to their places of origin, these local affiliates could grow stronger and more militant. They will be the potential terrorists who quietly plot the next big attack in their home countries.

Hunting Affiliates as Strategy

As Washington continues to strike at the core leadership of pre-9/11 al-Qaeda, it must also consider a sustained campaign against the network's dangerous periphery, which will constitute the bulk of the future al-Qaeda threat. If affiliates around the world are allowed to operate unchecked, they could become main centers of al-Qaeda activity. The examples of al-Gamaa al-Islamiyya and al-Jihad in Upper Egypt demonstrate how groups on the periphery can grow to embody the center. Furthermore, while al-Qaeda's centers of operation in Sudan and Afghanistan were not covered in this book, they are obvious examples of how local bases can grow to become deeper threats.

Low-Hanging Fruit

Fortunately, although affiliates threaten American interests, the U.S. and its allies can also threaten them. Clandestine al-Qaeda cells are hard to identify and very difficult to dismantle. By contrast, al-Qaeda affiliates are al-Qaeda's soft targets. U.S. intelligence services often know exactly where these groups are based (for targeting) and who commands them (for financial operations or even arrests). As such, they represent the "low hanging fruit" in the war against al-Qaeda – both in the Middle East and throughout the world.

At a time when the U.S. military is spread thin in Afghanistan, Iraq, and elsewhere, small-scale operations against these groups may prove a less complicated, less time-consuming, and less expensive mode of fighting terrorism. While Special Forces continue to pursue the core of the al-Qaeda leadership, other tangible victories – both military and political – in the war on terror can be scored by attacking the periphery. This two-pronged approach would weaken the al-Qaeda network's leadership, and also chip away at the network's future capacity for executing attacks.

This approach would put al-Qaeda at a psychological disadvantage. Al-Qaeda and its affiliates are effective because they strike at different Western and Muslim targets randomly. This often causes the desired effect of fear and confusion. By attacking different al-Qaeda affiliates methodically around the globe, but in a way that appears to be random, the United States and its allies have the opportunity to cause the same fear and confusion within the al-Qaeda's enclaves. In this way, the U.S. and its allies can begin to go on the offensive and attack the network in the way that they have attacked the West.

A Strategy Already Employed?

Smaller operations – including conventional attacks or

commando assaults – against affiliate groups in the Yemen, Algeria and Iraq have already marked substantial gains in the war on terror. The U.S. and cooperative host governments scored other successes in the Philippines, Georgia, and parts of Africa – areas that lie outside the scope of this book. These advances were achieved without the burdens that accompany regime change in places such as Iraq or Afghanistan. For example, the predator drone attack in the badlands of Yemen on November 5, 2002, a product of careful coordination between Yemeni and U.S. intelligence, resulted in the termination of several high-ranking al-Qaeda lieutenants. Months later, in June 2003, a U.S.-assisted assault by Yemeni forces on an IAA base in the Hattat region also resulted in a blow to al-Qaeda in Yemen.

Similarly, the U.S. military, with help from Kurdish peshmerga, decimated the Ansar al-Islam enclave during the spring 2003 Iraq war. Within eight days, the entire base was wiped out, more than 200 fighters were killed, and several were brought into custody. U.S. assistance to governments in North Africa eliminated the threat of several high-ranking leaders of the GSPC, including Nabil Sahrawi and the notorious Abd ar-Rezzak al-Para.

Cooperation is the Key

Some might ask, "Why must the U.S. get involved in the first place? Can't Washington simply demand that other countries take more of an active role in the war on terror?" The answer lies in the lessons learned from the attacks of September 11, 2001. Those attacks demonstrated that the United States can no longer allow states to struggle with the toothless counterterrorism methods of their choice.

The case of Yemen is perhaps the most salient. Lack of attention enabled al-Qaeda to successfully attack the U.S.S. *Cole* in 2000. Lack of coordination with Washington allowed Yemeni counterterrorism operations to remain in disarray until the financially devastating *Limburg* attack of 2002. Increased cooperation and oversight since then has led to a significant drop in successful terrorist attacks.

The recent successes against the GSPC in Algeria and its neighbors are also instructive. When Algeria was left to its own devices in its campaigns against the GIA and the GSPC, the result was disastrous. Algiers hobbled these groups, but never defeated them. In the process, the Algerian government alienated its people through egregious human rights violations and coercive political controls. Recent pinpoint operations with the U.S., however, have led to small but decisive victories over GSPC leaders and their supporting fighters. Washington must continue to forge cooperative relationships in the region if it wants to produce similar results.

Cooperation will be crucial on a strategic level, as well. While al-Qaeda and those who subscribe to its radical Islamist vision have declared war on America, it is not only America's war to fight. Nor is it the war of America's Western allies. At its very core, this conflict is a battle within the religion of Islam. Radical Islam can only truly be defeated as an ideology if moderates discredit it enough to change the tide of public opinion. As such, this will increasingly be a battle between moderate Islam and radical Islam. Moderate Islamic governments in the Middle East and elsewhere must begin to take the lead, with support from America.

Strengthening Areas of Weak Central Authority

In addition to international ties that can contribute to ideological victories and joint counterterrorism operations, the challenge ahead is to assist states in bringing areas of weak central authority under their control so that more affiliates cannot develop.

Across the board, Middle Eastern al-Qaeda affiliates originated in areas of weak central authority. Because Beirut (and occupying Syria) does not govern Ein al-Hilweh, Asbat al-Ansar emerged. In Yemen, the IAA exploited areas that exist outside of Sanaa's loose political control. Egypt's two radical groups grew out of the relative void in Upper Egypt, where Cairo's presence is weaker. Algeria's GSPC and Iraq's Ansar al-Islam, for their part, developed amidst the weak central authority that accompanies internecine violence. Failure to tackle these problem areas quickly enabled local Islamist groups to thrive. Al-Qaeda then exploited the problem by furnishing financial, military, and/or logistical assistance to these local groups, which became far more dangerous as affiliates.

The National Strategy for Combating Terrorism of 2003 stresses that one of Washington's top priorities must be to "diminish the underlying conditions that terrorists seek to exploit." Rather than forwarding another tired allusion to the eradication of poverty, the U.S. government sees the need to help weaker states "develop the military, law enforcement, political and financial tools necessary" to fight terrorism effectively.[3]

The necessary tools will differ in each case. On a military level, they could include the sharing of intelligence, military training, combined special operations, or satellite imagery. On a political level, Washington can provide financial assistance for special projects that would actually strengthen the position of the local government in the weaker areas. This might include contributions to the host country's education, transportation, or hospital system, as well as other critical areas of physical infrastructure that are commonly lacking in gray areas around the world. The challenge for Washington will be to find the right combination of assistance based on a country-by-country assessment, and then to oversee implementation. Proper oversight will ensure that the resources Washington dedicates are actually used in the fight against al-Qaeda affiliates, and that they are not squandered by governments that have been traditionally less than transparent in their use of foreign aid.

A Light Footprint

In the cases when Middle Eastern states are willing to

cooperate fully with the U.S., it will be important to ensure that the U.S. role is not a heavy-handed one. Indeed, a light footprint is necessary for successful cooperation in states such as Algeria, Yemen and elsewhere. Overzealous U.S. activity in the Middle East, a part of the world that begrudges U.S. power (if it does not plainly exude hatred for America), can lead to disaster, both in the fight against al-Qaeda affiliates and, more broadly, in U.S.-Middle East relations.

For instance, direct and open cooperation between the U.S. and the Kurds before the 2003 Iraq war and during the subsequent U.S.-led occupation did not go unnoticed by al-Qaeda and radical Sunni leaders in Iraq. The resentment of this relationship has arguably led to increased attacks against the Kurds in Iraq. Conversely, quiet U.S. cooperation with the Yemeni government has contributed to successful counterterrorism operations and an overall perception that Yemen remains fiercely autonomous.

Thus, as the U.S. State Department and military begin to engage with the Algerian government, caution is paramount. Open activity between the highly unpopular government in Algiers and Washington, which continues to decline in popularity throughout the Middle East, will not go unnoticed by an Algerian public prone to distrust and conspiracy theories. If progress is to be made in countering the threat of the GSPC, it should be done quietly and behind the scenes. Over time, if stability and transparency result from U.S.-Algerian cooperation, a heavier footprint could be achieved.

The Challenges of Foreign Support

The U.S. will likely run into more resistance in its efforts to garner allies in the war against al-Qaeda and the jihadi movement. Paul Pillar, former deputy chief of the CIA's counterterrorist center, asks an important question: "How will governments respond to a U.S. appeal to move against groups that have never inflicted comparable horrors on the United States or on any other nation or against groups that do not conspicuously pose [a dangerous] threat...?" Pillar believes that some "foreign governments may be a little slower to act, a little less forthcoming with information, or slightly more apt to cite domestic impediments to cooperation."[4] In other words, some governments may not recognize the looming threat of al-Qaeda affiliates – even the ones on their soil. One of the greatest diplomatic challenges that Washington will face in the months and years to come will be to maintain steadfast allies in the region in this battle against al-Qaeda's peripheral players. It will be imperative to prod them to rigorously pursue their local affiliates, and to maintain a high level of intensity, even after Osama bin Laden is captured or killed, and even after dealing serious blows to the al-Qaeda network.

When to Use the Stick

If a country, such as Syria (and by default Lebanon) refuses to take steps against affiliate groups and the lawless environments in which they operate, intense diplomacy is the first step. According to the U.S. National Strategy for Terrorism, when states are unwilling to do their part to fight terrorism, the U.S. will work to "convince them to change course and meet their international obligations."[5] If diplomacy fails, tough penalties and sanctions can be imposed. Threat of force may even be necessary. After all, harboring terrorists amounts to aiding and abetting them.

Countries that allow affiliates to operate openly within their borders may dig in their heels at first and ignore U.S. demands. Indeed, some may initially become more sympathetic to the affiliates in reaction to U.S. pressure. But a steadfast commitment to a policy that forbids states to harbor al-Qaeda affiliates will eventually yield positive results.

As discussed in Chapter Three, Damascus prevents Beirut from policing its own refugee camps, which has led directly to the establishment and expansion of Asbat al-Ansar. Syria already suffers from U.S. sanctions because it has been listed as a state sponsor of terrorism. More recently, the United States Congress passed the Syria Accountability and Lebanese Restoration Act, which calls upon Syria to end its occupation of Lebanon, and to sever ties with terrorist groups on its soil. Washington must now make it clear to Damascus that it sees Asbat al-Ansar as a critical component of this recent legislation, and that failure to allow Beirut to fully dismantle this group could result in further penalties.

Conclusion

Fighting al-Qaeda's armies will require a great deal of nimble coordination between Washington and dozens of countries spanning the Middle East, Asia and Europe in order to adapt to the amorphous nature of affiliate groups. The strategies, tactics, positions, and leaders of affiliate groups change fast and often, requiring real-time intelligence and quick decision making. If employed successfully, an aggressive strategy of smaller battles against affiliates can yield a series of unequivocal victories in a short amount of time. These victories, which will be perceived as both military and political blows to the al-Qaeda movement, can be shared by more than one nation.

Moreover, the small operations inherent to this strategy can take immense pressure off of an increasingly overburdened American military. Small victories could invigorate a public that has already grown weary of the war on terror, just three years after the most devastating terrorist attack in U.S. history.

More importantly, targeting affiliates will demonstrate to al-Qaeda and the jihadi movement that the entire world, not just the West, is actively engaged in this war on terror. With the help of cooperative Muslim governments, this strategy will also demonstrate that the real battle has begun: the battle between moderate Islam and the radicals.

Notes

1 "Palestinian Killed in Attack on US Forces in Iraq," AP, December 21, 2003.
2 Basel Muhammed, "Kurdish Official: Members from al-Qaeda are in Baghdad with Iraqi Identities," *al-Hayat*, October 29, 2003.
3 National Strategy for Combatting Terrorism, (February 2003), pp. 11-12. http://usinfo.state.gov/topical/pol/terror/strategy/
4 Paul Pillar, "Counterterrorism after Al Qaeda," *Washington Quarterly*, Summer 2004, pp. 101-114.
5 National Strategy for Combatting Terrorism, (February 2003), p. 12. http://usinfo.state.gov/topical/pol/terror/strategy/

Appendix A

Al-Qaeda's Middle East affiliate groups, as described in the U.S. State Department's "Patterns of Global Terrorism 2003."

Ansar al-Islam (AI)

a.k.a. Partisans of Islam, Helpers of Islam, Supporters of Islam, Jund al-Islam, Jaish Ansar al-Sunna.

Description

Ansar al-Islam is a radical Islamist group of Iraqi Kurds and Arabs who have vowed to establish an independent Islamic state in Iraq. It was formed in December 2001 and is closely allied with al-Qaede. Some of its members trained in al-Qaeda camps in Afghanistan, and the group provided safehaven to al-Qaeda fighters before Operation Iraqi Freedom (OIF). Since OIF, it has been one of the leading groups engaged in anti-Coalition attacks. (Ansar al-Islam was designated on 20 February 2003, under E.O. 13224. The UNSCR 1267 Committee designated Ansar al-Islam pursuant to UNSCRs 1267, 1390, and 1455 on 27 February 2003.) First designated in March 2004.

Activities

The group has primarily fought against one of the two main Kurdish political factions— the Patriotic Union of Kurdistan (PUK)—and has mounted ambushes and attacks in PUK areas. AI members have been implicated in assassinations and assassination attempts against PUK officials and work closely with both al-Qaeda operatives and associates in Abu Mus'ab al-Zarqawi's network. Before OIF, some AI members claimed to have produced cyanide-based toxins, ricin, and alfatoxin.

Strength
Approximately 700 to 1,000 members.

Location/Area of Operation
Central and northern Iraq.

External Aid
The group receives funding, training, equipment, and combat support from al-Qaeda and other international jihadist backers.

Source: http://www.state.gov/s/ct/rls/pgtrpt/2003/31711.htm
Patterns of Global Terrorism- 2003 (U.S. Department of State) Appendix B — Background Information on Designated Foreign Terrorist Organizations

Armed Islamic Group (GIA)

Description
An Islamic extremist group, the GIA aims to overthrow the secular Algerian regime and replace it with an Islamic state. The GIA began its violent activity in 1992 after the military government suspended legislative elections in anticipation of an overwhelming victory by the Islamic Salvation Front, the largest Islamic opposition party. First designated in October 1997.

Activities
Frequent attacks against civilians and government workers. Since 1992, the GIA has conducted a terrorist campaign of civilian massacres, sometimes wiping out entire villages in its area of operation, although the group's dwindling numbers have caused a decrease in the number of attacks. Since announcing its campaign against foreigners living in Algeria in 1993, the GIA has killed more than 100 expatriate men and women—mostly Europeans—in the country. The group uses assassinations and bombings, including car bombs, and it is known to favor kidnapping victims.

The GIA highjacked an Air France flight to Algiers in December 1994. In 2002, a French court sentenced two GIA members to life in prison for conducting a series of bombings in France in 1995.

Strength
Precise numbers unknown; probably fewer than 100.

Location/Area of Operation
Algeria and Europe.

External Aid
None known.

Source: http://www.state.gov/s/ct/rls/pgtrpt/2003/31711.htm
Patterns of Global Terrorism- 2003 (U.S. Department of State) Appendix B — Background Information on Designated Foreign Terrorist Organizations

Asbat al-Ansar

Description
'Asbat al-Ansar—the League of the Followers or Partisans' League—is a Lebanon-based, Sunni extremist group, composed primarily of Palestinians and associated with Usama bin Ladin's al-Qaeda organization. The group follows an extremist interpretation of Islam that justifies violence against civilian targets to achieve political ends. Some of those goals include overthrowing the Lebanese government and thwarting perceived anti-Islamic and pro-Western influences in the country. First designated in March 2002.

Activities
'Asbat al-Ansar has carried out multiple terrorist attacks in Lebanon since it first emerged in the early 1990s. The group assassinated Lebanese religious leaders and bombed nightclubs, theaters, and liquor stores in the mid-1990s. The group raised its

operational profile in 2000 with two attacks against Lebanese and international targets. It was involved in clashes in northern Lebanon in December 1999 and carried out a rocket-propelled grenade attack on the Russian Embassy in Beirut in January 2000. 'Asbat al-Ansar's leader, Abu Muhjin, remains at large despite being sentenced to death in absentia for the murder in 1994 of a Muslim cleric.

In 2003, suspected 'Asbat al-Ansar elements were responsible for the attempt in April to use a car bomb against a McDonald's in a Beirut suburb. By October, Lebanese security forces arrested Ibn al-Shahid, who is believed to be associated with 'Asbat al- Ansar, and charged him with masterminding the bombing of three fast food restaurants in 2002 and the attempted attack in April 2003 on the McDonald's. 'Asbat forces were involved in other violence in Lebanon in 2003, including clashes with members of Yassir Arafat's Fatah movement in the 'Ayn al-Hilwah refugee camp and a rocket attack in June on the Future TV building in Beirut.

Strength
The group commands about 300 fighters in Lebanon.

Location/Area of Operation
The group's primary base of operations is the Ayn al-Hilwah Palestinian refugee camp near Sidon in southern Lebanon.

External Aid
Probably receives money through international Sunni extremist networks and Usama bin Ladin's al-Qaeda network.

Source: http://www.state.gov/s/ct/rls/pgtrpt/2003/31711.htm
Patterns of Global Terrorism- 2003 (U.S. Department of State) Appendix B — Background Information on Designated Foreign Terrorist Organizations

Al-Gama'a al-Islamiyya (Islamic Group, IG)

Description
Egypt's largest militant group, active since the late 1970s, appears to be loosely organized. Has an external wing with supporters in several countries worldwide. The group issued a cease-fire in March 1999, but its spiritual leader, Shaykh Umar Abd al-Rahman—sentenced to life in prison in January 1996 for his involvement in the World Trade Center bombing of 1993 and incarcerated in the United States—rescinded his support for the cease-fire in June 2000. The IG has not conducted an attack inside Egypt since August 1998. Senior member signed Usama bin Ladin's *fatwa* in February 1998 calling for attacks against the United States.

Unofficially split in two factions: one that supports the cease-fire led by Mustafa Hamza, and one led by Rifa'i Taha Musa, calling for a return to armed operations. Taha Musa in early 2001 published a book in which he attempted to justify terrorist attacks that would cause mass casualties. Musa disappeared several months thereafter, and there are conflicting reports as to his current whereabouts. In March 2002, members of the group's historic leadership in Egypt declared use of violence misguided and renounced its future use, prompting denunciations by much of the leadership abroad. In 2003, the Egyptian government released more than 900 former IG members from prison.

For members still dedicated to violent jihad, the primary goal is to overthrow the Egyptian government and replace it with an Islamic state. Disaffected IG members, such as those potentially inspired by Taha Musa or Abd al-Rahman, may be interested in carrying out attacks against U.S. interests. First designated October 1997.

Activities

Group conducted armed attacks against Egyptian security and other government officials, Coptic Christians, and Egyptian opponents of Islamic extremism before the cease-fire. From 1993 until the cease-fire, IG launched attacks on tourists in Egypt— most notably the attack in November 1997 at Luxor that killed 58 foreign tourists. Also claimed responsibility for the attempt in June 1995 to assassinate Egyptian President Hosni Mubarak in Addis Ababa, Ethiopia. The IG never has specifically attacked a U.S. citizen or facility but has threatened U.S. interests.

Strength

Unknown. At its peak the IG probably commanded several thousand hard-core members and a like number of sympathizers. The cease-fire of 1999 and security crackdowns following the attack in Luxor in 1997 and, more recently, security efforts following September 11, probably have resulted in a substantial decrease in the group's numbers.

Location/Area of Operation

Operates mainly in the Al-Minya, Asyut, Qina, and Sohaj governorates of southern Egypt. Also appears to have support in Cairo, Alexandria, and other urban locations, particularly among unemployed graduates and students. Has a worldwide presence, including in the United Kingdom, Afghanistan, Yemen, and various locations in Europe.

External Aid

Unknown. The Egyptian Government believes that Iran, Usama bin Ladin, and Afghan militant groups support the organization. Also may obtain some funding through various Islamic nongovernmental organizations.

Source: http://www.state.gov/s/ct/rls/pgtrpt/2003/31711.htm
Patterns of Global Terrorism- 2003 (U.S. Department of State)

Appendix B — Background Information on Designated Foreign Terrorist Organizations

Islamic Army of Aden (IAA)

a.k.a. Aden-Abyan Islamic Army (AAIA)

Description

The Islamic Army of Aden (IAA) emerged publicly in mid-1998 when the group released a series of communiqués that expressed support for Usama bin Ladin, appealed for the overthrow of the Yemeni Government, and called for operations against U.S. and other Western interests in Yemen. Designated under EO 13224 in September 2001.

Activities

Engages in bombings and kidnappings to promote its goals. The group reportedly was behind an attack in June 2003 against a medical assistance convoy in the Abyan governorate. Yemeni authorities responded with a raid on a suspected IAA facility, killing several individuals and capturing others, including Khalid al-Nabi al-Yazidi, the group's leader.

Before that attack, the group had not conducted operations since the bombing of the British Embassy in Sanaa in October 2000. In 2001, Sanaa found an IAA member and three associates responsible for that attack. In December 1998, the group kidnapped 16 British, American, and Australian tourists near Mudiyah in southern Yemen.

Although Yemeni officials previously have claimed that the group is operationally defunct, their recent attribution of the attack in 2003 against the medical convoy and reports that al-Yazidi was released from prison in mid-October 2003 suggest that the IAA, or at least elements of the group, have resumed activity.

Strength
Not known.

Location/Area of Operation
Operates in the southern governorates of Yemen—primarily Aden and Abyan.

External Aid
Not known.

Source: http://www.state.gov/s/ct/rls/pgtrpt/2003/31759.htm
Patterns of Global Terrorism- 2003 (U.S. Department of State)
Appendix C — Background Information on Other Terrorist Groups

Al-Jihad
a.k.a. Jihad Group, Egyptian Islamic Jihad [EIJ]

Description
This Egyptian Islamic extremist group merged with Usama bin Ladin's al-Qaeda organization in June 2001. Active since the 1970s, the EIJ's primary goals traditionally have been to overthrow the Egyptian Government and replace it with an Islamic state and to attack U.S. and Israeli interests in Egypt and abroad. EIJ members who didn't join al-Qaeda retain the capability to conduct independent operations. First designated in October 1997.

Activities
Historically specialized in armed attacks against high-level Egyptian government personnel, including cabinet ministers, and car bombings against official U.S. and Egyptian facilities. The original Jihad was responsible for the assassination in 1981 of Egyptian President Anwar Sadat. Claimed responsibility for the

attempted assassinations of Interior Minister Hassan al-Alfi in August 1993 and Prime Minister Atef Sedky in November 1993. Has not conducted an attack inside Egypt since 1993 and has never successfully targeted foreign tourists there. Responsible for Egyptian Embassy bombing in Islamabad in 1995, and in 1998 an attack against U.S. Embassy in Albania was thwarted.

Strength
Unknown, but probably has several hundred hard-core members.

Location/Area of Operation
Historically operated in the Cairo area, but most of its network is outside Egypt, including Yemen, Afghanistan, Pakistan, Lebanon, and the United Kingdom, and its activities have been centered outside Egypt for several years.

External Aid
Unknown. The Egyptian Government claims that Iran supports the Jihad. Received most of its funding from al-Qaeda after early 1998—close ties that culminated in the eventual merger of the two groups. Some funding may come from various Islamic nongovernmental organizations, cover businesses, and criminal acts.

Source: http://www.state.gov/s/ct/rls/pgtrpt/2003/31711.htm
Patterns of Global Terrorism- 2003 (U.S. Department of State) Appendix B — Background Information on Designated Foreign Terrorist Organizations

Al-Qaeda
a.k.a. Qa'idat al-Jihad

Description
Established by Usama bin Ladin in the late 1980s to bring together Arabs who fought in Afghanistan against the Soviet

Union. Helped finance, recruit, transport, and train Sunni Islamic extremists for the Afghan resistance. Current goal is to establish a pan- Islamic Caliphate throughout the world by working with allied Islamic extremist groups to overthrow regimes it deems "non-Islamic" and expelling Westerners and non-Muslims from Muslim countries—particularly Saudi Arabia. Issued statement under banner of "the World Islamic Front for Jihad Against the Jews and Crusaders" in February 1998, saying it was the duty of all Muslims to kill U.S. citizens—civilian or military—and their allies everywhere. Merged with Egyptian Islamic Jihad (Al-Jihad) in June 2001. First designated in October 1999.

Activities

In 2003, carried out the assault and bombing on 12 May of three expatriate housing complexes in Riyadh, Saudi Arabia, that killed 20 and injured 139. Assisted in carrying out the bombings on 16 May in Casablanca, Morocco, of a Jewish center, restaurant, nightclub, and hotel that killed 41 and injured 101. Probably supported the bombing of the J.W. Marriott Hotel in Jakarta, Indonesia, on 5 August that killed 17 and injured 137. Responsible for the assault and bombing on 9 November of a housing complex in Riyadh, Saudi Arabia, that killed 17 and injured 100. Conducted the bombings of two synagogues in Istanbul, Turkey, on 15 November that killed 23 and injured 200 and the bombings in Istanbul of the British Consulate and HSBC Bank on 20 November that resulted in 27 dead and 455 injured. Has been involved in some attacks in Afghanistan and Iraq.

In 2002, carried out bombing on 28 November of hotel in Mombasa, Kenya, killing 15 and injuring 40. Probably supported a nightclub bombing in Bali, Indonesia, on 12 October that killed about 180. Responsible for an attack on U.S. military personnel in Kuwait, on 8 October, that killed one U.S. soldier and injured another. Directed a suicide attack on the MV *Limburg* off the coast of Yemen, on 6 October that killed one and injured four. Carried out a firebombing of a synagogue in Tunisia on 11 April that killed 19 and injured 22. On 11 September 2001, 19 al-Qaeda suicide attackers hijacked and crashed four U.S. commercial jets—two into the World Trade Center in New York City, one into the Pentagon near Washington, D.C., and a fourth into a field in Shanksville, Pennsylvania, leaving about 3,000 individuals dead or missing. Directed the attack on the *USS Cole* in the port of Aden, Yemen, on 12 October 2000 killing 17 US Navy members and injuring another 39.

Conducted the bombings in August 1998 of the U.S. Embassies in Nairobi, Kenya, and Dar es Salaam, Tanzania, that killed at least 301 individuals and injured more than 5,000 others. Claims to have shot down U.S. helicopters and killed U.S. servicemen in Somalia in 1993 and to have conducted three bombings that targeted U.S. troops in Aden, Yemen, in December 1992.

Al-Qaeda is linked to the following plans that were disrupted or not carried out: to assassinate Pope John Paul II during his visit to Manila in late 1994, to kill President Clinton during a visit to the Philippines in early 1995, to bomb in midair a dozen U.S. transpacific flights in 1995, and to set off a bomb at Los Angeles International Airport in 1999. Also plotted to carry out terrorist operations against U.S. and Israeli tourists visiting Jordan for millennial celebrations in late 1999. (Jordanian authorities thwarted the planned attacks and put 28 suspects on trial.) In December 2001, suspected al-Qaeda associate Richard Colvin Reid attempted to ignite a shoe bomb on a transatlantic flight from Paris to Miami. Attempted to shoot down an Israeli chartered plane with a surface-to-air missile as it departed the Mombasa airport in November 2002.

Strength
Al-Qaeda probably has several thousand members and associates. The arrests of senior-level al-Qaeda operatives have interrupted some terrorist plots. Also serves as a focal point or umbrella organization for a worldwide network that includes many Sunni Islamic extremist groups, some members of al-Gama'a al-Islamiyya, the Islamic Movement of Uzbekistan, and the Harakat ul-Mujahidin.

Location/Area of Operation
Al-Qaeda has cells worldwide and is reinforced by its ties to Sunni extremist networks. Was based in Afghanistan until Coalition forces removed the Taliban from power in late 2001. Al-Qaeda has dispersed in small groups across South Asia, Southeast Asia, and the Middle East and probably will attempt to carry out future attacks against U.S. interests.

External Aid
Al-Qaida maintains moneymaking front businesses, solicits donations from likeminded supporters, and illicitly siphons funds from donations to Muslim charitable organizations. U.S. and international efforts to block al-Qaeda funding has hampered the group's ability to obtain money.

Source: http://www.state.gov/s/ct/rls/pgtrpt/2003/31711.htm
Patterns of Global Terrorism- 2003 (U.S. Department of State) Appendix B — Background Information on Designated Foreign Terrorist Organizations

Salafist Group for Call and Combat (GSPC)

Description
The Salafist Group for Call and Combat (GSPC), an outgrowth of the GIA, appears to have eclipsed the GIA since approximately

1998 and is currently the most effective armed group inside Algeria. In contrast to the GIA, the GSPC has gained some popular support through its pledge to avoid civilian attacks inside Algeria. Its adherents abroad appear to have largely co-opted the external networks of the GIA and are particularly active throughout Europe, Africa, and the Middle East. First designated in March 2002.

Activities

The GSPC continues to conduct operations aimed at government and military targets, primarily in rural areas, although civilians are sometimes killed. A faction within the GSPC held 31 European tourists hostage in 2003 to collect ransom for their release. According to press reporting, some GSPC members in Europe maintain contacts with other North African extremists sympathetic to al-Qaeda. In late 2003, the new GSPC leader issued a communiqué declaring the group's allegiance to a number of jihadist causes and movements, including al-Qaeda.

Strength

Unknown; probably several hundred fighters with an unknown number of support networks inside Algeria.

Location/Area of Operation

Algeria, Northern Mali, Northern Mauritania, and Northern Niger.

External Aid

Algerian expatriates and GSPC members abroad, many residing in Western Europe, provide financial and logistic support. In addition, the Algerian Government has accused Iran and Sudan of supporting Algerian extremists in years past.

Source: http://www.state.gov/s/ct/rls/pgtrpt/2003/31711.htm
Patterns of Global Terrorism- 2003 (U.S. Department of State) Appendix B — Background Information on Designated Foreign Terrorist Organizations

Appendix B

Al-Qaeda's Middle East affiliate groups, as listed in Executive Order 13224 on September 23, 2001, and subsequent additional designations.

Executive Order 13224 blocking Terrorist Property and a summary of the Terrorism Sanctions Regulations (Title 31 Part 595 of the U.S. Code of Federal Regulations), Terrorism List Governments Sanctions Regulations (Title 31 Part 596 of the U.S. Code of Federal Regulations), and Foreign Terrorist Organizations Sanctions Regulations (Title 31 Part 597 of the U.S. Code of Federal Regulations).

EXECUTIVE ORDER 13224 - BLOCKING PROPERTY AND PROHIBITING TRANSACTIONS WITH PERSONS WHO COMMIT, THREATEN TO COMMIT, OR SUPPORT TERRORISM

By the authority vested in me as President by the Constitution and the laws of the United States of America, including the International Emergency Economic Powers Act (50 U.S.C. 1701 et seq.) (IEEPA), the National Emergencies Act (50 U.S.C. 1601 et seq.), section 5 of the United Nations Participation Act of 1945, as amended (22 U.S.C. 287c) (UNPA), and section 301 of title 3, United States Code, and in view of United Nations Security Council Resolution (UNSCR) 1214 of December 8, 1998, UNSCR 1267 of October 15, 1999, UNSCR 1333 of December 19, 2000, and the multilateral sanctions contained therein, and UNSCR 1363 of July 30, 2001, establishing a mechanism to monitor the implementation of UNSCR 1333, I, GEORGE W. BUSH, President of the United States of America, find that grave acts of terrorism and threats of terrorism committed by foreign terrorists, including the terrorist attacks in New York, Pennsylvania, and the Pentagon committed on September 11, 2001, acts recognized and condemned in UNSCR 1368 of September 12, 2001, and UNSCR 1269 of October 19, 1999, and the continuing and immediate threat of further attacks on United States nationals or the United States constitute an unusual and extraordinary threat to the national security, foreign policy, and economy of the United States, and in furtherance of my proclamation of September 14, 2001, Declaration of National Emergency by Reason of Certain Terrorist Attacks, hereby declare a national emergency to deal with that threat. I also find that because of the pervasiveness and expansiveness of the financial foundation of foreign terrorists, financial sanctions may be appropriate for those foreign persons that support or otherwise associate with these foreign terrorists. I also find that a need exists for further consultation and cooperation with, and sharing of information by, United States and foreign financial institutions as an additional tool to enable the United States to combat the financing of terrorism.

I hereby order:

Section 1.   Except to the extent required by section 203(b) of IEEPA (50 U.S.C. 1702(b)), or provided in regulations, orders, directives, or licenses that may be issued pursuant to this order, and notwithstanding any contract entered into or any license or permit granted prior to the effective date of this order, all property and interests in property of the following persons that are in the United States or that hereafter come within the United States, or that here-after come within the possession or control of United States persons are blocked:

(a) foreign persons listed in the Annex to this order;

(b) foreign persons determined by the Secretary of State, in consultation with the Secretary of the Treasury and the Attorney General, to have committed, or to pose a significant risk of committing, acts of terrorism that threaten the security of U.S. nationals or the national security, foreign policy, or economy of the United States;

(c) persons determined by the Secretary of the Treasury, in consultation with the Secretary of State and the Attorney General, to be owned or controlled by, or to act for or on behalf of those persons listed in the Annex to this order or those persons determined to be subject to subsection 1(b), 1(c), or 1(d)(i) of this order;

(d) except as provided in section 5 of this order and after such consultation, if any, with foreign authorities as the Secretary of State, in consultation with the Secretary of the Treasury and the Attorney General, deems appropriate in the exercise of his discretion, persons determined by the Secretary of the Treasury, in consultation with the Secretary of State and the Attorney General;

(i) to assist in, sponsor, or provide financial, material, or technological support for, or financial or other services to or in support of, such acts of terrorism or those persons listed in the Annex to this order or determined to be subject to this order; or

(ii) to be otherwise associated with those persons listed in the Annex to this order or those persons determined to be subject to subsection 1(b), 1(c), or 1(d)(i) of this order.

Sec. 2. Except to the extent required by section 203(b) of IEEPA (50 U.S.C. 1702(b)), or provided in regulations, orders, directives, or licenses that may be issued pursuant to this order, and notwithstanding any contract entered into or any license or permit granted prior to the effective date:

(a) any transaction or dealing by United States persons or within the

United States in property or interests in property blocked pursuant to this order is prohibited, including but not limited to the making or receiving of any contribution of funds, goods, or services to or for the benefit of those persons listed in the Annex to this order or determined to be subject to this order;

(b) any transaction by any United States person or within the United States that evades or avoids, or has the purpose of evading or avoiding, or attempts to violate, any of the prohibitions set forth in this order is prohibited; and

(c) any conspiracy formed to violate any of the prohibitions set forth in this order is prohibited.

Sec. 3. For purposes of this order:

(a) the term "person" means an individual or entity;

(b) the term "entity" means a partnership, association, corporation, or other organization, group, or subgroup;

(c) the term "United States person" means any United States citizen, permanent resident alien, entity organized under the laws of the United States (including foreign branches), or any person in the United States; and

(d) the term "terrorism" means an activity that —

(i) involves a violent act or an act dangerous to human life, property, or infrastructure; and

(ii) appears to be intended —

(A) to intimidate or coerce a civilian population;

(B) to influence the policy of a government by intimidation or coercion; or

(C) to affect the conduct of a government by mass destruction, assassination, kidnapping, or hostage-taking.

Sec. 4. I hereby determine that the making of donations of the type specified in section 203(b)(2) of IEEPA (50 U.S.C. 1702(b)(2)) by United States persons to persons determined to be subject to this order would seriously impair my ability to deal with the national emergency declared in this order, and would endanger Armed Forces of the United States that are in a situation where imminent involvement in hostilities is clearly indicated by the circumstances, and hereby prohibit such donations as provided by section 1 of this order. Furthermore, I hereby determine that the Trade Sanctions Reform and Export Enhancement Act of 2000 (title IX, Public Law 106-387) shall not affect the imposition or the continuation of the imposition of any unilateral agricultural sanction or unilateral medical sanction on any person determined to be subject to this order because imminent involvement of the Armed Forces of the United States in hostilities is clearly indicated by the circumstances.

Sec. 5.   With respect to those persons designated pursuant to subsection 1(d) of this order, the Secretary of the Treasury, in the exercise of his discretion and in consultation with the Secretary of State and the Attorney General, may take such other actions than the complete blocking of property or interests in property as the President is authorized to take under IEEPA and UNPA if the Secretary of the Treasury, in consultation with the Secretary of State and the Attorney General, deems such other actions to be consistent with the national interests of the United States, considering such factors as he deems appropriate.

Sec. 6.   The Secretary of State, the Secretary of the Treasury, and other appropriate agencies shall make all relevant efforts to cooperate and coordinate with other countries, including through technical assistance, as well as bilateral and multilateral agreements and arrangements, to achieve the objectives of this order, including the prevention and suppression of acts of terrorism, the denial of financing and financial services to terrorists and terrorist organizations, and the sharing of intelligence about funding activities in support of terrorism.

Sec. 7. The Secretary of the Treasury, in consultation with the Secretary of State and the Attorney General, is hereby authorized to take such actions, including the promulgation of rules and regulations, and to employ all powers granted to the President by IEEPA and UNPA as may be necessary to carry out the purposes of this order. The Secretary of the Treasury may redelegate any of these functions to other officers and agencies of the United States Government. All agencies of the United States Government are hereby directed to take all appropriate measures within their authority to carry out the provisions of this order.

Sec. 8. Nothing in this order is intended to affect the continued effectiveness of any rules, regulations, orders, licenses, or other forms of administrative action issued, taken, or continued in effect heretofore or hereafter under 31 C.F.R. chapter V, except as expressly terminated, modified, or suspended by or pursuant to this order.

Sec. 9. Nothing contained in this order is intended to create, nor does it create, any right, benefit, or privilege, substantive or procedural, enforceable at law by a party against the United States, its agencies, officers, employees or any other person.

Sec. 10. For those persons listed in the Annex to this order or determined to be subject to this order who might have a constitutional presence in the United States, I find that because of the ability to transfer funds or assets instantaneously, prior notice to such persons of measures to be taken pursuant to this order would render these measures ineffectual. I therefore determine that for these measures to be effective in addressing the national emergency declared in this order, there need be no prior notice of a listing or determination made pursuant to this order.

Sec. 11. (a) This order is effective at 12:01 a.m. eastern daylight time on September 24, 2001.
(b) This order shall be transmitted to the Congress and published in the Federal Register.

THE WHITE HOUSE, September 23, 2001.

ANNEX
*Al-Qaeda/Islamic Army
Abu Sayyaf Group
*Armed Islamic Group (GIA)
Harakat ul-Mujahedin (HUM)
*Al-Jihad (Egyptian Islamic Jihad)
Islamic Movement of Uzbekistan (IMU)
*Asbat al-Ansar
*Salafist Group for Call and Combat (GSPC)
Libyan Islamic Fighting Group
Al-Itihaad al-Islamiya (AIAI)
*Islamic Army of Aden
Usama bin Laden
Muhammad Atif (aka, Subhi Abu Sitta, Abu Hafs Al Masri)
Sayf al-Adl
Shaykh Sai'id (aka, Mustafa Muhammad Ahmad)
Abu Hafs the Mauritanian (aka, Mahfouz Ould al-Walid, Khalid Al-Shanqiti)
Ibn Al-Shaykh al-Libi
Abu Zubaydah (aka, Zayn al-Abidin Muhammad Husayn, Tariq)
Abd al-Hadi al-Iraqi (aka, Abu Abdallah)
*Ayman al-Zawahiri
Thirwat Salah Shihata
Tariq Anwar al-Sayyid Ahmad (aka, Fathi, Amr al-Fatih)
Muhammad Salah (aka, Nasr Fahmi Nasr Hasanayn)
Makhtab Al-Khidamat/Al Kifah

Wafa Humanitarian Organization
Al Rashid Trust
Mamoun Darkazanli Import-Export Company

NAMES OF THOSE DESIGNATED ON 04-19-02
Abdelkader Mahmoud Es Sayed (a.k.a. Kader Es Sayed)
***Abu Hamza Al-Masri (a.k.a. Abu Hamza Al-Misri; a.k.a.
Adam Ramsey Eman; a.k.a. Mustafa Kamel Mustafa; a.k.a.
Mustafa Kamel)**
Ahmed Idris Nasreddin (a.k.a. Ahmad I. Nasreddin; a.k.a. Hadj
Ahmed Nasreddin; a.k.a. Ahmed Idriss Nasreddine)
Khalid Al-Fawaz (a.k.a. Khaled Al-Fauwaz; a.k.a. Khaled A. Al-
Fauwaz; a.k.a. Khalid Al-Fawwaz; a.k.a. Khalid Al Fawwaz; a.k.a.
Khaled Al Fawwaz; a.k.a. Khaled Al-Fawwaz)
Lased Ben Heni
Mohamed Ben Belgacem Aouadi (a.k.a. Mohamed Ben Belkacem
Aouadi)
Mokhtar Bouchoucha (a.k.a. Mokhtar Bushusha)
Sami Ben Khemais Essid
Tarek Charaabi (a.k.a. Tarek Sharaabi)
The Aid Organization of the Ulema (a.k.a. Al Rashid Trust; a.k.a.
Al Rasheed Trust; a.k.a. Al-Rasheed Trust; a.k.a. Al-Rashid Trust)

NAME OF ENTITY DESIGNATED ON 02-20-03
***Ansar Al-Islam (a.k.a. "Devotees of Islam;" a.k.a. "Followers
of Islam in Kurdistan;" a.k.a. Jund Al-Islam; a.k.a.
"Kurdistan Supporters of Islam;" a.k.a. "Kurdistan Taliban;"
a.k.a. "Soldiers of Islam;" a.k.a. "Soldiers of God;" a.k.a.
"Supporters of Islam in Kurdistan")**

NAMES OF INDIVIDUALS DESIGNATED ON 09-23-03
Mohamed Abu Dhess (a.k.a. "Abu Ali;" a.k.a. Yaser Hassan)
Shabdi Abdallah (a.k.a. Emad Abdekhadi; a.k.a. "Al Falistini;"

a.k.a. "Emad the Palestinian;" a.k.a. "Zidan")
Aschraf Al-Dagma (a.k.a. "Noor")
*Abu Mus'ab Al-Zarqawi (a.k.a. 'Abd Al-Karim; a.k.a. Abu Al-Mu'taz; a.k.a. Al-Habib; a.k.a., Ahmad Fadil Nazzal Al-Khalaylah; a.k.a. Al-Muhajir; a.k.a. Gharib; a.k.a., Ahmed Fadeel Khalailah; a.k.a. Fedel Nazzel Khalaylen; a.k.a. "Mouhanad;" a.k.a. "Mouhannad;" a.k.a. "Muhannad;" a.k.a. "Rashid")
Djamel Moustfa (a.k.a. "Ali Barkani;" a.k.a. "Moustafa;" a.k.a. Belkasam Kaled)
Ismail Abdallah Sbaitan Shalabi

NAMES OF THOSE LISTED ON 10-24-03
*Al-Bakoun ala al-Ahd Organization (a.k.a. Faithful to the Oath)
*Mokhtar Belmokhtar
*Dhamat Houmet Daawa Salafia (a.k.a. Djamaat Houmat Ed Daawa Es Salafiya; a.k.a. Djamaat Houmat Eddawa Essalafia; a.k.a. Djamaatt Houmat Ed Daawa Es Salafiya; a.k.a. El-Ahoual Battalion; a.k.a. Group of Supporters of the Salafist Trend; a.k.a. Group of Supporters of the Salafiste Trend; a.k.a. Group Protectors of Salafist Preaching; a.k.a. Houmat Ed Daawa Es Salifiya; a.k.a. Houmat Ed-Daaoua Es-Salafia; a.k.a. Houmate Ed-Daawa Es-Salafia; a.k.a. Houmate El Da'Awaa Es-Salafitta; a.k.a. Katibat El Ahoual; a.k.a. Katibat El Ahouel; a.k.a. Protectors of the Salafist Call; a.k.a. Protectors of the Salafist Predication; a.k.a. Salafist Call Protectors; a.k.a. The Horror Squadron)
Mustapha Nasri Ait el Hadi
Djamel Lounici

NAME OF INDIVIDUAL DESIGNATED ON 12-05-03
*Saifi Ammari (a.k.a. "Abdalarak;" a.k.a. "Abderrezak Le Para;" a.k.a. "Abderrezak Zaimeche;" a.k.a. "Abdul Rasak ammane Abu Haidra;" a.k.a. "Abou Haidara;" a.k.a. "El Ourassi;" a.k.a. "El Para")

NAME OF INDIVIDUAL DESIGNATED ON 02-24-04
*Shaykh Abd-al-Majid Al-Zindani (a.k.a. Abdelmajid Al-Zindani; a.k.a. Shaykh 'Abd Al-Majid Al-Zindani)

Source: http://www.treasury.gov/offices/eotffc/ofac/sanctions/t11ter.pdf

Appendix C

Testimony of George J. Tenet, former Director of Central Intelligence, before the Senate Select Committee on Intelligence, discussing al-Qaeda, the affiliate phenomenon, and "stateless zones."

The Worldwide Threat 2004: Challenges in a Changing Global Context.

24 February 2004

Good morning, Mr. Chairman, Mr. Vice Chairman, Members of the Committee.

Mr. Chairman, last year I described a national security environment that was significantly more complex than at any time during my tenure as Director of Central Intelligence. The world I will discuss today is equally, if not more, complicated and fraught with dangers for United States interests, but one that also holds great opportunity for positive change.

TERRORISM

I'll begin today on terrorism, with a stark bottom-line:

The al-Qaeda leadership structure we charted after September 11 is seriously damaged—but the group remains as committed as ever to attacking the U.S. homeland.

But as we continue the battle against al-Qaeda, we must overcome a *movement*—a global movement infected by al-Qaeda's radical agenda.

In this battle we are moving forward in our knowledge of the enemy—his plans, capabilities, and intentions.

And what we've learned continues to validate my deepest concern: that this enemy remains intent on obtaining, and using, catastrophic weapons.

Now let me tell you about the war we've waged against the al-Qaeda organization and its leadership.

Military and intelligence operations by the United States and its allies overseas have degraded the group. Local al-Qaeda cells are forced to make their own decisions because of disarray in the central leadership.

Al-Qaeda depends on leaders who not only direct terrorist attacks but who carry out the day-to-day tasks that support operations. Over the past 18 months, we have killed or captured key al-Qaeda leaders in every significant operational area—logistics, planning, finance, training—and have eroded the key pillars of the organization, such as the leadership in Pakistani urban areas and operational cells in the al-Qaeda heartland of Saudi Arabia and Yemen.

The list of al-Qaeda leaders and associates who will never again threaten the American people includes:

Khalid Shaykh Muhammad, al-Qaeda's operations chief and the mastermind of the September 11 attacks.

Nashiri, the senior operational planner for the Arabian Gulf area.

Abu Zubayda, a senior logistics officer and plotter.

Hasan Ghul, a senior facilitator who was sent to case Iraq for an expanded al-Qaeda presence there.

Harithi and al-Makki, the most senior plotters in Yemen, who were involved in the bombing of the *USS Cole*.

Hambali, the senior operational planner in Southeast Asia.

We are creating large and growing gaps in the al-Qaeda hierarchy.

And, unquestionably, bringing these key operators to ground disrupted plots that would otherwise have killed Americans.

Meanwhile, al-Qaeda central continues to lose operational safe-havens, and bin Ladin has gone deep underground. We are hunting him in some of the most unfriendly regions on earth. We follow every lead.

Al-Qaeda's finances are also being squeezed. This is due in part to takedowns of key moneymen in the past year, particularly the Gulf, Southwest Asia, and even Iraq.

And we are receiving a broad array of help from our coalition partners, who have been central to our effort against al-Qaeda.

Since the 12 May bombings, the Saudi government has shown an important commitment to fighting al-Qaeda in the Kingdom, and Saudi officers have paid with their lives.

Elsewhere in the Arab world, we're receiving valuable cooperation from Jordan, Morocco, Egypt, Algeria, the UAE, Oman, and many others.

President Musharraf of Pakistan remains a courageous and indispensable ally who has become the target of assassins for the help he's given us.

Partners in Southeast Asian have been instrumental in the roundup of key regional associates of al-Qaeda.

Our European partners worked closely together to unravel and disrupt a continent-wide network of terrorists planning chemical, biological and conventional attacks in Europe.

So we have made notable strides. But do not misunderstand me. I am not suggesting al-Qaeda is defeated. It is not. We are still at war. This is a learning organization that remains committed to attacking the United States, its friends and allies.

Successive blows to al-Qaeda's central leadership have transformed the organization into a loose collection of regional networks that operate more autonomously. These regional components have demonstrated their operational prowess in the past year.

The sites of their attacks span the entire reach of al-Qaeda— Morocco, Kenya, Turkey, Jordan, Saudi Arabia, Kuwait, Afghanistan, Pakistan, Indonesia.

And al-Qaeda seeks to influence the regional networks with operational training, consultations, and money. Khalid Shaykh Muhammad sent Hambali $50,000 for operations in Southeast Asia.

You should not take the fact that these attacks occurred abroad to mean the threat to the US. homeland has waned. As al-Qaeda and associated groups undertook these attacks overseas, detainees consistently talk about the importance the group still attaches to striking the main enemy: the United States. Across the operational spectrum—air, maritime, special weapons—we have time and again uncovered plots that are chilling.

On aircraft plots alone, we have uncovered new plans to recruit pilots and to evade new security measures in Southeast Asia, the Middle East, and Europe.

Even catastrophic attacks on the scale of 11 September remain within al-Qaeda's reach. Make no mistake: these plots are hatched abroad, but they target U.S. soil or that of our allies.

So far, I have been talking only about al-Qaeda. But al-Qaeda is not the limit of terrorist threat worldwide. Al-Qaeda has infected others with its ideology, which depicts the United States as Islam's greatest foe. Mr. Chairman, what I want to say to you now may be the most important thing I tell you today.

The steady growth of Usama bin Ladin's anti-U.S. sentiment through the wider Sunni extremist movement and the broad dissemination of al-Qaeda's destructive expertise ensure that a serious threat will remain for the foreseeable future—with or without al-Qaeda in the picture.

A decade ago, bin Ladin had a vision of rousing Islamic terrorists worldwide to attack the United States. He created al-Qaeda to indoctrinate a worldwide movement in global jihad, with America as the enemy—an enemy to be attacked with every means at hand.

In the minds of bin Ladin and his cohorts, September 11 was the shining moment, their "shot heard 'round the world," and they want to capitalize on it.

And so, even as al-Qaeda reels from our blows, other extremist groups within the movement it influenced have become the next wave of the terrorist threat. Dozens of such groups exist. Let me offer a few thoughts on how to understand this challenge.

One of the most immediate threats is from smaller *international* Sunni extremist groups who have benefited from al-Qaeda links. They include groups as diverse as the al-Zarqawi network, the Ansar al-Islam in Iraq, the Libyan Islamic Fighting Group, and the Islamic Movement of Uzbekistan.

A second level of threat comes from small local groups, with limited *domestic* agendas, that work with international terrorist groups in their own countries. These include the Salifiya Jihadia, a Moroccan network that carried out the May 2003 Casablanca bombings, and similar groups throughout Africa and Asia.

These far-flung groups increasingly set the agenda, and are redefining the threat we face. They are not all creatures of bin Ladin, and so their fate is not tied to his. They have autonomous leadership, they pick their own targets, they plan their own attacks.

Beyond these groups are the so-called "foreign jihadists"—individuals ready to fight anywhere they believe Muslim lands are under attack by what they see as "infidel invaders." They draw on broad support networks, have wide appeal, and enjoy a growing sense of support from Muslims are not necessarily supporters of terrorism. The foreign jihadists see Iraq as a golden opportunity.

Let me repeat: for the growing number of jihadists interested in attacking the United States, a spectacular attack on the U.S. Homeland is the "brass ring" that many strive for—with or without encouragement by al-Qaeda's central leadership.

To detect and ultimately defeat these forces, we will continually need to watch hotspots, present or potential battlegrounds, places where these terrorist networks converge. Iraq is of course one major locus of concern. Southeast Asia is another. But so are the backyards of our closest allies. Even Western Europe is an area where terrorists recruit, train, and target.

To get the global job done, foreign governments will need to improve bilateral and multilateral, and even inter-service cooperation, and strengthen domestic counterterrorist legislation and security practices.

Mr. Chairman, I have consistently warned this committee of al-Qaeda's interest in chemical, biological, radiological and nuclear weapons. Acquiring these remains a "religious obligation" in bin Ladin's eyes, and al-Qaeda and more than two dozen other terrorist groups are pursuing CBRN materials.

We particularly see a heightened risk of poison attacks. Contemplated delivery methods to date have been simple but this may change as non-al-Qaeda groups share information on more sophisticated methods and tactics.

Over the last year, we've also seen an increase in the threat of more sophisticated CBRN. For this reason we take very seriously the threat of a CBRN attack.

Extremists have widely disseminated assembly instructions for an improvised chemical weapon using common materials that could cause a large numbers of casualties in a crowded, enclosed area.

Although gaps in our understanding remain, we see al-Qaeda's program to produce anthrax as one of the most immediate terrorist CBRN threats we are likely to face.

Al-Qaeda continues to pursue its strategic goal of obtaining a nuclear capability. It remains interested in dirty bombs. Terrorist documents contain accurate views of how such weapons would be used...

IRAQ

Mr. Chairman, we are making significant strides against the insurgency and terrorism, but former regime elements and foreign jihadists continue to pose a serious threat to Iraq's new institutions and to our own forces...

...Mr. Chairman, the situation as I've described it—both our victories and our challenges—indicates we have damaged, but not yet defeated, the insurgents.

The security situation is further complicated by the involvement of terrorists—including Ansar al-Islam (AI) and al-Zarqawi—and foreign jihadists coming to Iraq to wage jihad. Their goal is clear. They intend to inspire an Islamic extremist insurgency that would threaten Coalition forces and put a halt to the long-term process of building democratic institutions and governance in Iraq. They hope for a Taliban-like enclave in Iraq's Sunni heartland that could be a jihadist safehaven.

AI—an Iraqi Kurdish extremist group—is waging a terrorist campaign against the coalition presence and cooperative Iraqis in a bid to inspire jihad and create an Islamic state.

Some extremists go even further. In a recent letter, terrorist planner Abu Mus'ab al-Zarqawi outlined his strategy to foster sectarian civil war in Iraq, aimed at inciting the Shia.

Stopping the foreign extremists from turning Iraq into their most important jihad yet rests in part on preventing loosely connected extremists from coalescing into a cohesive terrorist organization.

We are having some success—the Coalition has arrested key jihadist leaders and facilitators in Iraq, including top leaders from Ansar al-Islam, the al-Zarqawi network, and other al-Qaeda affiliates.

The October detention of AI's deputy leader set back the group's ambition to establish itself as an umbrella organization for jihadists in Iraq...

THE OTHER TRANSNATIONAL ISSUES

Let me conclude my comments this morning by briefly considering some important transnational concerns that touch on the war against terrorism.

We're used to thinking of that fight as a sustained worldwide effort to get the perpetrators and would-be perpetrators off the street. This is an important preoccupation, and we will never lose sight of it.

But places that combine desperate social and economic circumstances with a failure of government to police its own territory can often provide nurturing environments for terrorist groups, and for insurgents and criminals. The failure of governments to control their own territory creates potential power vacuums that open opportunities for those who hate.

We count approximately 50 countries that have such "stateless zones." In half of these, terrorist groups are thriving. Al-Qaeda and extremists like the Taliban, operating in the Afghanistan-Pakistan border area, are well known examples.

As the war on terrorism progresses, terrorists will be driven from their safe havens to seek new hideouts where they can undertake training, planning, and staging without interference from government authorities. The prime candidates for new "no man's lands" are remote, rugged regions where central governments have no consistent reach and where socioeconomic problems are rife...

Source: http://www.cia.gov/cia/public_affairs/speeches/2004/dci_speech_02142004.html

Bibliography

Books

Alexander, Yonah and Swetnam, Michael S., *Usama bin Laden's al-Qaeda: Profile of a Terrorist Network*. (NY: Transnational Publishers, 2001).

Anonymous, *Through Our Enemies Eyes: Osama Bin Laden, Radical Islam, and the Future of America*, (Washington, DC: Brassey's, 2002).

Benjamin, Daniel and Simon, Steven, *The Age of Sacred Terror: Radical Islam's War Against America*, Revised Edition (NY: Random House, 2003).

Bergen, Peter, *Holy War, Inc. Inside the Secret World of Osama bin Laden*, (NY: Free Press, 2001).

Burke, Jason, *Al-Qaeda: Casting a Shadow of Terror*, (NY: I.B. Taurus, 2003).

Chaliand, Gerard, *The Kurdish Tragedy*, (London: Zed Books, 1994).

Dictionnaire Mondial de L'Islamisme. (France: Plon, 2002).

Dresch, Paul, *A History of Modern Yemen*. (Cambridge, UK: Cambridge University Press, 2000).

El Khazen, Farid, *The Breakdown of the State in Lebanon, 1967-1976*. (Cambridge, MA: Harvard University Press, 2000).

Gunaratna, Rohan, *Inside Al Qaeda: Global Network of Terror*, (NY: Columbia University Press, 2002).

Ismael, Tareq Y., *Middle East Politics Today: Government and Civil Society*, (Gainesville, FL: University Press of Florida, 2001).

Kepel, Gilles, *Jihad: The Trail of Political Islam*, (Cambridge, MA: The Belknap Press of Harvard University Press, 2002).

Kepel, Gilles, *Muslim Extremism in Egypt: The Prophet and Pharaoh*, (Berkeley: University of California Press, 1986).

Lesser, Ian O., et al. *Countering the New Terrorism*, (Santa Monica, CA: RAND, 1999).

al-Masri, Abu Hamza, *The Khawaarij and Jihaad*, (London: Finsbury Park Mosque, 2000).

Martinez, Luis, *The Algerian Civil War: 1990-1998*, (NY: Columbia University Press, 2000).

McDowall, David, *A Modern History of the Kurds*, (NY: I.B. Taurus, 1996).

Miller, Judith, *God Has Ninety-Nine Names*, (NY: Touchstone, 1996).

Mohaddessin, Mohammed, *Islamic Fundamentalism: The New Global Threat*, (Washington, DC: Seven Locks Press, 1993).

Munib, Muhammed, *Difa'an an Huquq al-Insan: Al-Juz' al-Khaamis*, (Cairo: The Egyptian Organization for Human Rights, 1997).

Mustafa, Hala, *Al-Islam as-Siyasi fi Masr: Min Haraka al-Islah ila Gama 'at al-Unf*. (Al-Qahira: Gamiya Huquq at-Tab' al-Mahfoutha liMarkaz al-Mahrousa, 1999).

Noman, Ahmed and Almadhagi, Kassim, *Yemen and the United States: A Study of a Small Power and Super-State Relationship, 1962-1994*, (NY: I.B. Taurus, 1996).

O'Balance, Edgar, *Islamic Fundamentalist Terrorism, 1979-1995: The Iranian Connection.* (NY: NYU Press, 1997).

Pipes, Daniel, *In the Path of God: Islam and Political Power*, (New Delhi: Voice of India, 1983).

Ranstorp, Magnus (ed), *In the Service of al-Qaeda: Radical Islamic Movements*, (NY: Hurst Publishers and New York University Press) forthcoming.

Reeve, Simon, *The New Jackals: Ramzi Yousef, Osama bin Laden and the Future of Terrorism*, (Boston: Northeastern University Press, 1999).

Ressa, Maria, *Seeds of Terror: An Eyewitness Account of al-Qaeda's Newest Center of Operations in Southeast Asia*, (NY: Free Press, 2003).

Reudy, John, (ed.), *Islamism and Secularism in North Africa* (NY: St. Martin's Press, 1994).

Roberts, Hugh, *The Battlefield, Algeria 1988-2002: Studies in A Broken Polity*, (London: Verso, 2003).

Sela, Avraham (ed.), *Political Encyclopedia of the Middle East.* (NY: Continuum, 1999).

Stern, Jessica, *Terror in the Name of God: Why Religious Militants Kill*, (NY: HarperCollins, 2003).

Terror in Yemen: Where To? (Sanaa: 26th September Publications, December 2002).

The Al-Qaeda Documents, Volume 2, (Alexandria, VA: Tempest Publishing, 2003).

Weaver, Mary Anne, *A Portrait of Egypt: A Journey Through the World of Militant Islam*, (NY: Farrar Straus and Giroux, 2000).

Weber, Max, *The Theory of Social and Economic Organization*, (Ed: Talcott Parsons), (NY: Free Press, 1964).

Zabarah, Mohammed Ahmad, *Yemen: Traditionalism vs. Modernity*, (NY: Praeger Publishers, 1982).

al-Zayyat, Montasser, *The Road to al-Qaeda: The Story of Bin Laden's Right-Hand Man.* (London: Pluto Press, 2004).

Newspaper and Magazine Articles

"17 European Tourists Freed from al-Qaeda Linked Group in Algeria," AFP, May 14, 2003.

"A Book About al-Qaeda Mistakes," *ash-Sharq al-Awsat*, August 6, 2003.

"Aden Islamic Army Threatens the American and British Ambassadors if they do not Leave Yemen," March 12, 1999.

"Afghani Terrorism Around the World," *Executive Intelligence Review*, October 13, 1995.

"Al-Balagh: Yemen: five Islamic groups merged in 'al-Jihad base'," Arabic News.com, Oct 1, 2003.

"Algeria captures Sahara terrorists," Deutche Presse-Agentur, September 23, 2003.

"Algeria Gives Germany Names of Tourists' Suspected Kidnappers: Paper," AFP, September 24, 2003.

"Algeria: Hattab Faction Announces Split from GIA," *ash-Sharq al-Awsat*, September 17, 1998 (FBIS).

"Algerian Appeals Paris Bomb Sentence," *ash-Sharq al-Awsat*, November 5, 2003.

"Algerian Army Kills 150 Islamists in Search Operation: Press," AFP, September 27, 2003.

"Algerian Islamic Extremist Group Pledges Allegiance to al-Qaeda," AFP, October 22, 2003.

"Algerian Leader, Hassan Hattab, Still Alive: Report," AFP, May 24, 2004.

"Algerian Terror Suspect Held in Germany Pending Extradition," AP, January 7, 2004.

"Al-Qaeda Man Behind Murder of US Diplomat Hiding in Northern Iraq: Jordan," AFP, December 18, 2002.

"Al-Qaeda Wing Rejects Truce that its Branch Was Offered in Yemen," *al-Hayat*, October 21, 2003.

"Al-Qaeda-linked Group in Algeria Replaces Founder: Reports," AFP, October 12, 2003.

"Al-Qaeda Feud Continues in Lebanese Camp," Middle East Newsline, March 2, 2003.

"Al-Qaida, Fatah Engage in Heavy Fighting," Middle East Newsline, May 20, 2003.

"Ansar Al-Islam Suicide Bomber was from Saudi Arabia," *Kurdish Media News*, March 25, 2003.

"Ansar al-Islam," Iraq News Wire, No.8, Part II, MEMRI, September 1, 2002.

"Ansar al-Islam's European Base," AFPC email update, October 31, 2003.

"Ansar al-Islam's Krekar Cited on 1988 Meeting with Bin Laden in Pakistan," *ash-Sharq al-Awsat*, March 1, 2003 (FBIS).

"Ansar Allah Claim Missile Attack on F-TV, Hariri Unconvinced," *an-Nahar*, June 16, 2003.

"Anti-terror Campaign Sparks Biggest Probe Ever," AFP, October 1, 2001.

"Arab Figures Implicated in Al-Qaeda Funding," Reuters, December 6, 2003.

"Arrest of Two Tunisians in the 'Italian Cell' for their Relations with the Ansar al-Islam Group," *ash-Sharq al-Awsat*, April 3, 2003.

"Arresting the Third Person from Ansar al-Islam," *ash-Sharq al-Awsat*, October 15, 2003.

"Asbat al-Ansar Suspected in McDonald's Bombing," *Lebanon Daily Star*, April 17, 2003.

"Ash-Sharq Al-Awsat Publishes Extracts from Al-Jihad Leader Az-Zawahiri's New Book," *ash-Sharq al-Awsat* (London), December 1, 2002.

"Australia Works with Lebanon on Terror Suspect," Reuters, September 6, 2003.

"Australian 'Sent Cash' to Terror Suspect," *The Advertiser* (Australia), September 29, 2003.

"Australian Islamic Leaders Tied to Alleged al-Qa'ida Leader Jailed in Spain," AFP, September 3, 2003.

"Australian Islamic Leaders Tied to Alleged al-Qa'ida Leader Jailed in Spain," AFP, September 3, 2003.

"Australian Terror Suspect Allowed Bail Again Despite New Laws," AFP, June 24, 2004.

"Az-Zindani Invites the American Ambassador to Visit Him," *al-Hayat*, April 1, 2004.

"Bin Laden Held to be Behind an Armed Algerian Islamic Movement," AFP, February 15, 2002.

"Blast at Yemeni Court," BBC World Service, May 14, 2003.

"Blasts and Intermittent Clashes Return to Ein al-Hilweh," *al-Hayat*, October 28, 2002.

"Bomb Damages Coffee Shop in Lebanon's Largest Palestinian Camp," AP, November 4, 2002.

"Bombing Number 19 in Ein al-Hilweh," *ash-Sharq al-Awsat*, November 6, 2002.

"Calm Restored After Clashes in Palestinian Camp in Lebanon," AFP, May 20, 2003.

"Car Bomb Kills Accused al-Qaeda Man in Lebanon Camp," Reuters, March 2, 2003.

"Cease-Fire Called to Allow Burial of Dead in Ein al-Hilweh," *an-Nahar*, May 20, 2003.

"Court Upholds Verdict Against Abu al-Hassan's Successor," *Yemen Times*, No. 14, Vol. 11, April 2-8, 2001.

"Dutch Police Detain Suspected Iraqi Radical Wanted in Germany," AFP, December 8, 2003.

"Egyptian Islamist Leaders Fault al-Qa'ida's Strategy," *ash-Sharq al-Awsat*, January 11, 2004 [FBIS].

"European Hostages' Mediator Back in Mali Capital from Desert Talks," AFP, August 6, 2003.

"Fatah Official Targeted in Ein al-Hilweh Bomb Attack," *Lebanon Daily Star*, October 21, 2002.

"Fatah Turns in to Lebanese Army Suspected North Korean Terrorist," *Lebanon Daily Star*, February 6, 2003.

"Fateh Accuses Palestinians, Kurds and Lebanese for the Series of Explosions in Ein al-Hilweh Refugee Camp in Lebanon," *ash-Sharq al-Awsat*, October 22, 2002.

"Founder of Biggest Muslim Group Executed-Report," Jordan Times (AFP), May12, 2004.

"Four Killed by Extremists in Eastern Algeria: Security Forces," AFP, June 19, 2003.

"French Intelligence Note Outlines Islamic Fundamentalists' Activities," *LeMonde*, January 25, 2002 [FBIS].

"Guilty Plea From One Of 'Lackawanna Six'," AP, January 10, 2003.

"Hattab Still Head of Biggest Algerian Extremist Group: Report," AFP, October 16, 2003.

"Hassan and the Islamic Army of Aden-Abyan," Al-Bab.com, January 1999,

"Heavy Clashes Rage Between Islamists, Arafat's Loyalists in S. Lebanon," *an-Nahar*, May 19, 2003.

"Hunting Islamists in Northern Iraq Coming From Pakistan with Support from Bin Laden," *al-Hayat*, August 7, 2003.

"I Met Bin Laden," *Newsweek*, October 13, 2003.

"Interview with Algerian Terror Leader Associated with Al-Qa'ida: The Islamic State Will Arise Only Through Blood and Body Parts," MEMRI, No. 642, January 13, 2004.

"Iran: FM Spokesman Rejects Allegations of Assisting Ansar al-Islam," IRNA, March 24, 2003.

"Iraq War 'Swells al-Qaeda Ranks'," Reuters, October 15, 2003.

"Islamic Extremist Threat Forces Cancellation of Two Stages of Dakar Rally," AP, January 29, 2004.

"Islamic Group Uses Mercenaries for Attacks," Middle East Newsline, July 9, 2003.

"Islamic Militant Group is Spreading Across Iraq," *Los Angeles Times*, September 3, 2003.

"Islamic Militants Harassing Iraqi Kurds; Group in North Iraq Backed by Iran and Bolstered by al-Qaeda, Opposition Leaders Say," *Washington Post*, September 5, 2002.

"It is Disclosed that the Yemeni was Trying to Escape from Lebanon Just before his Detention," *an-Nahar*, December 9, 2003.

"Italy Arrests Two People Who Funded the Algerian GSPC," *ash-Sharq al-Awsat*, October 30, 2003.

"Kurdish Leader Calls for the Elimination of Ladenite Ansar Al-Islam," *Kurdistan Newsline*, July 23, 2002.

"Kurdish Party Says it Captures Iraqi Islamists," Reuters, August 12, 2003.

"Lebanese Citizenship: Will it Last?" *Jerusalem Times*, May 22, 2003.

"Lebanon Announces New Arrest of "Terrorists" Targeting US Interests," AFP, July 15, 2003.

"Lebanon Blames Palestinian Extremists for Future TV Attack," AP, July 17, 2003.

"Lebanon Charges 10 for U.S. Fast-Food Bombings," Reuters, December 8, 2003.

"Lebanon Charges Six More in Anti-Western Bombings," Reuters, May 17, 2003.

"Lebanon: 25 Years of Prison for the Yemeni Ibn ash-Shahid," *al-Hayat*, March 9, 2004.

"Lebanon: A New Explosion in Ein al-Hilweh Refugee Camp," *ash-Sharq al-Awsat*, October 15, 2002.

"Lebanon: Rumors Revive Emergency Situation in Ein al-Hilweh Between the Fatah Movement and Islamic Asbat al-Ansar," *ash-Sharq al-Awsat* (London), August 18, 2002.

"Lebanon: Two Detainees Not Al-Ansar Members; 'Dismay' at Jordan's Position Noted," *as-Safir*, October 17, 2001 [FBIS].

"Libya mediated Mali hostage release,"Al-Jazeera.net. August 19, 2003.

"Libyan Ransom Raises Terror Fears," *The Australian*, August 29, 2000.

"Links Between Ansar al-Islam with Al-Qaeda and Iraq," PUK Information Department, July 30, 2002.

"Man in Yemen Says He Killed Three American Missionaries," AP, April 21, 2003.

"Milan-Based Islamist on 'Abduction' of his Deputies, Denies Links to al-Qaeda," *ash-Sharq al-Awsat*, June 19, 2003. [FBIS].

"Militant Group Puts Battle on the Web," AP, December 15, 2002.

"Militant Groups Merging in Yemen," AFP, October 2, 2003.

"Moroccan is Convicted on Terrorism Charges, Another Defendant is Cleared," AP, January 22, 2004.

"New Hardline Palestinian Group Jund al-Sham Appears in Lebanese Camp," *an-Nahar*, June 26, 2004.

"Oil pipeline explosion in Marib," Arabic News.com, July 13, 1998.

"On Sidon's court shootings," Arabic News.com, June 9, 1999.

"Osbat al Noor Vows to Murder Arafat's Top Lebanon Representative," *an-Nahar*, February 12, 2004.

"Palestinian Killed in Attack on US Forces in Iraq," AP, December 21, 2003.

"Profile of Bilal Khazal," *ash-Sharq al-Awsat*, June 13, 2003.

"PUK Forces Reportedly Repulse a Major Attack by Ansar al-Islam Forces," *Iraqi Kurdistan Dispatch*, July 5, 2002.

"Raid Finds al-Qaida Tie to Iraq Militants," AP, March 31, 2003.

"Sanaa Prepares to Present 200 Arrested Men to Court After Ending their Investigations," *Al-Hayat*, July 17, 2003.

"Scenarios to Bomb the American Embassy and the Convoy of the Ambassador and the Execution of Attacks on Syrian and Lebanese Military Positions," *Al-Hayat*, July 4, 2003.

"Six Algerians Allegedly Linked to Bin Laden Arrested in Spain," *Xinhua* (Beijing), September 27, 2001 [FBIS].

"Suspected Algerian Extremists Held in the Netherlands," AFP, April 24, 2002.

"Syria Hands Over 'Terrorist Network' Suspect to Lebanese Authorities," *Lebanon Daily Star*, May 9, 2003.

"Talbani's Forces Restore Their Positions from Ansar al-Islam in Armed Clashes that Resulted in the Death of 35 from Both Sides," *ash-Sharq al-Awsat*, December 6, 2002.

"Terror Handbook Found at Ansar al-Islam Camp: Report," AFP, April 9, 2003.

"The Environment of the Takfiri Fatwas in 'Bab Altbana' Broadens and Turns the Region into an Exporter of Jihad," *al-Hayat*, December 1, 2003.

"The Yemeni Government Studies the Enforcement of Regulation of Activities of Mosques and Preachers," *al-Hayat*, June 9, 2003.

"Three Wounded in Inter-Palestinian Fighting in Lebanon Refugee Camp," AP, August 4, 2002.

"Twelve Dead, Including Three Children, In More Algeria Unrest," AFP, June 22, 2003.

"Two Dead, More than 20 Wounded in Inter-Palestinian Clashes in Lebanon Camp," AFP, May 19, 2003.

"Two More Blasts in Southern Palestinian Refugee Camp," AP, October 16, 2002.

"Two Yemenis Wanted for Attack on French Tanker Extradited from Saudi," AFP, September 25, 2003.

"U.S. Freezes Assets of 15 in Italy," CNN.com, November 12, 2003.

"U.S. Warns of New Terror Threat in Yemen, Calls for 'Exceptional' Security," AFP, September 29, 2003.

"U.S.S. Cole Deployed; Prosecution of Suspects Delayed," *Yemen Observer*, December 4, 2003.

"UK expands freeze on terror funds," BBC.com, October 12, 2001.

"US Forces Capture Senior Ansar al-Islam Leader: Defense Official," AFP, October 14, 2003.

"US Official Pledges Aid to Algeria," AP, October 27, 2003.

"US Troops Kill Three in Battle with Ansar al-Islam," AFP, January 1, 2004.

"US Warns German al-Qaeda Extradition May Lead to 'Repercussions' in Yemen," AFP, November 17, 2003.

"USWAR/Ansar al-Islam Attacks PUK Positions," IRNA, March 26, 2003.

"Videotape Shows Desert hostages Now in Mali-Paper," Reuters, July 30, 2003.

"World in Brief," *Washington Post*, October 17, 2003.

"Yemen Arrests Five Members from Al-Qaeda and Unveils Money Transfers from an Arab African State," *ash-Sharq al-Awsat*, October 14, 2003.

"Yemen Captures 32 Militants from Qaeda and the Escape of the Most Wanted," *ash-Sharq al-Awsat*, March 10, 2004.

"Yemen Detains 17 al-Qaida Suspects," UPI, October 16, 2003.

"Yemen Foils Attacks on British Embassy," AFP, December 14, 2003.

"Yemen Frees or Pardons 146 Suspected of al-Qaeda Links," AFP, November 17, 2003.

"Yemen Reportedly Nabs Second Militant in Days," Reuters, March 4, 2004.

"Yemen Seeks Cole Attack Suspects After Jailbreak," Reuters, April 11, 2003.

"Yemen Terrorist Offers Deal to Stop Action," *ash-Sharq al-Awsat*, July 27, 1999 [FBIS].

"Yemen: Background on Aden-Abyan Islamic Army," *ash-Sharq al-Awsat*, January 5, 1999 [FBIS].

"Yemen: Release of Most of Those Accused of Terror," *Al-Hayat*, October 28, 2003.

"Yemen: Report on Confession of Yemeni Kidnapper," *ash-Sharq al-Awsat*, January 14, 1999 [FBIS].

"Yemeni Authorities Arrest Extremists, and Investigated with Harithi," *ash-Sharq al-Awsat*, September 25, 2003.

"Yemeni Authorities Arrest Militants from Jaysh Aden Abyan al-Islami," *ash-Sharq al-Awsat*, July 10, 2003.

"Yemeni Kills 3, Including U.S., Canadian Workers," Reuters, March 18, 2003

"Yemeni Official Accuses Leaders in Islah of Involvement in Terrorism and Criminal Sponsorship," *al-Hayat*, April 28, 2004.

Abbas, Dhikra, "Yemeni Aide on Islamic Army, Threats," *al-Majallah*, Nov 21, 1999 [FBIS].

Abd al-Latif al-Manawi, "The Egyptian Gamaa Islamiyya Requests the Leaders of al-Qaeda to Apologize to the Parents of the Victims," *ash-Sharq al-Awsat*, November 14, 2003.

Aichoune, Farid, "GSPC: Les Meandres de la Piste Terroriste," *Le Nouvel Observateur* (France), May 8, 2003.

Aqil, Radwan, "Report on Formation, Growth of Usbat al-Ansar Group in Palestinian Refugee Camp in Lebanon," *Al-Wasat* (London), October 1, 2001 [FBIS].

ash-Shafi', Muhammed, "Ansar al-Islam Group Threatens to Fight Americans, Seculars in Iraq," *ash-Sharq al-Awsat*, June 13, 2003 [FBIS].

Beauge, Florence, "Armed Islamists in Algeria have Reorganized into Three Groups," *Le Monde* (Paris), October 31, 2002 [FBIS].

Bennet, Brian, and Ware, Michael, "Life Behind Enemy Lines," *Time Magazine*, December 15, 2003.

Bergman, Lowell, "Qaeda Trainee is Reported Seized in Yemen," *New York Times*, January 29, 2004.

Blanford, Nicholas, "Lebanon Targets Islamic Radicals," *Christian Science Monitor*, May 20, 2003.

Bremner, Charles and McGrory, Daniel, "Bin Laden Cell Plotted French Poison Attack," *The Times* (London), November 30, 2001.

Brummitt, Chris, "Iran: We've Deported al-Qaida Suspects," AP, October 17, 2003.

Burns, Robert, "Iraq Group Said Main Threat to U.S. Forces," AP, October 23, 2003.

Butler, Desmond and Van Natta Jr, Don., "Trail of Anti-U.S. Fighters Said to Cross Europe to Iraq," *New York Times*, December 6, 2003.

Ceaux, Pascal, " Intelligence Note Describes Breakthrough of Fundamentalist Movement in Seine-Saint-Denis, *LeMonde* (Paris), January 25, 2002.

Chivers, C.J., "Kurdish Leader is Assassinated in Militant Raid," *New York Times*, February 10, 2003.

Chivers, C.J., "Kurds Face a Second Enemy: Islamic Fighters on Iraq Flank," *New York Times*, January 13, 2003.

Connolly, Kate, "Germany accused of buying hostages' release," *London Daily Telegraph*, August 20, 2003.

Crawford, David, "Prosecution Suffers Blow in Dutch al-Qaeda Trial," *Wall Street Journal*, May 21, 2003.

Crumley, Bruce, "Uncle Osama Wants You: A journalist infiltrates a radical network in Paris, and gets a rare glimpse of a terror recruiter in action," *Time*, March 24, 2003.

de Bendern, Paul, "Sources: Last 15 European Tourists Freed in Algeria," Reuters, May 19, 2003.

Decamps, Marie-Claude, "Spain, Logistic Base," *LeMonde*, March 12, 2002 [FBIS].

Defghanpisheh, Babak "Inside Al Ansar: Jailed Militants Tell Newsweek how their Group has Adapted to Fight U.S. Occupation," *Newsweek*, October 13, 2003.

Diab, Yousef, "Beirut Considers Extraditing the Two Australian Brothers of Lebanese Origin Accused of Financing a Terrorist Network," *ash-Sharq al-Awsat*, December 23, 2003.

Durukan, Namik, "Al-Qaida of Northern Iraq, Ansar al-Islam Says Confidently: If America Hits, Jihad Will Begin," *Milliyet* (Turkish), January 7, 2003.

Eberhart, Dave, "Iraqi Terrorist Detail Ties to Bin Laden," NewsMax, March 18, 2002.

Eggen, Dan, "Cleric Charged with Aiding al-Qaeda; U.S. Says Yemeni Raised More than $20 Million," *Washington Post*, November 18, 2003.

Ensor, David, "Yemen Arrests al-Qaeda Leader," CNN.com, November 25, 2003.

Evans, Michael, "Al-Qaeda in Secret Talks with Lebanon Terror Group," *The Times* (London), February 1, 2002.

Farah, Douglas, "Al Qaeda's Finances Ample, Say Probers," *Washington Post*, December 14, 2003.

Filkins, Dexter and Oppel, Richard A., Jr. "Huge Suicide Blast Demolishes U.N. Headquarters in Baghdad; Top Aid Officials Among 17 Dead," *New York Times*, August 20, 2003.

Finn, Peter, "Sting Hints at U.S. Tactics on Terror," *Washington Post*, February 28, 2003.

Fisher, Ian, "Recent Attacks in Yemen seen as Sign of Large Terror Cell," *New York Times*, January 3, 2003.

Fleishman, Jeffrey, "Hinting at Hussein's Links to Al Qaeda," *Los Angeles Times*, February 5, 2003.

Galbraith, Peter, "The Wild Card in a Post-Saddam Iraq," *Boston Globe*, December 15, 2002.

Gallagher, Paul, "Algerian Militants the Main Terror Threat to Britain, Experts Warn," *The Scotsman*, January 16, 2003.

Gellman, Bart "U.S. Suspects Al Qaeda Got Nerve Agent From Iraqis; Analysts: Chemical May Be VX, And Was Smuggled Via Turkey," *Washington Post*, December 12, 2002.

Gertz, Bill, "Al Qaeda Recruits Oil-Field Attackers," *Washington Times*, March 11, 2003.

Gertz, Bill, "Eroded al Qaeda Still a Threat," *Washington Times*, January 16, 2004.

Gertz, Bill, "September 11 Report Alludes to Iraq-al Qaeda Meeting," *Washington Times*, July 30, 2003.

Goldberg, Jeffery, "The Great Terror," *The New Yorker*, March 25, 2002.

Gunaratna, Rohan, "Terror From the Sky," *Janes Intelligence Review*, September 24, 2001.

al-Haj, Ahmed, "Yemen Pursuing Another al-Qaida Member Following Arrest of Mastermind of Attacks on USS Cole, French Tanker," AP, November 26, 2003.

Halawi, Jailan, "Time for a Historic Reconciliation," *Al-Ahram Weekly*, No. 592, June 27-July 3, 2002.

Harris, Paul, "Algeria Faces the Challenges of Peace." *Jane's Intelligence Review*, vol. 12, no.3 (March 2000).

Hauptmeier, Carsten, "Al-Qaeda Trial Underway in Germany," AFP, April 17, 2002.

Hendawi, Hamza, "Fear Among Copts Intensifies in Egypt Over Muslim Militants' Bloody Campaign," AP, March 22, 1997.

Higgins, Andrew and Cooper, Christopher, "A CIA-Backed Team Used Brutal Mean to Crack Terror Cell: Albanian Agents Captures Egyptians Who Alleged Torture Back in Cairo," *Wall Street Journal*, November 20, 2001.

Higgins, Andrew and Cullison, Alan, "The Story of A Traitor to al Qaeda," *Wall Street Journal*, December 12, 2002.

Horne, Alistair, "The Algerian Connection: What it Means and What it has Done," *National Review*, February 10, 2003.

Howard, Michael, "Militant Kurds Training al-Qaida Fighters," *The Guardian*, August 23, 2002.

Ibrahim, Youssef M., "Algeria is Seen Edging Toward Breakup," *New York Times*, April 4, 1994.

Jiwa, Salim, "Terror Targets: A Look at Radical Islamic Groups Targeted by Bush's Order," ABC News Online, September 25, 2001.

Judah, Tim, "London Arrest is Boost for Iraqi Kurd Nationalists," *Jerusalem Report*, November 18, 2002.

Kaplan, David E., "Playing Offense: The Inside Story of how U.S. Terrorist Hunters are Going After al-Qaeda," *U.S. News and World Report*, June 2, 2003.

Kaplan, Robert D., "A Tale of Two Colonies," *Atlantic Monthly*, April 2003.

Kaplan, Roger, "Democracy in Algeria: Singer-Activist Ferhat Mehenni's Campaign for Liberal Self-Government," *Weekly Standard*, Vol.8, No. 9, June 16, 2003.

Kelley, Matt, "Saddam Confidant Linked to al-Qaida Group," AP, October 30, 2003.

Kole, William J., "Czechs coming under fire for secretive arms deals to Yemen," AP, December 1, 2003.

Lake, Eli J., "US Negotiates Trade Terror Suspects," UPI, May 9, 2003.

Lamb, Christina, "British Forces Hunt Bin Laden in Yemen," *Washington Times*, November 18, 2002.

Leppard, David, "MI5 Knew for Years of London Mosque's Role," *Sunday Times* (London), November 25, 2001.

Love, Brian, "Libyan Agents Discover Camp Linked to al-Qaeda," AFP, July 5, 2004.

Macfarquhar, Neil, "Iraq Drawing a New Tide of Islamic Militants," *New York Times*, August 13, 2003.

al-Mahdi, Khaled, "Yemen Foils Car Bomb Attacks," Arab News.com, October 1, 2003.

Makram, Faisel, "Ali Saleh: Let us shave our heads before others shave theirs," *al-Hayat*, January 12, 2004.

Manresa, Andreu, "Algiers Accuses the Saudi Millionaire Bin Laden of Paying the GIA Terrorists," *El Pais* (Madrid), October 8, 1998.

Mantash, Ahmed, "Clashes in Lebanon Refugee Camp Kill 5," AP, May 19, 2003. *Al-Hayat*, October 15, 2003.

Marie, Jego, "L'Islam Radical S'est Implante Dans L'est du Kurdistan Irakien," *Le Monde*, November 13, 2002.

Martin, Paul, "Suspect in Attacks Said to be Very Ill," *Washington Times*, October 31, 2003.

McElroy, Damien, "Al-Qaeda Fighters Set Up Base in Lebanese Refugee Camp," *Daily Telegraph*, June 22, 2003.

Mcelroy, Damien, "US Extends the War on Islamic Terror to the Sahara Desert," *Telegraph* (UK), June 6, 2004.

McGrory, Daniel, "Clerics Aid Secret Fight Against Islam Terror Gangs," *The Times* (London), January 26, 2004.

Muhammed, Basel "Kurdish Official: Members from al-Qaeda are in Baghdad with Iraqi Identities," *al-Hayat*, October 29, 2003.

Muqaddam, Muhammad, "Algeria: Reports of Arresting "The Emir of the GIA," *al-Hayat*, November 20, 2003.

Nasif, Nicholas, "Nature of Cooperation Between Lebanon, US To Combat Terror Explained," *An-Nahar*, October 11, 2001 [FBIS]

Nasrawi, Salah, "Egyptian Militants Kill 14 in Attack on Mostly Christian Village," AP, March 14, 1997.

Panossian, Joe, "Lebanon Arrests Suspected Terrorist," AP, October 20, 2003.

Panossian, Joe, "Security Forces Arrest Yemeni Member of al-Qaida Group Indicted in Bombings of Western Targets in Lebanon," AP, October 18, 2003.

Parker, Ned, "Ansar al-Islam, The Vanguard of Radical Islam in Iraq," AFP, August 14, 2003.

Patterson, Mike, "Iraq Operations Providing Intelligence on al-Qaeda: Myers," AFP, July 30, 2003.

Perry, Tom, "Egyptian Islamist Group Drops Guns, Turns to Print," Reuters, November 29, 2003.

Peterson, Scott, "Algeria's Real War: Ending the Cycle of Violence," *Christian Science Monitor*, June 24, 1997.

Peterson, Scott, "Iraqi Funds, Training Fuel Islamic Terror Group," *Christian Science Monitor*, April 2, 2002.

Peterson, Scott, "The Rise and Fall of Ansar al-Islam," *Christian Science Monitor*, October 16, 2003.

Peterson, Scott, "US vs. Iraq: Saddam May Have Fired the First Shot," *Christian Science Monitor*, April 9, 2002.

Phillips, John, "Assassins Pierce Heart of Algeria," *Sunday Times* (London), December 1, 1996.

Pipes, Daniel and Schanzer, Jonathan, "Is America Winning?" *New York Post*, April 8, 2002.

Pisik, Betsy "108 Nations Decline to Pursue Terrorists," *Washington Times*, December 2, 2003.

Purvis, Andrew and Turgut, Pelin "Al-Qaeda's Tracks?" *Time*, December 8, 2003.

Rashwan, Dia, "A New Rapprochement?" *Al-Ahram Weekly*, No. 593, July 4-10, 2002.

Reeve, Simon, "The Worldwide Net: is bombing effective against terrorism?" *The Ecologist*, November 22, 2001.

Rotella, Sebastian, "3 Terror Network Suspects Arrested," *Los Angeles Times,* November 29, 2003.

Rotella, Sebastian, "A Road to Ansar Began in Italy: Wiretaps are said to show how al-Qaeda sought to create in Northern Iraq a substitute for training camps in Afghanistan," *Los Angeles Times*, April 28, 2003.

Sachs, Susan, "An Investigation in Egypt Illustrates Al Qaeda's Web," *New York Times*, November 21, 2001.

Schanzer, Jonathan, "Saddam's Ambassador to al Qaeda: An Iraqi prisoner details Saddam's links to Osama bin Laden's terror network," *The Weekly Standard*, March 1, 2004.

Schemm, Paul, "Algeria's Return to its Past: Can the FIS Break the Vicious Cycle of History?" *Middle East Insight*, vol. 11, no. 2 (1995).

Schmidt, Susan and Farah, Douglas, "Al Qaeda's New Leaders; Six Militants Emerge From Ranks to Fill Void," *Washington Post*, October 29, 2002.

Schmidt, Susan, "Yemen Recovers Huge Cache of Explosives from Blast Site," *Washington Post*, September 11, 2002.

Smiles, Sara and Morris, Linda, "Islamic Youth Leader Charged with Terrorist Links," *Sydney Morning Herald*, September 13, 2003.

Smith, Craig S., "Militant Slain in Algeria; Ties to Qaeda are Reported," *New York Times*, June 21, 2004.

Smith, Craig S., "Terror Suspect Said to be Held by Algeria," *New York Times*, June 5, 2004.

Smith, Craig S., "U.S. Training African Forces to Uproot Terrorists," *New York Times*, May 11, 2004.

Stoichevski, William, "Former Leader of Kurdish Guerrilla Group Says Ansar al-Islam Unlikely Responsible for Attacks on Americans in Iraq," AP, August 12, 2003.

Stout, David, "2 Yemeni Fugitives Indicted in Qaeda Attack on U.S.S. Cole," *New York Times*, May 15, 2003.

Taher, Abdel Salaam, "Yemen Arrests Four Suspects, and Strikes at the Remaining Elements of the Hattat Group," *Ash-Sharq al-Awsat*, July 29, 2003.

Tasgart, Osman, "Report on Bin Laden's Sleeper Networks in Europe," *Al-Majallah*, November 4, 2001 [FBIS].

Tattersall, Nick, "U.S.-Trained Malian Troops Ready for Desert Battle," Reuters, March 18, 2004.

Taylor, Catherine, "Taliban-Style Group Grows in Iraq," *Christian Science Monitor*, March 15, 2002.

Tremlett, Giles, "Muslim Cleric Faces Extradition: Spanish Court Charges Qatada with al-Qaida Membership," *The Guardian* (UK), September 18, 2003.

Tyler, Patrick E., "Intelligence Break let Powell Link Iraq and Qaeda," *International Herald Tribune*, February 7, 2003.

Ulfkotte, Udo, "Refuge Lebanon," *Frankfurter Allgemein* (German), February 6, 2002 [FBIS].

Vick, Karl, "Iran Turns Away Militant Group: Halt in Aid to Kurdish Faction Comes After Missile Attacks," *Washington Post*, March 25, 2003.

Walsh, Courtney C., "Italian Police Explore Al Qaeda Links to Cyanide Plot," *Christian Science Monitor*, March 7, 2002.

Whitaker, Brian, "Yemen Bombers Hit UK Embassy," *Guardian*, October 14, 2000.

Williams, Daniel, "Islamic Militants Harassing Iraqi Kurds; Group in North Iraq Backed by Iran and Bolstered by al-Qaeda, Opposition Leaders Say," *Washington Post*, September 5, 2002.

Williams, Daniel, "Italy Targeted by Recruiters for Terrorists; Attacks Tied to New Alliance," *Washington Post*, December 17, 2003.

Williams, Daniel, "Italy Targeted by Recruiters for Terrorists; Attacks Tied to New Alliance," *Washington Post*, December 17, 2003.

Wright, Lawrence, "The Man Behind Bin Laden: How an Egyptian Doctor Became a Master of Terror," *New Yorker*, September 16, 2002.

Wright, Robin, "Wanted Iraqi May Be Al-Qaeda Link," *Los Angeles Times*, Dec 9, 2002.

Yehia, Ranwa, "Islamists on a Rampage in Lebanon," *Al-Ahram Weekly*, No. 464, January 13-19, 2000.

Yousef Diab, "The Verdict on a Terrorist Network in Lebanon that Exploded Restaurants and Enterprises with American Names," *Ash-Sharq al-Awsat*, December 21, 2003.

Zaatari, Mohammed, "Ain al-Hilweh Leaders Take Steps to Contain Recent Violence," *Lebanon Daily Star*, June 5, 2002.

al-Zaidi, Hassan, "Prospects of Releasing 70 Terror-Linked Detainees," *Yemen Times*, September 22, 2003.

Zayir, Ismail, "Ansar al-Islam Group Accuses Talabani of Spreading Rumors about its Cooperation with al-Qaeda," *al-Hayat* (London), August 22, 2002.

Government Reports and Legal Documents

"Africa Overview," *Patterns of Global Terrorism 1995*, (Washington, DC: United States Department of State, April 1996).

"Ansar al-Islam Named to SDGT List," (Bulletin from the Office of Foreign Assets Control), February 20, 2003.

"Asbat al-Ansar," *Patterns of Global Terrorism 2003*, (Washington, DC: United States Department of State, April 2004).

"Background Briefing with Traveling Press Corps, Santiago, Chile," November 18, 2002.

"Background Information on Other Terrorist Groups," Appendix C, *Patterns of Global Terrorism 2001*, (Washington, DC: United States Department of State, 2002).

"Background Notes: Yemen, October 1996," Bureau of Public Affairs, U.S. Department of State.

"Designation of Dhamat Houmet Daawa Salafia Under Executive Order 13224," U.S. Treasury Press Release, October 20, 2003.

Italian Court Brief Regarding the Arrests of: El Ayashi Radi Abd El Samie Abou El Yazid, Ciise Maxamed Cabdullah, Mohammed Tahir Hammid and Mohamed Amin Mostafa, March 31, 2003.

Joint Inquiry into Intelligence Community Activities Before and After the Terrorist Attacks of Spetember 11, 2001 The Senate and House Report of the U.S. Senate Select Committee on intelligence and U.S. House Permanent Select Committee on Intelligence. December 2002.

"Lebanon Refugee Camp Profiles," http:\\www.un.org\unwra\refugees\lebanon.html

"Lebanon," CIA Factbook, html:\\www.cia.gov\cia\publication\factbook\geos\le.html

"Links Between Ansar al-Islam with Al-Qaeda and Iraq," PUK Information Department, July 30, 2002.

"Middle East Overview," *Patterns of Global Terrorism* 2001, (Washington, DC: United States Department of State, 2002).

"Middle East Overview," *Patterns of Global Terrorism*, 2000, (Washington, DC: United States Department of State, 2001).

National Strategy for Combatting Terrorism, February 2003, http://usinfo.state.gov\topical\toll\terror\strategy\

"Press Briefing with Algerian Foreign Minister Abdelaziz Belkhadem," December 3, 2003, http://\www.state.gov\secretary\rm\2003\2673.htm

Report of the Panel of Experts in Somalia pursuant to Security Council resolution 1474 (2003).

"Salafist Group for Call and Combat (GSPC)," Patterns of Global Terrorism 2001, (Washington, DC: United States Department of State, 2002).

Spanish Cell Documents, Folio 11811 and Folio 11730.

Spanish Court Document 35/2000, Central Trial Court #5, Madrid Spain, July 19, 2002.

"Terrorism: Reported Planning by an Australian-Based al-Qaeda Associate to Attack the U.S. Embassy in Venezuela and U.S. Interests in the Philippines; Presence of al-Qaeda Members in Australia." CIA Document dated "Mid-June 2002."

"The Kurdish Regional Government: The Story of Rehabilitating Iraq," (Kurdistan Regional Government – Winter 2002).

"Treasury Designates Six Al-Qaida Terrorists," U.S. Treasury Press Release, September 24, 2003.

"U.S. Designated Three Individuals and One Organization Involved in Terrorism in Algeria," U.S. Treasury Press Release, October 24, 2003.

"U.S. Designates Additional Members of Italian Al Qaida Cell," U.S. Treasury Press Release, June 24, 2004.

"U.S.-Algerian Relations, Past and Future," Statement by Ambassador Idriss Jazairy, Middle East Institute, Washington, DC, May 6, 2003.

USA vs. Usama bin Laden, Trial Transcript, Day 2, http:\\cryptone2.org\usa-v-ubl-02.htm

"United States Designates Bin Laden Loyalist," U.S. Treasury Press Release, February 24, 2004. .

"War on Terrorism," United States European Command, February 14, 2002.

Bush, George W., September 17, 2002, http://www.whitehouse.gog\nsc\nscintro.html

Cronin, Audrey, "Al-Qaeda After the Iraq Conflict," Congressional Research Service, May 23, 2003.

Katzman, Kenneth, "Iraq: U.S. Regime Change Efforts and Post-Saddam Governance," Congressional Research Service, November 18, 2003.

Powell, Colin, Remarks to the United Nations Security Council, February 5, 2003, http://www.state.gov\secretary\rm\2003\17300.htm

Tenet, George J., "The Worldwide Threat 2004: Challenges in a Changing Global Context," Testimony before the Senate Select Committee on Intelligence, February 24, 2004, http:\\www.cia.gov\cia\public_affairs\ speeches\2004\dci_speech_02142004.html

Journal Articles and Think Tank Reports

"Civil Concord: A Peace Initiative Wasted," International Crisis Group Africa Report, No. 31, July 9, 2001.

"Islamism in North Africa II: Egypt's Opportunity," International Crisis Group, Middle East and North Africa Briefing, April 20, 2004.

"Palestinian Non-Government Organizations in Lebanon," Ajial Center, November 5, 2001, http://www.arts.mcgill.ca/MEPP/PRRN/papers/ajial_center/ngo_lebanon.html

"The Algerian Crisis: Not Over Yet," International Crisis Group, No. 24, October 20, 2000.

"Yemen: Coping with Terrorism and Violence in a Fragile State," International Crisis Group, No. 8, January 8, 2003.

Auda, Gehad and Ali Hasan, Ammar, "The Globalization of the Radical Islamic Movement: The case of Egypt," Strategic Papers #120 (Cairo: Al-Ahram Center for Political and Strategic Studies, 2002).

Raman, B. "Attack on USS Cole: Background," South Asia Analysis Group, No. 152, October 16, 2000.

Bengio, Ofra, "Iraqi Kurds: Hour of Power?" *Middle East Quarterly*, Volume 10, Number 3, Summer 2003.

Brackman, Nicole," Palestinian Refugees in Lebanon: A New Source of Cross-Border Tension?" The Washington Institute for Near East Policy, Peacewatch 263, May 30, 2000.

Delpech, Therese, "International Terrorism and Europe," Institute for Security Studies (European Union), Chaillot Papers, No. 56, December 2002.

Gambill, Gary, "Ain al-Hilweh: Lebanon's Zone of Unlaw," *Middle East Intelligence Bulletin*, June 2003, Vol.5, No.6.

Gunaratna, Rohan, "The Post-Madrid Face of Al Qaeda," *Washington Quarterly*, Summer 2004.

Hoffman, Bruce, *Al-Qaeda, Trends in Terrorism and Future Potentialities: An Assessment*, (Washington, DC: RAND, 2003).

al-Khazen, Farid, "Permanent Settlement of Palestinians in Lebanon: A Recipe for Conflict," *Journal of Refugee Studies*, Vol. 10, No. 3, 1997.

Kassem, Hashem, "Understanding the Significance of Ain al-Hilweh," *Eastwest Record* (2003).

Katz, Mark N., "Breaking the Yemen-al-Qaeda Connection," *Current History*, January 2003.

Khashan, Hilal, "Palestinian Resettlement in Lebanon: Behind the Debate," April 1994, http://www.arts.mcgill.ca\MEPP\PRRN\papers\khashan.html

Knights, Michael, "Algeria's Security Situation Declines Precipitously," *Defense & Foreign Affairs' Strategic Policy*, January/February 2003.

Knights, Michael and Schanzer, Jonathan "Algeria's GSPC: Dichotomy and Anomaly," Forthcoming.

Layachi, Azzedine, "Algeria: Flooding and Muddied State-Society Relations," MERIP Press Information Note 79, December 11, 2001.

Levitt, Matthew, "Untangling the Terror Web: The Need for a Strategic Understanding of the Crossover Between International Terrorist Groups to Successfully Prosecute the War on Terror," Testimony before the Committee on Banking, Housing, and Urban Affairs, United States Senate, October 22, 2003.

Levitt, Matthew, "Placing Iraq and Zarqawi in the Terror Web," Policywatch. no. 710, Washington Institute for Near East Policy, February 13, 2003.

Lloyd, Cathie, "Multi-Causal Conflict in Algeria: National Identity, Inequality and Political Islam," QEH Working Paper, No. 104, April 2003

Moghadam, Asaf and Levitt, Matthew, "Radical Islamist Groups in Germany: A Lesson in Prosecuting Terror in Court," Policywatch #834, Washington Institute for Near East Policy, February 19, 2004.

Nassif, Daniel, "Al-Ahbash," *Middle East Intelligence Bulletin*, Vol. 3, No.4, April 2001.

Pillar, Paul, "Counterterrorism after Al Qaeda," *Washington Quarterly*, Summer 2004.

Pollack, Josh, "Saudi Arabia and the United States, 1931-2002," *MERIA Journal*, Vol. 6. No. 3, September 2002.

Radu, Michael, "Hostages, Terrorism and the West," *Foreign Policy Research Institute E-Notes*, August 27, 2003.

Raufer, Xavier, "New World Disorder, New Terrorisms: New Threats for the Corporate, Computer and National Security," Center for the Study of Contemporary Criminal Menace, November 1998.

Rotberg, Robert I., "Failed States in A World of Terror," *Foreign Affairs*, July/August 2002 (81:4).

Rubin, Michael, "Ansar al-Sunna: Iraq's New Terrorist Threat," *Middle East Intelligence Bulletin*, Vol.6, No. 5, May 2004.

Rubin, Michael, "Are Kurds a Pariah Minority?" *Social Research*, Spring 2003.

al-Sayyid, Kamel, Mustafa, "The Other Face of the Islamist Movement," *Working Papers* (Carnegie Endowment for International Peace), Number 33, January 2003.

Shahar, Yael, "Al-Qaida's Links to Iranian Security Services," International Policy Institute for Counterterrorism, January 20, 2003.

Tal, Nachman, "Islamic Terrorism in Egypt: Challenge and Response," Strategic Assessment, April 1998 (1:1), Jaffee Center for Strategic Studies.

Toth, James, "Islamism in Upper Egypt: A Case Study of a Radical Religious Movement," *International Journal of Middle East Studies*, No. 35 (2003).

Wiktorowicz, Quintan, "Centrifugal Tendencies in the Algerian Civil War," *Arab Studies Quarterly*, Volume 23, Number 3, Summer 2001.

Yacoubian, Mona, "Algeria's Struggle for Democracy," Occasional Paper Series, No. 3, Council on Foreign Relations, 1997.

Acknowledgements

I would like to thank a number of individuals for their contributions to this book. Merissa Khurma, Joyce Karam and other research assistants were invaluable in their capacity as Arabic language translators. I could never, in such a short time span, have digested all of that Arabic material on my own. Christi Cuffee, Ben Fishman, Naysan Rafati, and Barak Seener also provided other valuable research assistance. Avi Jorisch, Matthew Levitt, Chris Verbeek and Janine Zacharia read various incarnations of this book, and provided sound advice on how to make this work more accessible. I would particularly like to thank Jeff Cary, Cliff Carle, Elana Harris, Rick Levinson and Esther Kustanowitz for their editing. Readers of individual chapters at varying stages included Ghalib Bradosti, Soner Cagaptay, Patrick Clawson, Steven Cook, Gary Gambill, Mark Katz, Habib Malik, Dave Romano and Michael Rubin. Their comments were greatly appreciated. Special thanks to Reda Hassaine for several long discussions about Algeria from London, to Gehad Auda for enlightening chats about Egypt, and to Paul McGuire for continued encouragement. The flexibility of Alicia Gansz, Alexis Luckey and the Washington Institute for Near East Policy publications team helped make working with Ian Shapolsky at SPI books a reality. I would like to express my gratitude to many other individuals, spanning more than ten countries and four continents, who helped provide invaluable information for this book, but who have asked to remain anonymous.

Finally, I would like to thank Dennis Ross and Robert Satloff for bringing me to the Washington Institute for Near East Policy. My experiences here have been invaluable.

Jonathan Schanzer
Washington, DC
September 2004

About the Author

Jonathan Schanzer is a research fellow at the Washington Institute for Near East Policy, America's foremost think tank on Middle Eastern affairs. Prior to joining the Institute, Mr. Schanzer was a research fellow for the Middle East Forum, a Philadelphia-based think tank. Mr. Schanzer has also worked at the Truman Institute for the Advancement of Peace in Jerusalem, the *Atlanta Journal Constitution*, and CNN.

Mr. Schanzer holds a BA in International Studies from Emory University, and a master's degree in Middle Eastern Studies from the Hebrew University of Jerusalem. He also studied Arabic at the American University in Cairo.

Mr. Schanzer's Middle East writings have appeared in the *Weekly Standard*, *New Republic*, *Los Angeles Times*, *New York Post*, *Wall Street Journal*, *Jerusalem Post* and *Middle East Quarterly*. He appears as a frequent guest analyst on the Fox News Channel, as well as CNN, CNBC, al-Hurra, and al-Jazeera.

Mr. Schanzer has traveled extensively in Iraq, Yemen, Turkey, Egypt, Jordan, the Palestinian territories and Israel. He speaks Arabic and Hebrew.

Index